Advance Praise for **True Fan**

"I really appreciate how this book begins with a deep look at the individual, who they are and what they want from life, then doing the same for the family. We are all wealth creators, so the question is what do we want to create? I loved the sections on charitable foundations and the Life Energy Quotient. Chris Clark is right, time is our greatest treasure."

—*Caroline Mulroney Lapham, CIM*

"Regardless of your current position in life, anyone can benefit from the thought-provoking guidance and practical advice offered throughout Chris's book. This book will reframe your perceptions about wealth and the pursuit of wealth while providing you with hands-on tools to realize True Family Wealth. This isn't a 'get rich quick' book; this is a 'how to build and live a fulfilling life' book."

—*Doug Arscott, President, The Juice Plus+ Company Canada*

"As a money coach, I speak with families daily about their money hopes, concerns, and worries. Every family should use this informative book as a useful resource to facilitate money conversations and to develop their family wealth strategy."

—*Janet Gray, Certified Financial Planner,*
Money Coaches Canada

"The emotions of money and the relationship issues created around money have had a profound impact on our health, our family, and our society. This is the most comprehensive assessment of what it takes to have a healthy relationship with money and each other that I have come across so far."

—*Sandra Stewart, CCS, Advisor & Cash Flow Specialist,*
High Road Financial Planning

"Truly inspiring. The mix between spiritualism and wealth creation is very empowering. Chris's explanation of the value of the meditative practice as a profound experience that helps us all build wealth within and without was one of the best descriptions I have read."

—*Barry Mills, CPCA, EPC, CAFA*

"We will forever be grateful for the financial structure Chris and her team have built and supported for our family for so many years."

—*Brent Hollister, Retired President and CEO,*
Sears Canada

"Informed, friendly, timely, and effective ... in many ways, part of our family."

—*John Wetmore, former President and CEO,*
IBM Canada Ltd.

"Wise advice from a trusted adviser and friend."

—*Sinan Akdeniz, President, East Coast Fund Management,*
and former Vice Chair and COO, TD Securities

"Too often I encounter families whose wealth growth and succession plans have become threatened or even destroyed because the money itself was seen as the ultimate goal. Chris Clarke's book attacks this premise head on, seeking to show that wealth, family, and personal— and dare I say spiritual—growth should be looked at as a unit to achieve financial, family, and life success. This thought-provoking book is highly recommended for people seeking to grow in all these ways with their families into the future."

—*Brian Cohn, Partner, Gowling WLG*

TRUE FAMILY

Wealth

Money, Love, and An Inspired Life

Chris Clarke

BARLOW BOOKS

fine books for enterprising authors

Library and Archives Canada Cataloguing in Publication data available upon request.

ISBN 978-1-988025-19-3 (paperback)
ISBN 978-1-988025-26-1 (ebook)

Printed in Canada

TO ORDER:
In Canada:
  Georgetown Publications
  34 Armstrong Avenue, Georgetown, ON L7G 4R9

In the U.S.A.:
  Midpoint Book Sales & Distribution
  27 West 20th Street, Suite 1102, New York, NY 10011

Publisher: Sarah Scott
Project manager: Zoja Popovic
Cover design: Soapbox
Cover illustration: Jeannie Phan
Interior design: Kyle Gell Design
Page layout: Kyle Gell Design
Copy editing: Eleanor Gasparik
Proofreading: John Copping
Marketing & publicity: Marjorie Wallins

For more information, visit **www.barlowbooks.com**

Barlow Book Publishing Inc.
96 Elm Avenue, Toronto, ON
Canada M4W 1P2

**BARLOW
BOOKS**

For my parents, Doug and Carol Clarke,
who love me unconditionally.

For my children, Stefan, Erik, and
Rachele Mortveit. It is a great honour
to be your mother.

For my husband, Karl Mortveit.
My hero, my teacher, my soul mate,
and my best friend.

CONTENTS

▲　▼　▲

In July 2015, I retreated to a private villa overlooking the Pitons in St. Lucia with the idea I might write a book. I'd never written a book before and I needed to be inspired, so I chose an inspiring place. But when I got on the plane, I had only a vague notion of what I wanted to get down on paper. It wasn't until I sat down to write that I discovered there was a great deal I wanted to say. In fact, I was astounded by the experience—the writing took over while "I" slipped into the background. Everything that had happened in my past brought me to this perfect place where I had something meaningful to share with you.

I have been part of the private wealth management industry for thirty years. During this time, I have witnessed confusion, ambiguity, and fear—as well as joy and elation—about money, both in my own life and the lives of my clients. But never before, not even when I first sat down to write this book, have I seen such polarization over money and its role in our society as I do now.

I hear the media, politicians, and everyday people judge each other, using labels like "elites," "working class," "privileged," and the "populace." The perceived lack or abundance of money is at the root of all this dysfunction and blame. Yet dig a little deeper and you will see that the real dysfunction lies with people and their relationship with themselves and each other, not money. People are blaming each other for the choices they have or have not made.

Behaving like toddlers is not going to get us very far.

We must grow up. Our relationships, our planet, and our bank accounts depend on it. We are all equals on the path of life, trying to find peace and contentment. We are all at different points of the path, but it is the same path. We are in this together. Let's collaborate, not compete. Let's be vulnerable and true, not phony and disloyal. Let's be kind and respectful, not cruel and resentful. If we can heal our relationships with ourselves and each other, I believe there is plenty of money to go around. More importantly, we must remember our kids are watching! How we handle these times of change will influence their well-being in so many ways.

I hope this book, *True Family Wealth*, can help. It is certainly a different kind of book. The first half is philosophical, and

and the second half is financially practical. The first half seeks to shed light on and eliminate the polarizing and limiting belief systems many people—sometimes unknowingly—have about money and family relationships, and to help readers develop a neutral mindset where they can better utilize the tools offered in the second half. There is no quick fix, and my suggestion is to reread the book a couple of times as you experience in real life the systems presented. You will discover something new each time you do.

I humbly offer this book to you in the hopes that you will receive it with an open mind and heart. Thank you in advance for reading it. I hope you like it, and I hope it is like nothing you've read before. I would love to hear your thoughts, ideas, and questions. You can reach me through my website (www. truefamilywealth.ca), Facebook page (www.facebook.com/ truefamilywealth.ca), and via LinkedIn.

The more we collaborate to resolve family and money issues, the faster we will find our way through and beyond.

Chris Clarke

How *True* Wealth Enriched My Family

▲ ▼ ▲

Most of us think wealth is just money: the cash in our bank, the value of our home, or the size of our financial portfolio. Some people chase it; others hoard it; still others fear it. For most, money represents safety and security, and we spend a considerable chunk of our lives trying to accumulate it. And we worry about it—some of us, almost constantly. As a consequence, and all too often, families break up over money distress.

Money no longer goes as far as it once did. For most people, the promise of a retirement pension after long-term employment has gone the way of the dodo bird. As more people live past the average life expectancy (79 years for men and 83 for women in Canada),[1] they have an even greater challenge

1

funding their retirement years from personal savings. Only an exceptional few will be able to do so while maintaining the lifestyle they live today.

As the co-owner and CEO of a family office[2] wealth management firm, I have been fortunate to work with families of wealth for the past thirty years. I can tell you that many of these folks have trouble with the idea of money too. These wealth creators have millions of dollars at their disposal, and yet they're often afraid it will be lost, which makes them feel insecure about their and their children's future (the more you have, the more you have to lose in so many ways). As well, they are frequently highly stressed by their complex, multi-faceted, and at times confusing and burdensome wealth management issues. Some struggle with guilt about their financial abundance and often feel resented by those with less money. And even the most financially confident and astute individuals find that money worries cause trouble on the home front. Being "rich" means little if you do not feel "enriched."

Most young adults are worried about money too, which distorts the choices they make in life. Even if they grew up with money, they too often don't know how they'll ever afford a home of their own or the lifestyle they once had. In their eyes, opportunities are few, competition is fierce, money is scarce, and hope is drying up. They often feel they have to choose between a career that makes good money and one that would be inspiring and fulfilling to them. Why must they choose one at the expense of the other?

Wealthy or not, we all have something in common. We all (except for the enlightened few) struggle with our relationships to money and to each other. Clearly, our attitude toward money is all wrong. Too many of us accumulate money only to feel safe rather than use it for the joy of creation. It's time to remember what money is meant for: *as a tool of exchange between people who care about each other's well-being, to equalize everyone's right to a good life, and to play with in the act of creation.*

It's also time to rethink wealth. Wealth is having an abundance of what we most treasure. That, is *True* wealth. Yes, it includes money, but it also includes a loving group of people who support us. We call that group "family," whether related by blood or not. *True* wealth is good health, self-confidence, and high self-esteem. It is having an education and continued opportunities for lifelong learning. *True* wealth is having a personal mission and clarity of life direction. It is the opportunity to give our unique talents to the world and create. *True* wealth is our experiences and life lessons, our traditions and memories. It is our hopes, dreams, and challenges. In other words, a life of *True* wealth is built upon a clear and great purpose, loving relationships, and many achievements. *Money without loving relationships is shallow. Loving relationships without money is wasted potential.* A family is *truly* wealthy only when each member thrives. Many parents will agree with me when I say we are only as happy as our least happy child.

I learned about *True* wealth in my own life when a thief came to visit and revealed the power of a man I now see is a warrior. But a bit of backstory first. I was born into a family that wasn't "rich" but that believed in the importance of education. With my parents' assistance, I pulled the funds together to attend university and graduate with a business degree. I earned my C.A. designation and at age twenty-six launched what would ultimately become my own financial planning business. Prior to that, at age sixteen, I had already met my soul mate (who later became my husband). Like me, he was born into a family that wasn't "rich" but that believed in a strong work ethic and self-reliance. His dad owned a small construction company, so it made sense that my husband would study civil engineering. Yet upon completing that education, in his heart, he knew he wanted to fly. So he borrowed some money and went back to school. By age twenty-five, he became a pilot for a charter airline.

So here we were in the early 1990s, living what was then referred to as the "yuppie" lifestyle in a wealthy suburban town outside Toronto. By 1993, we had one son and I was pregnant with our second. Having my own business gave me freedom to manage my time. Having a pilot in the family allowed us to fly anywhere for almost free, so we travelled all over the world, often at the drop of a hat. Being a pilot also allowed my husband time to work in my financial planning business. He would often arrive at the office straight from the airport, still in his pilot uniform, and put in time problem-solving business issues. Before long, my business became our business. We had a lovely home decorated to perfection. We had no financial worries. We were living the North American dream. But it was someone else's dream—we just didn't know it yet.

My husband's family had a ski chalet two hours north of Toronto. Realizing what a wonderful place this was for a young family to play together, we bought a charming antique log home on sixty-eight acres. Our "cabin" was on the mountainside overlooking the ski hills, valley, and crystal-clear waters of Georgian Bay. We were surrounded by hundreds of acres of pristine meadows, forests, rivers, and streams with not a house or concrete building in sight. This became our getaway. For the next ten years, we packed up the three kids (our daughter was born in 1996) and loaded the car to head to our corner of paradise every weekend. We spent the summers hiking, cycling, swimming, and kayaking and the winters skiing, skating, and snowshoeing right out our front door. At night we saw a show of stars that I had not known existed. Deer, foxes, and coyotes commonly wandered our fields, with the odd sighting of a wolf or bald eagle. The kids played games outside that they had created from their imaginations, falling into bed at night exhausted and happy. Grandparents, aunts and uncles, cousins, and friends regularly joined in the family fun.

It wasn't long before we realized that *this* was our dream and we were living it ... but only on the weekends. When Sunday night came around, we packed with heavy hearts, locked up the little cabin, and drove back to the city. I remember one

stormy winter night when our three-year-old son started wail-
ing as we got ready to head back to the city. He told us he
didn't want to leave the cabin so we should just go without
him. That broke my heart.

My husband and I had talked for years about living full-
time at the cabin. However, we had a limiting belief that
this was just "not done." After all, life in the country was
for country folk. Professionals like us with big goals and big
money expectations would never move away from where all
the action was. That would be professional suicide, wouldn't
it? We had a thriving business in the city. We had employees
and clients who depended on us. They wouldn't tolerate us
moving to the country because surely they would think we
weren't serious about our business—or so we thought. If we
threatened our business like that, we could lose everything:
our house, our beloved cabin, our money, and our lifestyle—
all of which we had worked so hard to obtain. It would be
downright irresponsible of us to follow this dream full-time.
Our fears entrapped us, although we were stuck in a beautiful
prison. Then cracks began to appear in the foundation of our
"successful life." By the age of thirty-five, I was wiped out,
and so was my husband. I had developed a hypothyroid condition that left me running on empty most of the time. Once,
I actually had to crawl up the stairs to reach my toddler on
the second floor since my legs couldn't carry me. And my
husband was flying almost all the time then. Cost-cutting measures at the airline required the pilots to be away more often

and for longer. He was always jet-lagged, and when he came home at the oddest of times, he couldn't rest with a house full of kids who wanted to play and do what kids do. He had to keep plugging, though, as we had a family to support.

As our kids grew older, education was critical, and we started their schooling as early as possible. We enrolled them in what we felt were the best schools in our area: at one point, each child was in a different school. It took us and their other caregivers up to an hour and a half each morning and each evening to do the drop-off and pick-up loop. We didn't have time to spend with friends or to travel much anymore because we were juggling the business, the flying, the schools, homework, soccer practice, swimming lessons, gymnastics, and music lessons—not to mention the groceries, cleaning, cooking, laundry, and bills that had to be paid to all the good people who were helping us to do all this. Our lifestyle took more and more money to support, and we soon realized that we, too, were caught on the production tread-mill. It was just not sustainable! We knew that what this sick mother, exhausted father, and hyper-scheduled kids needed was a different way of life. Yet our limiting beliefs still prevented us from taking action. We were living successfully by societal norms, but not according to our true passions. Our relationships were beginning to suffer, and our achievements were unravelling.

Then, in only a moment, it seemed like everything we had worked for was gone. My husband and I arrived at the office one morning to find the front windows smashed and all our computers stolen. Our business was now in the hands of a thief who would likely never be caught. I remember sitting down on the curb outside the broken windows with my head in my hands. It was a struggle just to breathe. It felt as though everything I thought to be true was a lie. I believed that if you worked really hard, only good things and success would be yours. If you were an honest, responsible, and kind person, bad things like this wouldn't happen to you. If you took really good care of other people, you would always be rewarded. How could any of this be true when we had just lost everything in a matter of minutes? Security appeared an illusion. I was devastated.

Something unexpected happened, though. I met a warrior, a man I had not previously truly known. He saved us all. How? Not by catching the thief—those computers were long gone. But he showed me that he had my back. He made me understand that nothing was permanent except for the love that surrounded me and ran through me. Not money, not possessions, not even the business. This warrior reminded me of the person I was, of the drive, determination, and sheer will I had deep within that could not be stolen. He helped me recall the great joy I experienced creating the life I was living. He inspired me that I could do it again. This was not the end. Not only that, but now I had the chance to make it even better, because I had so much more awareness about what I wanted from life. He told me he would protect me and lend me his power to rebuild my castle in any way I wanted. And that is exactly what he did.

This warrior was my husband. I had known him almost all my life but had not fully recognized who he really was. He saved our business and, with the help of our business partner and team members, rebuilt the systems. However, this warrior's biggest sacrifice was yet to come. In order to give the business and his family the attention we truly needed to thrive, he walked away from his flying career. He knew that not having control over his schedule and living with the exhaustion of jet lag would diminish his power to sculpt our lives the way we dreamed they could be. But it was not all sacrifice. The thief had also taught my husband what he truly valued most: his family and our business over his love of flying. And he treasured his freedom, which flying had paradoxically taken from him. We used this opportunity to discuss with our young children what we really wanted for our lives together. We dug deep to uncover our core values and began to understand what united us. We discovered how similar our passions and interests were, and what type of lifestyle made us feel joyous and alive. We decided that money was not a good enough reason not to live life the way we wanted. Money was not at the core of our identity. It could be taken away too easily, no matter how much we tried to protect it. Money was to be used to live the life we wanted; it was not itself the goal. Money would not rule us; we would rule it.

So we moved in 2001, and here we are today. We live full-time in our paradise. My husband and I remodelled the cabin into what would be better described as a lodge in the country. We also acquired another twenty-five adjoining acres of maple forest, which may produce maple syrup some day. We can do our sports seven days a week. Each of us has been rewarded for our athletic achievements with various awards. We have travelled the world together. We wake up each day to heart-stopping beauty right at our doorstep and never take it for granted. Two of our children have returned from post-secondary school to build successful businesses of their own, while the third finishes her university degree with the aim to join our business someday. Our relationships with each other, extended family, and friends nourish us. Our idea of fun remains "hanging out" with each other at the cabin or in town with friends. We are creating some new businesses together, and our foundational business has grown over five times in size since we moved, with clients across Canada and overseas.

Here we are twenty-five years later. My family and I are now *truly* wealthy, enriched by so many treasures and a life full of achievements. We live with excitement about what we will next create together, united in the spirit of independence, hard work, continual learning, and service to others. We are nourished daily by Mother Nature and live healthy, active lives. Together with our adult children, we are thriving and sharing our experiences and burdens, learning from one another as equals on the path of life. We celebrate our accomplishments and have created traditions that ground us. Oh yes, and we also help one another create money. We, as a family, have chosen to create money for ourselves rather than rely on others for it. We have enough of it to live life the way we dreamed, and then some. We are an Enriched Family.

However, I don't want to mislead you into thinking our relationships were and are always easy. They were and are the most challenging part of *True* wealth creation. We wouldn't be living this beautiful life were it not for a great deal of self-reflection, risk-taking, and many battles with ourselves and one another. In fact, as our children became teenagers, all hell broke loose. They did what teenagers are supposed to do: they pushed our buttons. And we pushed theirs. Let me be very clear. Despite the truly inspired life we live, it is not easy! There have been (and will be) really tough times. Every family experiences this. Evolution is happening and we have growing pains. But through all the emotional struggles, we as a family never lost sight of our deepest values and mission: to love each other, stay together, and co-create together. We communicated, communicated, and communicated some more. We practised forgiveness mostly and took self-responsibility always. We also employed the family team-building tools that I share with you in this book. When asked how we have come through the challenges together that so often break others apart, I respond that it was due to one key understanding. *We believe that everything that happens in relationships is a reflection of what is going on inside you; that the outer events or relationship conflicts are simply mirroring something in you that needs to be addressed.* So we worked—and still work—endlessly on ourselves in relation to one another.

This brings me to the purpose of *True Family Wealth*. I want to share with fellow wealth creators what I have learned and to inspire you to think differently about your resources, regardless of whether you find them currently lacking or abundant. Do you have to be financially wealthy to benefit from this book? No. But you do have to be interested in wealth creation, and see yourself as a wealth creator.

This book offers a different perspective on money and family. I also provide you a system that has helped me and my family thrive. It has given me the power to create and preserve the business I want, the family I want, and the life I want by *working with change* instead of *fearing it*. My goal with *True Family Wealth* is to provide a tool to empower *True* wealth creators so they can experience the life they really want for themselves and the next generations. This includes money, to be sure, but also the power of family relationships and our ability to create together. I call this system The Family Treasury™. It creates Enriched Families as it cultivates *True* wealth and helps sustain it for generations.

In *True Family Wealth*, I share the step-by-step Family Treasury process that will equip you to achieve the wealth you *truly* want and to keep it for future generations to enjoy. This system enables family leaders, successors, and follow-on generations to steward *True* family wealth in a sustainable way. Your family can be an Enriched Family today and into the future. But in the spirit of full disclosure, I must warn you that it will only work if you are prepared to accept what I've come to regard as three key principles:

1. This system will achieve results, but they will not be overnight. While it is a fairly simple process to follow, it is not an immediate fix. The Family Treasury takes commitment, the courage to self-reflect, and acceptance of self-responsibility for everything you've created in your life. The ride won't always be smooth, but there'll be much fun along the way. Results will depend on the time committed, participation achieved, and how "rigorously honest" you are with yourself (my friend came up with that one).

2. For The Family Treasury to work for you in the long term, you need to adopt the perspective that resources aren't only monetary and aren't limited. I am asking you to consider that conversations about finances and family should not be held separately, as they each affect the other profoundly. Money is NOT the responsibility of the "breadwinner" while everyone else gets to live in ignorance of matters financial. It makes the world go around so we must all be responsible and gain financial acumen, whether we "enjoy" it or not. I'm asking you to consider forming a new set of beliefs

to replace the old dysfunctional set. *We are all wealth creators.* You'll find the book most helpful if you read it with an open mind, as I'm going to invite you to work with both practical and abstract information (perhaps more abstract than you're used to).

3. You need to believe as I do that the only wealth worth having is one that allows opportunities for all your family members (and the others who support you) to thrive. Money is a wonderful blessing to be shared. *True* wealth is not just measured by the size of your financial portfolio; it's measured by your feeling of fulfilment and joy, and the quality of love and personal freedom in life. You need to believe that a family united is stronger than the separate self. When it comes to the act of creation, a family united by a common vision can accomplish so much more than individuals alone. Besides, it's no fun celebrating your successes alone.

True Family Wealth is about putting the power to create and preserve wealth back into the loving hands of family. Although I chose to focus on family because this is typically the place where people feel most free to express themselves, the system can just as easily be used by the individual, a business, or community groups.

We begin by challenging your beliefs about money and wealth, goals and dreams, creativity, and the resources available in abundance to all of us. Then I show you how to imagine your family as a business. If you do, you'll see that the "business of family" can be a profitable one. You'll develop an understanding of yourself and your family in order to recognize both your specific opportunities and the roadblocks in your way. You'll design both a personal and a family mission and set goals and objectives about what you'll create. It might be a business, or a philanthropic quest, or maybe a career or innovation that can change the world. You'll learn techniques to develop emotional maturity and financial knowledge within your family team and a culture of creativity and leadership. Then you'll learn about some specific tools you'll need to accomplish your family mission.

These all lead to a new holistic approach to wealth *stewardship* for the new age. For families that have achieved a certain measure of financial independence, this can lead to the "family bank," which you can use to invest in your family's well-being for generations to come. More importantly, as CEO of The Family Treasury, you will have the opportunity to mentor the next generations and pass on the values, experiences, and wisdom you have earned over the years.

I have tested parts of this model with some of our clients over the years. They report that their young people are confident and motivated wealth stewards. Together, they feel a sense of family unity and community responsibility. They sleep well knowing their finances are secure and available to create the life they truly want. I have also honed this process within my own family. My children will tell you they feel stronger and safer. They have gained inspiration through clarity of purpose, mission and vision, and joy in the shared experiences, rewards, and successes. They're empowered by financial strength and literacy, supported by conflict resolution and leadership skills. They feel as though they belong to something greater than themselves. They are expressing what it is to be *truly* wealthy, and money in the bank has little to do with it. I continue to gain inspiration from families who have used similar concepts to grow and preserve their money, relationships, and freedom of expression for generations. They live truly inspired lives.

For those of you expecting *True Family Wealth* to be a business book, you might be wondering at this point if you've picked up the wrong book. For those of you thinking this book would share tips on how to build a happy, thriving family, you might be asking yourself what this has to do with business. *True Family Wealth* has everything to do with both and more. It is about catalyzing our abundant resources through the selective use of our personal power to express our individual and collective potentials. The Family Treasury is about creating (and keeping) financial wealth while raising successful families and maintaining positive, meaningful relationships. It is about preserving and growing our totality of resources, including but not limited to money, for generations to come.

If you already consider yourself blessed with abundant financial wealth and professional success, this book is written for you. If you are, or want to be, a wealth creator this book is for you. If you consider yourself still stretching toward your own financial security, then this book is written for you. If you are somewhere in between, successful but not wealthy or wealthy but not successful, this book is—you guessed it—also written for you. But if you think you have all the money you want and need, both for your benefit and for the benefit of subsequent generations; you have no fear of losing it; your family relationships are warm, unconditionally loving, and supportive; and your future is even bigger and brighter than your past, then, please, still read this book. Why? Because you have a responsibility to teach what you know to your next generation, and The Family Treasury can help you do that.

Now it's time to start our journey. Can you imagine how money in the hands of love can change the world? Can you imagine how co-creating with your own family might change *your* world immeasurably?

A word before you begin

In chapters 4, 5, and 6, you will see the following icon: ▲**1**

The icon identifies the eleven specific processes that together form the three overarching Family Treasury systems: Stewardship through a Worthy Mission, Development through Loving Relationships, and Legacy of Achievements. These processes are reflected in The Family Treasury Balance Sheet (Figure 16), which is used to measure and chart the progress you and your family make toward the creation and preservation of *True* family wealth.

Rethinking Wealth
Challenging 4 Key Beliefs

▲ ▼ ▲

When we were kids, most of us were introduced to wealth through stories about *treasure*. What a sumptuous word, evoking visions of overflowing chests abundant with magnificent jewels and gold and silver coins. It triggered our cravings for fortune, riches, and lavish lifestyles. The fairy tales and adventure stories we read conditioned us to understand treasure as something extraordinary and coveted, yet illusive and rare, hidden from all but the luckiest or bravest. Yet as an adult, would you agree that the word *treasure* really refers to *that which we most cherish?*

What do you cherish most? Your family, friends, home, and health? How about your achievements and life lessons? Do you treasure your memories—those albums and hard drives filled with photos and home videos? Perhaps your family history and where you or your ancestors have come from is important to you? Or the country you live in and the earth you stand upon, the air you breathe, and the sun that warms you and brightens your day? Do you cherish those stolen moments when time seems to stand still? And, yes, there is also money and possessions. They are pretty cool too.

The Family Treasury is both a philosophical and practical wealth management process for preserving and continuing to grow our *many* treasures and resources in a sustainable, harmonious, respectful, and dynamic way. It is a system that celebrates what a family really could be, what a business really should be, and how the two can become one, transforming lives now and into the future. Done well, it can be an evolutionary next step for all of us, individually and collectively.

It stands in contrast to what we as a society focus the vast majority of our time and attention (and therefore our lives) on: the pursuit of money. Truth be told, that is not actually what we value most. How messed up is that? We tell ourselves we cherish the many treasurers in our lives, but our actions show the opposite. Our relationship with money is dysfunctional, and we need to fix it, or get a divorce. We need to challenge our current beliefs about money and success, reassess our goals and dreams, and rediscover our creativity and right to abundance.

Rethinking Money

Have you ever thought: *If I just had more money, I'd be happy?*
With more money, I could do more, be more, have more, and then,
finally, feel peace of mind. You're not alone. Most of the population, financially wealthy or not, believes that if they just had
more money, they'd be happier. Put simply, we have been
fooled into believing that we *get* happiness with money. We
think it can be bought.

Does Money Make Us Happy?

Most people feel they don't have enough money for an
acceptable standard of living, so I can see why they might
think money would be the solution to their troubles. Today,
less than 1% of the population has the majority of the money
while everyone else struggles to make ends meet. There is
no judgment here: it is simply the current condition we find
ourselves in. Given the broad range within that 1%, most
of them would say that they, too, struggle to make ends
meet. Often, the more you make, the more you spend. Many
wealthy folks would also agree that the money made them
happy for a while, then it lost its shine. They reached a certain point where money no longer had the same happiness
boost it once did.

But throwing more money at our problems won't resolve
them. We know that money doesn't necessarily guarantee
happiness, and it certainly doesn't make you content. While

material goals can perhaps be honourable, they often require giving up more time to make more money. We see evidence everywhere of how the relentless accumulation of money often destroys relationships, families, and our health and well-being. *It's easy to see the damage done by the relentless drive for money with too little time spent elsewhere.* We've all witnessed or experienced first-hand parent-and-child relationship breakdowns and family breakups where money had a role. We all know children (and adults too) who have become lost and unmotivated, and often abuse drugs or alcohol. In developed nations, the "lost generation" of our youth is as widespread among the wealthy as it is in the rest of the population. Life-threatening illnesses often associated with stress affect the affluent as much as anyone else, with "dis-ease" affecting most people in some way. There is a pervading sense of lack of meaningful purpose or a struggle to find clarity of direction affecting both young and old in our economically advanced nations. Of course, we can't blame all of this on money. It's not money's fault. However, we can blame our dysfunctional relationship with money, since it usually plays a significant role.

> *Throwing more money at our problems won't resolve them.*

When we understand that our resources are so much more than money, yet observe how those resources are often devalued, misused, misunderstood, and, at worst, ignored, it is no wonder that so many of us, whether rich or poor, feel discontented.

Is Money Scarce?

In western society, we've embraced capitalism and benefited enormously from the results. Generally speaking, even those of us with the lowest levels of income live a lifestyle of luxury compared with those in developing nations. For the most part, though, our pursuit of financial wealth is a singular enterprise narrowly focused on money, and that pursuit is competitive, volatile, consumptive, and divisive. When comparing geographically, demographically, culturally, and economically, it is easy to see that those with money have power—and those without it, don't. We observe how our society judges success—and, therefore, how worthy and important someone is—by their money or, more typically, by the perception that they have money. I bet you know someone who values money above all else in this world and aims to "win" at all costs. "The one who dies with the most toys wins" is a common expression. We often lie, cheat, steal, and even kill for money.

This behaviour can be partly blamed on the belief that money, as a primary resource, is scarce. Our entire supply-and-demand economic system is built on this scarcity principle, which we are taught at an early age in school and is part of the reason we have money hoarders and money spenders, the excessively rich and the excessively poor. *Most people also hold a well-ingrained belief that money is not for them: its scarcity ensures that only the very special can have it.* We constantly use it to measure our worthiness against another. In doing so, we can always find a comparison that makes us feel lack. *Money's perceived scarcity also causes us to compete for it, even in the way we invest.* Our investment marketplace was once an opportunity to buy into good companies that produced goods and services we needed in exchange for a share in their long-term success. Yet today's stock market has become a casino fuelled by greed and fear where, too often, capitalizing on short-term disparities for individual profit is more important than investing in long-term group success. We believe we need to compete to get money, and lots of it, fast in order to be safe and have power over our lives—and, frankly, the lives of others. How did we get here? I would like to suggest three linked causes.

1. Our limiting societal beliefs, fear, misunderstandings, and lack of education about money and how to use it means most of us do not realize our personal power to *create* money. Many of us do not see ourselves as wealth creators, so we begin from a place of disempowerment.

2. As a result, we often sacrifice our creative potential in exchange for perceived safety and security in an uninspiring job. We sell our time for a fixed

compensation with little to no upside potential. We are told what to do, when to do it, and how to do it with little freedom of personal expression.

3. And because there are so many people willing to do the same thing, we compete the jobs away from each other and drive compensation down each time we do so.

Sensational as it may sound, money itself is not scarce. It is our attitude toward it that make it seem so. So might the secret to having more money be to stop competing with each other? *Instead, can we learn to act on opportunities to bring unique value to each other? No scarcity, or limits, there.*

> " *So might the secret to having more money be to stop competing with each other?*

This may not be such a crazy idea. What if we were to collaborate rather than compete? Competition feeds isolation and fear. Collaboration breeds creativity and confidence. Would we not all be stronger and better prepared to take risks, as wealth creators should, if we knew our team was watching our back? *The Family Treasury supports wealth creation in a collaborative rather than competitive manner.* No one gets hurt, all members have equal opportunity, and dealings are honest, respectful, and transparent. The Family Treasury seeks to annihilate the belief that money is scarce by developing a right relationship with it. First, however, this requires an understanding that what we believe affects how we behave and how we behave will give us the result that reinforces what we believe.

Do We Relate Well to Money?

We often feel dissatisfied with where we are and what we don't have. No matter how financially "successful" we are, we personally know someone—or perhaps know of someone—who seems to have so much more than we do: more stuff, more money, more fun, more power, more fame. Do you ever wonder why they seem to have so much more than you? In exploring this, let's consider the financial context of our lives.

> " We have a pretty messed-up
> relationship with money.

For starters, our society is incredibly confused about money, and we all pick up on those convoluted beliefs. Various groups have widely differing beliefs about money. Some of this is generational: those who lived through the Great Depression have a very different approach to money than do baby boomers, who grew up in a time of plenty. I daresay that some of the confusion also stems from religion. Certain religious groups celebrate and revere money as a gift from God for good works. Certain others teach that money is shameful, or even evil, and that lack of it shows piety: to have money means they've sacrificed their morals because of a deeply held fundamental belief that people with money must be dishonest and/or greedy.

Then there are the folks who think that people with money must work all the time and, therefore, are terrible parents or lousy spouses. I have seen others take the opposite approach. They decide they don't need money or success to be happy and rebel against it, opting for a small life in a house made of tin cans and tires (it's true, I've actually seen it). Those with a lot of money, and a lot of stress, often bail out of the rat race, believing they've earned a life of leisure, only to find themselves bored and depressed. Then they begin nickel-and-diming everyone √ around them just for something to do or out of fear they might now lose their money.

If you are from Britain or Canada, you also most certainly do not discuss money openly in social settings, as that is considered poor taste. That is, unless you're at a cocktail party with your business associates where it's acceptable to boast about your last business deal, stock trade, or new expensive car. But "don't discuss money with the children"! We've also been told that if you want to make really good money, you must graduate from university with a degree. What university did Henry Ford, Mark Zuckerberg, and Richard Branson graduate from? That's right, they didn't.

And what about the obligations of those who are financially successful? Do you feel beholden to give to charity because you're "so fortunate"? Not to give back makes you feel guilty because why should you have so much when others do not? If you don't feel guilty enough already, most of the world resents you for having money and will only begin to forgive you if you give much of it away. We are told in the West that capitalism is our human right and the path to success; yet for many countries in the East, capitalism is considered evil and to be avoided. After all, debt is responsible for the demise of our society, is it not? But wait a minute—didn't debt build our society?

I think you get my point: we have a pretty messed-up relationship with money. People make excuses about money. They seem confused about money: how to make it, how to keep it, should they keep it, should they make it. And there just doesn't seem to be enough of it! No wonder money runs away from so many. Would you stay in a relationship with someone who had such a bewildering message regarding what they wanted from you?

If we keep looking to the outside world for the "right answer" about money and all we get is contradiction, confusion, and the same result over again, is it not insane to continue in this way? Where should we direct our attention instead? To the inside! The health of our internal beliefs about money will determine if it wants to stay with us. The practice of self-awareness is the key to recognizing our limiting, sabotaging beliefs and unlocking our potentials. But first, let's look at what money really is.

What Is the Truth about Money?

We seem to both love and fear money, as if it's a god. Who gave money all this power over our lives anyway? Oh, right. We did. Recalling from the Introduction the first of the three facts that we need to accept before applying The Family Treasury model—that we must take self-responsibility for everything we've created in our lives—well, that includes money and the power it has over us. We create either a lack or an abundance of money due to our beliefs about it. It is all in our perception.

What is money really? Money is not good and it is not evil. It's just a thing: neutral. What makes it good or bad depends on our attitudes toward it. It has no power over us other than what we choose to give it. It is simply an efficient unit of exchange meant to replace a cumbersome and awkward centuries-old barter system. Not so long ago in some cultures, seashells were used as a means of exchange. Would it seem absurd to get all worked up and emotional over seashells? To devote our entire life to accumulating seashells? Well, we do just that over bits of synthetic polymer! If we must assign power to money, then let's ensure we are not its slave. Instead, money should be our servant.

> We create either a lack or
> an abundance of money due
> to our beliefs about it. It is all
> in our perception.

Whether we earn money, buy money, or are given money, we all have something in common. We are born and we die. In between, we all have twenty-four hours each day that we live— we just don't know for how long. During that time, we put our life's energy to use in some way that most often involves earning, growing, preserving, and spending that money. Let's call it our Life Energy Quotient (LEQ), where one hour of life equals one unit of available life energy. When we use up LEQ in the pursuit of money, we are exchanging LEQ for money. Albert Einstein told us that energy can neither be created nor destroyed, it only changes form. Therefore, we alchemize LEQ into money each time we work. Every minute we spend working, whether framing a house, researching a point of law, or managing our investment portfolio, we are converting our LEQ to money. We are all equal in this regard, no matter who we are, where we live, or what our other resources are.

What differs between us is:

- how much of our LEQ we are prepared to convert to money (which is a function of our values, beliefs, and motivations)
- how much money we can get for our LEQ (which is a function of our education and circumstances)
- how good we are at converting LEQ to money (which is a function of our talents and appetite for risk)
- what we choose to spend our LEQ = money on (which is a function of choice)

Humans are the only creatures (that we know of) on this
planet who have the conscious, self-aware ability to make
choices and to direct actions based on those choices. As long
as you have the mental capacity, you can choose values and
beliefs that are either fearful or empowering. You can choose
education or ignorance in its many forms. You can choose
to take risks, grow, and evolve, or choose to stagnate com-
fortably. You can choose to consume your money or to be
a steward of that money. In other words, the differences in
our wealth experiences are mainly due to the consequences
of the choices we make. We are responsible for our money
experience.

How Does LEQ Work?

To demonstrate how LEQ works, I'd like to introduce Jack and
Jill. They will continue to make appearances throughout the
upcoming chapters to illustrate various points.

Jack works as a carpenter for $50 an hour, and Jill, works
as a senior lawyer for $500 an hour. Did you already assume
that Jill is the more successful one in life? She earns more
money than Jack and could likely afford a "better" car and
a "better" home than Jack. She'd be able to travel and have
the best things and finest wines, no doubt. But what makes
a "better" car or a "better" home? Is that not subjective? For
some, a better home is a mansion in the city full of fine fur-
nishings, while for others it would be a small log cabin tucked
away in the woods. Jill may feel that it is perfectly reasonable

to work 8,000 LEQ hours to pay for that $4 million mansion. On the other hand, Jack dreams of building and living in his own log cabin in the woods. It will cost him $400,000. He, like Jill, is sacrificing 8,000 LEQ hours for the home of his choice. Taxation ignored, in this example, they both achieved their dreams while sacrificing the same amount of LEQ. How perfect is that? No, really, do you get what this means? It means that more money is *not* the answer to achieving our dreams, as most people think. *The trick is matching the amount of LEQ we are willing to exchange for money to the price tag on our dream.* If not in balance, you either don't get the dream or when you do get it, you're exhausted and can't enjoy it!

What if the price tag on your dream exceeds the amount of LEQ you are willing to exchange? You can do one of two things. After considering your values and priorities, you may recognize that you don't really want that dream at all because you aren't willing to give up more LEQ to have it. That is contentment and gratitude in action. Or through education, risk-taking, and creativity, you can increase the amount of money you receive in exchange for your LEQ. Stretching for a big dream requires becoming a better LEQ alchemist, which builds your personal power. That is evolution in action. Both options are fabulous.

> 66 *The trick is matching the amount of LEQ we are willing to exchange for money to the price tag on our dream.*

Following up with a second example, let's say that in addition to being an experienced journeyman carpenter, Jack also has a college education in construction management and runs his own business. With more qualifications and broader experience, he can command a price of, say, $150 an hour. Then he could have that $400,000 dream home by sacrificing 67% less of his LEQ, again ignoring taxation. He would now only need to exchange 2,666 LEQ hours for the same dream home, while Jill had to sacrifice 8,000 LEQ hours. Through education and risk-taking, Jack increased the value of his LEQ exchanged for money—or put another way, he reduced the LEQ he had to sacrifice to reach the same dream. Would that not make Jack more successful than Jill? Well, that depends! *Getting more money for each LEQ hour you give certainly helps achieve your dream, but it still depends on how much LEQ you are prepared to convert to money in the first place.*

You may surmise that the time between birth and death is the only resource truly limited on this planet. Of course, science has proven this to be untrue, teaching us that time is, in fact, also an illusion. Human perception of dimensions through the five senses is what creates a past, present, and future. Science and ancient wisdom tell us there actually is no time; everything exists at once. You are born, alive, and dead at the same time. But since that's a topic for someone else's book—and I can't yet wrap my head around it anyway—let's keep our sanity and agree that our only present restriction is that there are twenty-four hours in the day, for that is our collective experience, our equitable gift.

With that consideration in mind, let's look at a third example. Jack and Jill have each chosen to exchange their equitable gift of LEQ for unequal amounts of money. Both are single. Jill earns $500 an hour and Jack earns $150 an hour. Jill works as a lawyer twelve hours a day, five days a week, and a further six hours on the weekend. Thus, she works sixty-six hours a week. Jack, on the other hand, works seven hours a day, five days a week, for a total of thirty-five hours a week. Jill has chosen to exchange sixty-six LEQ hours for $33,000 a week (sixty-six hours of life energy at $500 an hour). Jack has chosen to exchange thirty-five LEQ hours for $5,250 a week. If we look only at the money, one might say Jill made the smarter trade. But when you live your last LEQ, and take your last breath, are you likely to think of it as lost money? I hope not.

From the perspective of what we often call "trade-offs," some would say that Jack is the wiser as he has chosen a more balanced life. He chooses to work only thirty-five hours a week or, in other words, is exchanging only thirty-five LEQ hours of work for money, leaving more LEQ available for such activities as honing his craft and building his own log home, or perhaps socializing and having some fun. Some would say Jill is the wiser as, at a time when she is young, single, and energetic, before the obligations of family slow her down, she has chosen to focus her LEQ to accumulate money and create financial wealth. She may not be living a balanced life right now but has chosen that purposefully to focus and maximize one area of her life, empowering the other areas for a later time.

The reality is: it is simply a choice, and with each choice comes consequences. If Jill is passionate about what she does, looks forward to work, and moves creatively in flow throughout her day, it is likely a good investment of 59% of her available waking LEQ a week. For now, she has balance. Jack exchanges 31% of his available waking LEQ weekly; for him, it is just enough money to meet his needs, as he is unwilling to offer more. He prefers to leave LEQ for his sports/fitness activities and healthy eating habits, his family and friends, his woodworking, and time to laze around on the porch looking up at the sky. His spirit, body, and mind receive more balanced attention than does Jill's. His spirit is nurtured by unconditional love and security from family and friends; his body is becoming stronger; and his mind is growing with new knowledge and discoveries. Jack is contented, peaceful, and looking forward to tomorrow. There will be times in his life, too, where he will need to shift into high gear and direct, say, 60% of his LEQ to a worthy creative project, which could result in more money. That is perfectly appropriate, just not sustainable. *Both Jill and Jack have made equally wise choices for these periods in time, but to be truly sustainable the LEQ needs to renew itself.*

> " An inspired spirit, healthy body, and creative mind build more powerful LEQ per hour of life available.

It is important when expending our LEQ that we do so with as much balance as possible, because the *spirit, body, and mind* comprise the home in which the LEQ resides. These three elements feed off each other, regenerating more LEQ. How can this be, if there are only twenty-four hours a day? More LEQ is created by increasing the life energy available per hour of life available. An inspired spirit, healthy body, and creative mind build more powerful LEQ per hour of life available.

Let's look again at Jill, whose LEQ is heavily focused on activities of the mind to earn her money. Over the short term, Jill has been giving up LEQ that could otherwise have been used to nurture good health and improve her fitness, spend time with friends and family, maybe go on a few dates, and explore new interests. This is not a problem in that time frame and is often appropriate when a creative project of some kind is underway. Over the long term, however, Jill is going to be out of balance, so this heavy expense of LEQ is not sustainable. Jill will likely end up stressed, and uptight. She will suffer physically, emotionally, and psychologically as cortisol, the stress hormone, wreaks havoc on her body and she runs down her sympathetic nervous system. Her spirit will also suffer, as she has no time or energy to exchange for quality meaningful relationships or the passionate and creative pursuit of other interests. And what is the point of the $33,000 earned weekly if she doesn't have the time to buy that beautiful home and enjoy living in it? Jill is in danger of manifesting the "dis-ease" in her emotions and spirit into a disease in her body, further weakening her LEQ.

▲ ▼ ▲

We can take back control of our lives when we recognize that more money is not always the answer. Money is only our tool, a means to an end. LEQ is the real treasure. The attitude we have toward money can be so much different if we realize what we have or don't have is based on our choices, habits, and often self-imposed limitations. That is empowering, because we can do something about it. Also, our relationship with money can improve dramatically when we see it as something to be played with in the act of creation. *True* wealth is the ability to direct our LEQ toward magnificent creations using what I call the 3 Root Resources: will, relating, and action. (More on these terms later, but I wanted to introduce them to you here to bear in mind.)

Rethinking Success

When most of us think about success, we think of material goals or achievements. We think of the worldly things and experiences we *want* to have. Some *want* that promotion, cool car, or a nicer house. Others *want* to travel more or retire at age fifty-five. Another may *want* to learn to play the piano, or to climb Mount Everest. All of these require us to get and spend more money.

Our mind immediately takes us to a vision of what we want to see materialize in our life, that which we currently feel we don't have. We can be either motivated by that vision or deeply discouraged. I would suggest that the more intense our wants and desires for what we don't yet have, the more dissatisfied we can become. How unfortunate. What we really need to ask ourselves is: why do we want that goal at all?

Do We Want Things or Feelings?

Why do we want money anyway? Why are our goals so often materialistic? Well, we are a "consumer-driven" society. We are bombarded daily by advertisements for all the items we should buy and all the experiences we should have to improve our lives. Advertisers know we just want to feel good, which is why they appeal to our desires to be more, have more, and do more. We need money for this, and lots of it.

But what do most people consider their *greatest* desire? If you ask them to state the "big picture" of what they really want more of in life, they aren't going to say "stuff." Assuming they have good health, they are more likely to say money, love, or freedom—or all three. Money brings power. Love brings meaning. Freedom is having the time to enjoy both. Most of us think that with money, love, and freedom, we will be happy. So, then, isn't happiness really what we all want, even if it is fleeting? And if we dig deeper, isn't our fundamental goal a feeling of contentment and fulfilment?

Money brings power. Love brings meaning. Freedom is having the time to enjoy both.

So *money, love,* and *freedom* are simply resources to achieve those long-term states of contentment and fulfilment. As we determined earlier, it's not really money that makes us happy; it's the *feeling* we get when we use money to feel safe or to experience or create something awesome. It gives us choice to decide what that next awesome thing should be. It isn't really just any love we want, but meaningful, compassionate relationships where we know we aren't alone and that someone loves us just as we are, unconditionally. We want to belong, to matter, and to *feel* supported always. In the end, it's not really even freedom we want, is it? In western society, most of us already have that. We live in countries where we are free to be ourselves, to make choices. Is it not the *feeling* of freedom that we really want? That feeling when we aren't rushed and running on adrenaline, or having boundaries imposed on us when we would otherwise use our time differently. Do we really just crave a life created and lived according to our own choosing?

The drive to find contentment and fulfillment spurs us on. Our desire "nature" has a purpose. Our evolution! This is the essence of personal growth or, as some would say, spiritual growth. But if that term makes you uncomfortable, perhaps we can speak of it from a more scientific perspective. We are talking about *our innate drive to evolve.* Spiritual growth and our drive to evolve is one and the same, a path along which your self-awareness and personal power grows. You can have all the stuff in the world, but if you aren't evolving, you're contracting. If you aren't growing, you're withering and dying. It is the way of the universe. If you're growing and evolving, you're more likely to experience contentment and fulfilment, even if you don't always feel happy. After all, happiness is a temporary emotion, not a core feeling, just as its opposite, sadness, is also temporary. Fulfillment is a more permanent state of serenity, acceptance, curiosity, and gratitude. It is a joyous state of being. Even sorrow can be experienced at the same time as serenity, acceptance, and gratitude. It has a flow and ease to it. A certain sustainable level of gratitude and contentedness can even be present in the aftermath of great tragedy. I have seen it in action, and likely so have you. I have personally known a few people who have suffered horrendous tragedy, like the violent death of a child. Yet, despite their gut-wrenching heartache, you feel joy in their presence. What coexists within them, and seems to lead them forward, is their joyous nature and love of living. To me, they are spiritually evolved people.

> **" Spiritual growth and our drive to evolve is one and the same.**

So it seems pretty clear that we all want the same thing. We want to feel peace, contentment, fulfilment, and joy. Yet we keep thinking we will find it by chasing after money, love, and freedom. The very act of chasing means we think we still don't have it. Or maybe we already do have it in some form, but we don't perceive that we do? What if we stop chasing? What if, instead, we remind ourselves to generate the feelings we want through gratitude for what we do have? Better still, what if we trained ourselves to generate those feelings regardless of what we have, but simply because we are alive to experience another day? Is that not almost the same thing? If you experience joy, peace, contentment, and fulfillment, do you really care where it comes from? And bonus: because you are generating the joy from the inside, independent of having something on the outside, you can never lose it! Various spiritual teachings tell us that this is our ultimate evolutionary mandate. By developing this innate evolutionary ability, we attain *True* wealth.

How Do You Evolve Your Goals and Yourself?

If we feel fulfillment by following our innate drive to evolve, how does an evolved person look and behave? What do they act like? Psychologist Abraham Maslow, best known for his eponymous hierarchy of needs, developed a theory of psychological health that culminated through the evolution of the self, what he called "self-actualization." He defines a self-actualized person as one who is living creatively and fully using his or her potential. He suggests that at any given time, each of us will be working with one or two aspects of ourselves, developing that particular potential through some form of creation, and that we will grow and change dynamically throughout life toward self-actualization. This is evolution. The self-actualized person is an evolved person. Let's have a look at the characteristics of self-actualized people to better understand what it must *feel like* to be them.

The following list is adapted from Maslow's *Motivation and Personality*,[3] in which he published the results of his private study on self-actualization. Characteristics of self-actualized people include:

- A more efficient perception of reality: Self-actualizers are able to detect the disingenuousness and dishonesty of people and judge them correctly and honestly.

- An acceptance of self, others, nature: Self-actualizers not only accept their own flawed human nature with humour and tolerance but also the shortcomings and contradictions of others.

- Reliance on own experiences and judgment: Self-actualizers are independent, not reliant on culture and environment to form opinions and views.

- Spontaneous and natural: Self-actualizers are true to themselves and aren't hung up on being as others think they should be.

- Task centring: Most of Maslow's subjects were generally strongly focused on problems or issues outside of themselves.

- Autonomy: Self-actualizers tend to be resourceful, independent, and free from reliance on external authorities or other people.

- Continued freshness of appreciation: Self-actualizers seem to have an "innocence of vision," like that of an artist or a child, in which they constantly renew their joy in the simple and natural. A sunset or a flower will be experienced time and time again as intensely as if for the first time.

- Profound interpersonal relationships: Self-actualizers develop deep, loving bonds in their interpersonal relationships.

- Comfort with solitude: Despite their social-mindedness and satisfying relationships with others, self-actualizers need solitude and are comfortable being alone.

- Non-hostile sense of humour: Self-actualizers like to laugh and joke but not at the expense of others.

- Peak experiences: All Maslow's subjects reported frequent peak experiences (temporary moments of self-actualization), which were marked by feelings of ecstasy, harmony, and deep meaning. Self-actualizers reported feeling at one with the universe, stronger and calmer than ever before, filled with light, beauty, goodness, and so forth.

- Socially compassionate: Simply, self-actualizers possess humanity.

- Few friends: Self-actualizers prefer a few close friends rather than many surface relationships.

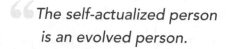

The self-actualized person is an evolved person.

In his preface, Maslow explains that the subjects of his study came from all walks of life. Geography, demography, and economic status were not relevant. *The monetary resources were unimportant. The number of toys, electronics, houses, and cars one had made no difference.* Included on the list were even those who experienced ill health or poverty. Maslow states that it was the attitude of the person that made the difference as to how they evolved. In other words, it was in their choices. *It was how they spent their LEQ.* It was in how they chose to react to the circumstances of their lives. In choosing to be empowered, and not to play the victim, they found this place of awesome feeling, this JOY, regardless of the things they did or did not have.

How did they do it? As I review the list, I see the following tools at work:

- Emotional maturity: They understand their emotions and the ability to flow with them, to not be absorbed by them or tell false stories about them.

- Awareness: They understand themselves and others. They use independent thought and are less tied to what is culturally accepted as the norm. Thus, they are evolutionary creators. They strive to live in truth and see the essential facts of situations while avoiding reactivity based on false beliefs about themselves or others.

- Gratitude: They are grateful for both the beautiful and the imperfect. They view life's challenges and sufferings as learning and growing opportunities.

- Profound relationships: Although they don't waste time on meaningless acquaintances, they still retain a compassion for all humanity. But if they can't be real with someone and share an energetically positive space, they will not engage. They develop and nurture deeply loving relationships with others (and themselves) and establish clear and respectful boundaries.

- Purpose: They have a reason for breathing, for getting out of bed in the morning, for living, for creating, for sharing.

So let me ask you: does it feel amazing to be evolved? To read the descriptions from Maslow's self-actualization study subjects—experiences of ecstasy, harmony, deep meaning, oneness with the universe, and so on—I don't know about you, but that sounds pretty awesome to me. I have never had a bank balance that made me feel like that (well, okay, maybe for a day or two, but certainly not in a sustainable way). I can't speak for you, but I am pretty clear that this is the goal I am going for in my life with my LEQ. It is how I intend to measure success.

I propose that the pinnacle of success for you and your family will be when each of you thrives. Some might achieve the highest levels of self-actualization in this lifetime, and others will still be on the path, working toward that point, at the end of their life. But perhaps, at the very least, we could all strive for what I think are very doable upward turns of the evolutionary spiral. You will learn more detail about the following in later chapters, but I want to introduce you now to the goals that form the basis of how your Family Treasury members will be encouraged to treat one another and themselves in developing these important self-actualization tools.

- Emotional maturity: Aim for detachment from emotions, meaning that you learn to feel and acknowledge them, respond where appropriate, and then let them go. Avoid creating family drama and stories over issues that are usually not about you yet may mirror something within you that needs to evolve.

- Awareness: Learn to calm the emotions so that your mind can perceive and you can respond with clarity about the truth of a situation, not what your reactivity would have you jump to assume is the situation.

- Gratitude: Nourish, appreciate, and even celebrate what you do have and value. When looking forward to how far you must go, remember to look back at how far you've come.

- Profound relationships: Strive for open, honest, vulnerable, and respectful communication with those you care about.

- Purpose: Strive for meaningful work that you are proud of and makes use of your unique talents and abilities. Find a purpose, regardless of whether or not you're paid for it, that is worthy of your life focus.

▲ ▼ ▲

Knowing that our fundamental goal is a sustained feeling of contentment, fulfilment, and joy helps us to understand that our life purpose is to evolve, not to chase money. In the act of evolving, we will generate all those incredible feelings that we think money will give us. Evolving empowers us to use money as a tool to create, knowing that it is the act of creating that will give us the most joy.

Rethinking Dreams

Having a great big dream is nature's way of pulling us into evolution. A big dream is not the same thing as a material goal, although it can include them. A dream is a big goal on steroids. We are meant to dream to evolve. Therefore, we must all have at least one, and it should be spectacular. It is the outer-stretch goal that helps us reach that fundamental inner goal of joy, peace, and fulfillment. It is expressed as a vision of your ultimate life expression. A dream imagines how you will be and what you will do, have, experience, and feel when you are living your potentials. When you stretch yourself for a dream, you leave your comfort zone and discover personal power you didn't know you had. You evolve to a new level, becoming a more whole person. Which is why we are all here. If you're not evolving, you're shrinking and dying. So dream big and stretch. Get comfortable being uncomfortable. The quality of your life, health, and bank account depends on it.

How much LEQ are you willing to put toward your dream? Probably most of it. How much LEQ are you prepared to convert to money to help you achieve that dream? That's hard to say, if you don't know the price of your dream.

As we've determined, money is a tool to create. And the very act of creating is a joyous process that helps us evolve into better versions of ourselves. Can we exchange our LEQ for money with sanity and harmony, knowing that the LEQ we invest is perfectly matched to what we want most out of life? Can we use our creativity and unique talents to naturally make more money? Yes, we can. How? By becoming clear about what we want most from life and then fearlessly directing our LEQ toward that in a focused way, step by step by step.

Whether or not you are financially wealthy, it's always a good time for some strategic planning.

Generally, most people have three main uses for their money. First, they want to fund their lifestyle, which includes their basic needs, of course, but preferably a little luxury too. Second, they may have a special dream they wish to achieve. Third, they wish to help their families do likewise.

> *Having a dream is nature's way*
> *of pulling us into evolution.*

To make achieving your dream possible, I suggest you answer these three questions:

1. What is your dream? It would be helpful to break down your "big picture" into goals and then objectives. Your dream should be a big stretch but also realistic, taking into consideration where you're starting from.

2. What is the price tag? Using the Capital Threshold technique (explained below), you can figure out not only the financial capital but also the human and social capital needed to achieve your dream, while maintaining a certain lifestyle.

3. What is your strategic plan? After comparing the price tag of your dream with your current resources, you can use strategic planning to close the gap.

What Is Your Dream?

What *is* your big dream? To help you articulate your dream in detail, ask yourself these two questions: What is the greatest vision for your life at this time, given your values and purpose? What do you want your future to look like? Your big dream should feel like a mountain you can't wait to climb.

To realize your big dream, of course you need to take action. To direct that action in a focused and efficient way, you need to set goals and objectives. Setting goals is part of the process of visualizing the realization of your dream. Picture yourself climbing that mountain and the landing points along the way. You need to have a clear vision of what the dream will look like, both the whole and its parts, for it to have a greater chance of manifesting. *Hint:* Your big dream has a higher likelihood of materializing if it is related to what you are passionate about. In setting goals, ask yourself ... when you realize your dream, what will it look like for you:

- spiritually

- financially

- physically

- relationally

- socially

These aspects are important parts of you as a whole person, so nothing but a holistic approach will do. In each of these categories, set goals that are specific, measurable, and realistic but still a stretch. They should fulfill your personal life desires, especially around money, love, and freedom. *Hint:* You have a much better chance of achieving your dream if it benefits not only you but others as well.

> *You have a much better chance of achieving your dream if it benefits not only you but others as well.*

Then, to ensure that you actually make the often-arduous climb up to that mountain peak, it is best to break down the journey into steps, and then take them one at time. Objectives are those steps, both short-term and long-term targets, that need to be met in order to achieve your goals. As the goals are achieved, so ultimately will be your dream. A strategic plan pulls all those objectives and goals together into a synergistic road map to guide you toward the big dream destination (more about this later).

Let's Look at Jack

Jack is a carpenter living in the city and working for a cabinetmaker. Yet he values fresh air, nature, and wide-open spaces. He dreams of building a log home and living a self-directed family life in the country. Yet he doesn't want to just up and leave his employer without giving him time to find a replacement. He knows he currently doesn't have the money to build the log home and support himself while he does so. You can see that Jack has been realistic about his starting point but is making himself stretch out of his comfort zone to visualize his dream.

In pursuit of his dream, Jack's list of goals might include: (1) become self-employed, (2) find the perfect homestead, and (3) create a cash reserve of $50,000. He is a darn good carpenter and could be of great benefit to the locals of a small town.

Here's how Jack broke down two of his more important goals into annual objectives:

- ✔ **Spiritual Goal:** Become self-employed (yes, this is a spiritual goal):

  - **Objective 1:** Build a website and use social media that clearly displays his abilities, talents, and offering, and keep it up to date.

  - **Objective 2:** Consider which towns he may wish to live in, research the competition, and use his network to create leads.

  - **Objective 3:** Complete competitively priced small contracts to establish a good reputation for his work in his chosen town, while transitioning out of his current employment.

✔ **Financial Goal:** Create a cash reserve of
$50,000:

- **Objective 1:** Evaluate his cash flow budget
  and cut discretionary spending to save
  enough dollars monthly into the reserve
  fund to meet the target in eighteen months.

- **Objective 2:** Set up a Tax Free Savings
  Account to protect the reinvested investment income on his savings from taxation.

To sketch out, or model, your big dream in such a way that you can grasp it quickly and view it regularly, a bubble chart is very useful. Businesses often use them. Figure 1 (see page 54) indicates some of the categories that you might consider when setting well-rounded goals and objectives. Of course, there are other ways of setting and documenting goals and objectives, so choose the method that suits you best.

▲ ▼ ▲

Whether the goal is to build a $400,000 log home, as Jack wants, or a $4,000,000 mansion, like Jill wants, the process is the same. Break the dream down into goals, and then the goals into short- and long-term objectives. *Then, let it go.*

Figure 1: Some categories of goals and objectives to consider when defining your dream

You might be surprised to hear me say that last bit—after all, I am a financial planner. But I say it deliberately and sincerely. Equally important to defining the plan in the first place is not fixating on the plan unfolding exactly as you imagined it. You have created the road map but won't know about the detours until you hit them. And there will be lots of those. The universe knows better than you do how to achieve your dream and get you to your destination, so hold the vision but be flexible about how and when you will get there.

What Is the Price Tag?

The price tag of your big dream comprises not only the necessary financial capital but also the human and social capital. ✓
Human capital refers to the value of a person's knowledge, experience, and talents. Social capital refers to a person's influential and supportive network. To begin, you first need to know the financial cost of your big dream in order to assess your ability to achieve it. We can get there by adding up the financial cost of each of your goals. Not all goals require money to achieve them, but frankly, most do. What is the cost to build and run that private school for special needs children? What is the cost to buy and renovate those buildings into office space? How much money will you need to take a family vacation together every year? And how much do you need to preserve for yourself (and your family) to live well while you strive for these goals? Of course, these estimates will be just that: estimates. The further out in time you go, the less accurate those estimates will be. Actual results will most certainly vary. But the inaccuracy of your initial estimates is not sufficient reason to bypass the exercise, since it lets you add another strategic layer of information to the road map you'll use to reach your destination, knowing that the detours you encounter along the way will help you refine those estimates.

Now having an estimate of the financial costs, special calculations take into account the future cash flows required to support your dream over time, inflation and tax adjusted, while meeting your lifestyle and financial security needs. In breaking down your future goals into separate cash flow streams, you are then able to assess the current financial capital required to meet each of them based on certain assumptions, such as inflation rates and investment asset returns. At my firm, we call these assessments *financial capital thresholds*. You can have a few of them. To say more about how these calculations work is beyond the scope of this book, yet it should be said that financial planners are best equipped to run these calculations as they have the necessary expertise and software systems.

Figure 2 is an example of how to price a family's big dream to leave work and focus full-time on charitable endeavours. Let's assume this is Jack, and he has a family. They want to set up and fund their own charitable foundation. They want to be able to support themselves but don't want to eat into the kids planned inheritance. Therefore, they need to know the capital thresholds (or price tags) to leave work, to set up the foundation, and to leave a bequest. We quantified their financial independence capital threshold (called lifetime living expenses), charitable giving capital threshold (called the charitable fund), and legacy capital threshold (called inheritance).

A bar chart shows the results. The vertical axis indicates the dollar amount: you can add as many zeros as you like, in that you could be talking about $16,000 or $16 million or $160 million; it works the same way. The two vertical bars compare a projection of Jack and his family's available financial capital

Figure 2: How to price a family's big dream

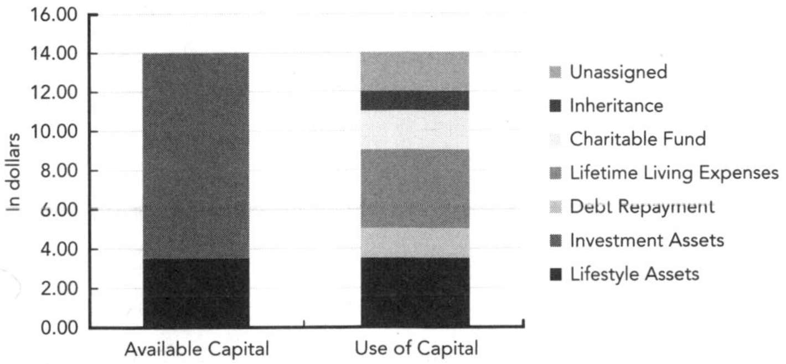

Source: Model designed by Brent Barrie, Family Office Director, First Affiliated Holdings Inc. By permission.

to the planned uses of that capital to meet debt obligations and each of the capital thresholds. Each capital threshold is expressed as either a one-time cost (for example, the donation establishing the charitable fund) or a cumulative capital requirement based on a stream of cash flows (for example, to fund debt repayment or lifetime living expenses). Thank goodness software is available to run these complex calculations, as they would be very difficult to do manually. This family now has the financial price tags on their big dream.

Let's Look at Jack and Jill

Let's assume that both Jack and Jill have families. We want to assess the financial price tag on their dream by looking at the capital thresholds of their various goals.

Over his working years, Jack has accumulated capital of $1,400,000. Of this, $350,000 is the value of his and his wife's log home. They have accumulated investment assets of $1,050,000. His wife is guaranteed a healthy teacher's pension when she retires. They want to know if they have the resources to pay off their debts, retire, set up a charitable fund, and leave behind some money for the kids. Figure 2 shows the results of running a series of cash flows to define their capital thresholds. This analysis shows them that they can keep their home for life while using their investment assets to pay off their debt, and set aside a financial independence capital threshold of $400,000 to supplement the pension and meet lifetime living expenses. They have sufficient monies to set up their charitable fund with $200,000 of funding and still leave an inheritance to the kids with a margin of safety left over.

Figure 2 can just as easily model a similar situation for Jill and her family, but with more zeros. Her financial independence capital threshold to fund her lifestyle living expenses is $4,000,000, and her philanthropic capital threshold to set up her charitable fund is $2,000,000. Of course, family dreams and goals will differ and their resources will be different;

> therefore, their capital threshold targets (and result-
> ing bar chart) will be unique to them.

Then let's consider the human capital needs to meet your big dream. What unique abilities are needed? What education might be required? What physical and spiritual goals need to be met? How much of your LEQ must be directed toward that?

And finally, look to your social capital needs. Who in your network of relationships can lend their support to your dream and how? Would seeking out new contacts, joining new associations, and developing new relationships be of value? Establish the goals and objectives and define how much of your LEQ will need to be directed toward that effort.

What Is Your Strategic Plan?

Now you're ready to document your financial, human, and social capital goals into a strategic plan. This plan lays out the specific objectives to be met along the way to achieving your big dream. Year by year, the strategic plan should assess how best to deploy your current financial resources, with your capital thresholds in mind, to meet your objectives. It should also address the dangers that could throw you off course and suggest methods to mitigate these risks. The strategic plan is a multi-faceted document and includes a financial plan that should consider the following:

- annual cash flow needs to meet your financial capital threshold goals, including securing financial independence, while at the same time achieving your human and social capital goals

- tax minimization strategies

- investment strategies, including establishing target returns needed to meet your goals

- risk management and insurance to protect your financial security

- estate planning to protect your legacy, including wills and powers of attorney

Figure 2 modelled a family that is projected to have enough financial capital currently to meet their lifetime needs (or is projected to meet them based on certain earnings and retirement assumptions). In fact, they are projected to have leftover capital not needed for their financial security needs. They can meet the financial price tag on their charitable giving goals, fund an inheritance, give up their full-time jobs, and not affect their current lifestyle. There is still an unassigned portion for them to use as they wish. How fortunate for them. They no longer need to direct a lot of their LEQ to manifesting money. The strategic plan will help them address where to spend their free LEQ, based on their values, toward the human and social capital needed to manifest their goals.

What if our scenario showed the family had a shortfall of financial capital compared with the price tag of their dream? That's the case for many people. The strategic plan would ask them to consider how much of their individual LEQ they are prepared to convert to money to reach the big dream. It would also look for ways to catalyze the conversion of LEQ to higher and higher amounts of money through education, risk-taking, savings, and investment strategy. In doing so, they would be growing their human and social capital at the same time. This is not about sacrificing your big dreams if your capital currently falls short. It is about reconsidering how badly you want those big dreams, what is most important to you, and then creating a strategic plan to achieve them using your LEQ in the most efficient manner possible.

We revisit these steps in more detail in Chapter 5 and 6, when applying them specifically to The Family Treasury processes. At that point, you will note that I speak more often in terms of vision, and less of the big dream. For many folks, the term "dream" reflects an unachievable reality, in other words, the stuff of dreams. The Family Treasury works with business concepts, and in business, we would use the word "vision" to reflect the same in a practical sense.

Rethinking Creativity

At the deepest levels of reality, you don't just "get" money, or love, or freedom. You *create* it. Although this thought might be a stretch for you right now, try to understand that you can create anything you want as long as you passionately *desire* it, *choose* to get it, and then take *action* to go after it. You create the money that begets more money. You create the good health that begets more good health. You create the love that begets more love. You create the time to beget more time and the freedom to beget more freedom. You create the imagination, knowledge, experiences, beliefs, and traditions that beget more of these but with an evolutionary upward turn of the spiral each time. As long as you *desire* something, make *choices*, and take *action*, you are in the act of creating. The quality of what you create depends entirely on how consciously you deploy what I call the 3 Root Resources: will, relating, and action. These concepts are discussed in depth in Chapter 3.

If you don't have what you want, it's because you haven't created it. You and you alone are responsible for applying your resources and creating the life you want.

> ❝ **If you don't have what you want, it's because you haven't created it.**

Now, perhaps you're thinking, "That's a pile of crap! I'm not responsible for losing my job when my employer went bankrupt. I'm not responsible for having cancer. I'm not responsible for being born with this disability. I'm not responsible for my addiction, it's a disease. I'm not responsible for being born into a family of poverty that can't afford to send me to school." Or you could just as easily be thinking, "That is ridiculous. I didn't create all this wealth. My parents did, and I simply inherited it." Or, "I didn't create this good health. I was born with good genes." So even those blessed with an abundance of a certain resource often don't feel empowered by it because they believe they have it out of luck. And they often feel a lack of resources in other areas.

I get it. The idea that we can create whatever we want may sound far-fetched. I myself am still trying to own it. Many of us face challenges that seem to impose boundaries on what we can achieve in this life. Plenty of real-world examples demonstrate how life can hand us circumstances beyond our control, situations we feel we didn't choose to create for ourselves. Esoteric philosophers and Buddhists would call it karma. Scientists would call it random bad luck. Religions would call it the consequence of sin. Whatever the cause, "shit happens." Did we somehow, back along the path of our lives, make choices that set things up for where we are today? Is there something significant for us to learn in every circumstance we face that can build our character and personal power? Is this shit we're dealing with really the growing pains of the act of creation? Is it possible we actually in some way did choose this for ourselves?

Well, that's a subject well handled in wonderful books written by other authors much wiser than me. My point is: I'm not talking about the circumstances of your life now, in the past, or in the future. I'm talking about your responses to them. *You have the innate ability to create whatever you really want, to have what you really want, working within, and regardless of, the circumstances of your life.* I am also suggesting that you can create anything you truly, really want. Please note that I said *truly, really want.* I did not say *kind of want.* I am not talking about cool things to do, have, or get either. I am not talking about genie-in-the-bottle stuff where—*poof!*—you think it and you have it. Creation takes commitment and effort. Therefore, you are not likely to achieve what you really want without a lot of time, effort, and courage—so you better really want it. It is also very important to know what you really want. Often we know what we don't want but have no clarity around what we do want. So, we get more of what we don't want because that is our focus.

> ❝*Creation takes commitment and effort.*

Let's consider what "a life worth creating" is for us. Is it possible that what we want to achieve, what we truly desire at the deepest level of ourselves, is not always what society and the advertisers tell us we should want? For example, let's look at health. Popular culture equates good health with high athletic-performance capability and perfectly tuned bodies. So for someone born with a severe physical disability who wants good health, is it realistic that he or she measure themselves against someone who wins the Ironman triathlon or climbs Mount Everest? Would that really even interest him or her? That person's benchmark for good health would be something quite different but still achievable.

Let's look at money. Society equates financial success with luxury cars and real estate. Is someone who just lost their job going to passionately dream of buying a lakefront cottage? No. They will likely focus on creating a stable and secure home for their family. Achieving that would feel like financial success to them, and appropriately so.

What if what we dream of is not just something "cool" that would temporarily make us feel "successful"? What if what we really and truly dream of is something that would bring us lasting joy, contribute to society, and, in its achievement, actually resonate with our talents and abilities?

The limitations and boundaries I highlighted above are merely examples of the reality many people find themselves in, usually through no fault of their own. What is their responsibility, however, is how they perceive that reality. Every single one of us has a choice: if not the ability to choose a different circumstance or a different body, then at least always the ability to choose how we will grow and evolve from where we find ourselves. The only people exempt from this responsibility are those who don't have a mature ability to choose or who are lacking the capability of mature self-direction, such as people with mental disabilities and children who have not yet matured into an understanding of cause, effect, and social responsibility. But make no mistake: even though they may lack the ability to self-direct with maturity, they can be very creative people.

When we stop feeling sorry for ourselves and the circumstances we have been dealt, when we choose to "make lemonade out of lemons," when we reject being a victim of the stories of our life—that is when the magic happens. That is when we take back our personal power and decide for ourselves what we want to create with what we have, and how that can give us more; then we can create still more with what we just created. No matter where we are, the 3 Root Resources (will, relating, and action) are always available to us.

It's important to understand that when I say "we can create anything we want," I'm not intending to be facetious. If we are honest with ourselves, we might all think it would be really cool to fly, but in all seriousness, it's not on our minds 24/7 as something to which we want to devote our time and energy. The person with a severe disability might think it would be cool to win a marathon, but if he was honest, that really isn't his dream. Maybe he passionately wants to be a surgeon. The person who just lost her job might think it would be fabulous to have a lakefront cottage, but if she were really self-aware she would realize that what she truly, really wants is to build financial independence. The person born into poverty might wonder about a life of great wealth and possessions but in reality is passionate about creating a home and foundation that can provide for the basic needs of life. *So we can all have what we truly, really want because what we really want is what we are here to manifest in the first place.* Despite our limitations, if we look closely, we'll see we already have certain talents and unique abilities that would support the creation of that higher reality for ourselves. We have all been given the ingredients (the 3 Root Resources) for success, and in putting together our strategic plan, we have created the recipe. How abundant our creations are depends on how good our recipe is. How good our recipe is depends on our level of consciousness and how well we understand the 3 Root Resources. Remembering always: *we alone are responsible for our creations.*

> " We already have certain
> talents and unique abilities that would
> support the creation of that higher
> reality for ourselves.

How Do We Create Abundance?

We need to better understand these ingredients—the 3 Root Resources—that we're using to create (or not create) our wealth of treasures. *How well you create with them, how abundant your manifestations become, depends entirely on you and how well you balance and harmonize them; how consciously you use them.* We go into that more in Chapter 3, but right now we are going to look at understanding *why* they are abundant, and yet why it often doesn't seem that way.

Everything Is Energy

Everything in the universe, including you and me, manifests from an infinite field of energy. The thing that lies around, within, and throughout everything is energy. All matter is made of vibrations, variations, and permutations of the energy field. At the deepest level—whether we're talking of a human, a tree, or a chair—we are all One, because we are all made of, and part of, the indivisible energy field. We only think we are separate because our five senses tell us so. In fact, we are a temporary conglomeration of vibrating particles all from the same bowl of soup.

Consider Albert Einstein's theory of relativity:

$$E \text{ (energy)} = m \text{ (mass)} \times c^2 \text{ (the speed of light squared)}$$

Einstein was telling us that mass and energy are each simply different aspects of the same thing. Mass is a tightly compressed manifestation of energy (measured by energy of motion of the object divided by the speed of light squared). What is energy, though? Energy is infinite. It has no beginning and no end. You are made of it and I am made of it. The trees, animals, rocks, Earth, and stars are made of it. Money is made of it. Since we are all made of it, we have it in us always. How it is compressed determines how it will manifest. A well-known definition in physics is that energy is a property of objects that can be transferred to other objects or converted into different forms but cannot be created or destroyed. If energy can't be created, and it can't be destroyed, then it is the only thing in the universe like that. All else is a temporary form, and comes and goes. Everything else is formed and then ultimately unformed. Even the granite rock of the Canadian Shield (some of which is 2.7 billion years old), black holes, stars, and our sun are gradually decaying back to their source. *So if energy can't be created, and it can't be destroyed, it was and is always present in infinite, unending amounts. We need only to shape it with our consciousness.* All your resources come from this abundant energy supply, so they, too, are limitless. The 3 Root Resources come from it. Will, manifesting as power, comes from it: a forceful expression of energy. Relating, manifesting as love, comes from it: a magnetic, drawing-together expression of energy. Action, manifesting as achievement, comes from it: a directional expression of energy. Money is a manifestation of energy. It is nothing more than concretized energy and so, too, is abundant and limitless. So why doesn't it appear that way?

> *We are all made of, and part of, the indivisible energy field.*

Mindfulness Is Awareness

Our resources don't appear abundant and limitless because of our limited consciousness. Ancient teachings speak of the Law of Mentalism, which tells us our individual experience is primarily mental. It is what we are conscious of. Our reality exists because of our thoughts about it. Our thoughts come from higher states of consciousness or lower "sleepier" ones.

For many of us, our consciousness is limited and therefore our perceptions are skewed.

A simple example is a warm sunny day. You want to go to the beach. The beach, the water, and the sunny day are there. You have a desire to go to the beach on the sunny day because of past experiences at the beach on sunny days that you decided, or *thought*, were good. Therefore, you will perceive this day as perfect and be happy—things are going your way. On the other hand, a road worker dealing with hot tar might perceive that same day as a bad day. He thinks of feeling very hot and uncomfortable from his past experiences, which have become memories. He will be troubled about it as he leaves for work, and his expectations will be fulfilled as his day unfolds.

Our life experience is due to our perceptions and beliefs about things. This is what the Law of Mentalism is about. People can and will have very different experiences from the very same occurrence—all due to thought forms, and which ones we choose to believe. A belief then moves energy to ultimately transform it into a manifest thing, like an emotion, a speech, or a skyscraper.

Most often, our thoughts go no further than emotion, which means we are operating at a lower form of consciousness. We all know what that's like, don't we? The emotion is usually fear-based and spirals downward into further limiting and destructive thoughts, leading to still more troublesome emotions. This leads to us feeling very limited. The good news is that we have choice. We can choose to practise mindfulness.

Mindfulness is the practice of paying attention to and acknowl-edging the present moment and noticing our thoughts and feelings about it. This brings awareness. With awareness, we can create whatever we *truly* wish by evolving our thoughts to higher and higher levels of consciousness. Our evolution is all about mastering our personal power by learning to watch and then redirect our thoughts into manifesting the lives we want to experience. I speak further on this in Chapter 5.

You are a body, emotions, thoughts, and a collection of beliefs and experiences. We call this a personality. Yet under all that, you recognize that there is "another you" in there, the one who observes the different parts of the self such as the body, emotions, mind, and behaviours. It is the knower, the witness, the inner wisdom, the inside voice that can be totally trusted because it speaks Truth. How conscious you are—and, therefore, how high the frequency of force that puts energy into motion—determines how creative you are and how innovative your creations will be.

> How conscious you are—and, therefore, how high the frequency of force that puts energy into motion— determines how creative you are and how innovative your creations will be.

That conscious knower gives us the vision pictured, our personality is the paintbrush, and pure energy is the canvas.

We have an unlimited supply of canvas, so you can create to your heart's content. The question is: what are we creating? The answer depends upon how evolved our personality and consciousness is.

A very wise lady—my meditation coach, Donna Mitchell-Moniak—pointed out something that helped me to understand the potentials that lie within the energy field. She said: "Science tells us that we are over 80% water. We feel very dense because of the density of the water. But within the water are the atoms with space in between. We are told that, in fact, we are 90% space. We are a coherent, temporary, collection of space and forces and particles. Think, therefore, how we can change to be physically, emotionally, and mentally whatever we truly want. We are one with the substance that creates everything so we can create anything. We are a coherent pool of awareness and power in that fluid space."

It is important to recognize here that Mitchell-Moniak speaks of our ability to change anything we want not only physically but also emotionally and mentally. This tells us, and science has shown, that we have an energetic field that is physical but also a higher vibrating field that is our "emotional body" and a still higher vibrational field that is our "mental body." Emotions and thoughts are things as well! They are manifestations, matter in a sense.

It's also important to make the distinction here between consciousness, self-conscious, and subconscious. Human beings are self-conscious; I mean this in the sense that we are aware of ourselves as conscious. There is enormous power in that. In addition, we have both the conscious and the subconscious parts of us. Our subconscious is considered to be the patterns, beliefs, programs, and memories that are deep within us, that we're not even aware of, that can often be the driving factor. Nevertheless, our subconscious affects the quality of our over-all consciousness and, therefore, the qualities of our creations. We can discover these unconscious patterns through, once again, mindfulness. Journaling can also help.

We are always creating, as we are always choosing—whether those choices are of a low or higher quality. It is true, then, that the energy of potential is all around us and endless. That is a good thing. Yet what an enormous respon-sibility we have when we finally understand that our level of consciousness will determine how everything around us manifests itself.

As we'll discuss in more detail in Chapter 3, the 3 Root Resources (will, relating, and action) are directed by the energy of consciousness. The quality of that consciousness—the level of frequency at which it puts energy in motion—will determine the qualities of the forms it produces. The more authentically tuned our consciousness is to our true poten-tials, the more evolutionary our creations will be.

To Think Is to Begin

The Universal Laws refer to the forces that without fail govern how everything works at its deepest levels. They are often also called the Laws of Nature. One of these, The Law of Correspondence, tells us that our outer world is nothing more than a reflection of our inner world. "As within, so without."[4] While Einstein thought energy changed form at the speed of light, later scientists have told us that energy transformation is instantaneous. Energy follows thought. *Therefore, our thoughts instantly create the energetic imprint of what we think about.* Yikes, how scary is that?! The more we think it, the more conscious we are of it, the more atoms and molecules gather together by resonating vibration to create the physical form. (Abundance in action!) So our outside life is a movie, a creation (some would say an illusion), reflecting what is going on inside with our thoughts. This is both inspiring and terrifying, is it not? If you think you are not worthy, not smart enough, not talented enough to have a big life, you will get a small one because you created that. If you think (and deeply believe) that you are brilliant, vibrant, and successful, your choices will come from there, and as a result, your outer life will reflect that.

Consciousness is the builder of form. The quality of the form is in direct relation to the quality of the consciousness, which is expressed through thought. If thought instantly imprints the scaffolding for the form to come, our way is cleared to begin the building process. What is not in our control, however, is how long that project might take. You must be patient and committed in following through with the significant responsibility we have within ourselves to determine how our dreams will manifest.

▲ ▼ ▲

Now that we've had the opportunity to rethink our beliefs about money, goals, dreams, and creativity, we have a better understanding that our personal resources and *True* wealth is so much more than just money. We know that *True* wealth exists when we develop our three forms of capital: financial, human, and social. We also know how to define our dream, assess its price tag, and develop a strategic plan of goals and objectives to realize it. *But what if your dream is so big that you won't be able to achieve it alone?* Have you ever considered how working with others in the act of creation, as a group united by a common vision, can enable you to accomplish so much more than the separate self can alone? Do you believe in "United we prosper, divided we fall"? Could that group be the people you care most about in this world? Next, let's challenge our definition of family and business to discover how the "business of family" can be a profitable one, especially when you apply the best practices of The Family Treasury model.

Rethinking Family
The Business of Family

▲ ▼ ▲

A Different Perspective

When it comes to the act of creation, a family united by a common vision can accomplish so much more than separate individuals alone. Also, true success is only achieved when all members of your family thrive. So whether you are a family without a business, are in business together now, or have never thought of being in business, you *are* already this—perhaps you've just never looked at it this way. Family business and the business of family can be the same thing. So to further prepare you for applying The Family Treasury model, let's define "family" and "business" in more detail and challenge you to look at your family from a different perspective.

The online edition of *Merriam-Webster Dictionary* defines family as "a group of individuals living under one roof and usually under one head."[5] Hmm, sounds much the same as most businesses. I usually define family as any group of two or more people who care deeply for each other (even if maybe they don't always get along!). This definition of family is not limited to blood ties. However, for simplicity I will refer to family throughout this book as the typical nuclear family, which includes grandparents (elders), parents, and children.

> *True success is only achieved when all members of your family thrive.*

So, what is business? In his book *The Leader Who Had No Title*, Robin Sharma defines business as a forum to bring "people together around some marvelous dream that inspires them to express the fullest of their talents and contribute rich value to those they serve."[6] Couldn't a family likewise hold some collective wonderful dream? Couldn't they also do their utmost to support each other, express their talents, and contribute value to the other family members? Sharma continues, "The main business of business is to connect with—and add value to—people."[7] Doesn't that also sound like a family? Whether or not you work together formally in your own commercial family business, you still have the core attributes of what makes up a business.

Also, business is not just a thing, it is an action. *Merriam-Webster Dictionary* online defines business as "the activity of making, buying, or selling goods or providing services in exchange for money."[8] Isn't pretty much everyone in your family over the age of eighteen "in business" then (or at least we would hope so)? So if every adult in your family is "in business," then perhaps all that is missing is your recognition that if you work together in a cohesive fashion toward some terrific dream, then you have become an enterprise—in other words, a "family in business."

If you need further proof of the parallels between family and business, let's look at *Merriam-Webster*'s definition of enterprise: "a project or activity that involves many people and that is often difficult."[9] Definitely sounds like a family to me!

We know that the long-term success of a business depends upon many factors:

- a clear group mission to give direction
- the motivation that comes from expressing unique talents
- teamwork to enhance results
- continuous attention and enormous effort
- policies and procedures to prevent chaos
- the excellence that comes from education, training, and best practices

- the continuous reinvestment of all of the above

So why should the long-term success of a family require anything less?

Whether or not your family is in business together, The Family Treasury can work for you because *it's not so much about families in business as it is about the business of family*. The cornerstone belief of The Family Treasury is that business is a beautiful thing. Your family need not work together in the same business to be in the business of family. The Family Treasury models itself after business while not necessarily being *a* business. Business creates the goods and services our society needs to function. It also generates the careers and jobs we hold and the money we earn. In business, we can grow as people, stretch our creativity, and work together as a team to realize a fabulous dream. We help one another to be the best we can be, learn life lessons, and find a place of belonging. When done well, business can be a sustainable success not just to benefit the current participants but also subsequent generations. This does not occur by luck. It happens when conscious attention is focused on implementing learned best practices and applying discipline and commitment to follow them through.

> *Your family need not work together in the same business to be in the business of family.*

Doesn't our family life deserve at least as much effort, concern, and care as our business life? I think so, which is why The Family Treasury was developed.

The Family Treasury seeks to turn the management of *all* your wealth resources into a sustainable, for-profit business enterprise, including:

- your money-making financial capital (such as operating businesses and investment portfolios)

- your just-as-valuable human capital (such as your will and creativity, the quality of your relationships, and the effectiveness of your family as a united team)

- your just-as-valuable social capital (honouring your networks and community impact)

You may be having trouble seeing your family working together in harmony toward some wonderful group mission. Perhaps many of your family relationships are less than functional. Dare I say it out loud? You may not even like some of your family members. We all have family relationship challenges, as it is the burning ground for our most dysfunctional behaviours and evolutionary impulses. So why do we think there is no place for best practices, mission and vision, strategic plans, and team-building exercises in family? Why do we allow family dysfunction to continue for years, causing ongoing damage, when we would not tolerate it in business? Could family dysfunction partly stem from the fact that the core principles that make a business successful are often misunderstood or simply ignored in the functioning of most families?

The State of Today's Family

A business manifests the three things most of us want more of: money, love, and freedom. If successful, a business makes *money*, which when reinvested creates more money and further opportunity. A thriving business has people working within it who *love* what they do and keep coming back each day with the aim to grow for the long term. They are committed to supporting each other in the expression of their unique talents for the good of the entire group, not just themselves alone. Even if they don't form deep friendships, they respect and care for each other's well-being. If sustainable, a business provides a supportive platform that allows its people the *freedom* to be creative, to sculpt their lives as they wish, and to create something of value for customers or clients.

Family is already structured much the same way as business, and serves pretty much the same function: it creates. Can we all agree that, in principle at least, we are stronger together than we are alone? Many hands make light work. United we stand. Do we not feel safer to express ourselves when we know someone has our back? We are more willing to take risks, to stretch into our potentials when the possible fall is well cushioned. Is a loving family network not then a super power? Strength and power comes from knowing you are loved—no matter what mistakes you make—and that you are valued. We are, at our very core, pack animals who need a group for protection and also to thrive. We need each other to create magnificence.

> " Can we all agree that, in principle
> at least, we are stronger together
> than we are alone?

Too often, though, family just creates a mess because its true potential is not understood in today's western society and, thus, is ignored and mismanaged. Despite the technology to keep us plugged in and interacting with each other, our culture has actually become divisive and isolating, and we all feel like we're "out of time" all the time. As parents, we are told to always set a fine example, avoid exposing our children to our crap, and to argue and fight in private or, preferably, not at all. It is expected that parents always have it together, make a great income, keep a clean home, have all the latest stuff, go to all the cool places, have perfect kids in clean clothes who get straight As in school while being superstars in music, athletics, and the sciences and who never do drugs, drink, or swear. Oh, and we've got to look great doing it all! No wonder we're exhausted and too busy to notice anything other than the to-do list.

But young people today might actually have it worse. In western society, those who grew up with baby-boomer parents experienced a lifestyle like no generation before them.

The vast majority of baby boomers made and spent money at an unprecedented level of abundance. Their homes have multiple TVs and computers, tablets, and smartphones, and they've travelled as a family to countries that just thirty years ago only a select few were lucky to experience. Their kids got new clothes whenever they liked, they participated in multiple activities and sports teams (often with the latest equipment), and many had the latest technology, digital media, and trendy gadgets at their fingertips. Baby boomers' kids grew up having so much. After the baby boomers came Generation X, and they and their kids lived pretty luxuriously too. But now as young people reach the age where they should leave home and live on their own, they're discovering (with a shock) that they can't afford a home (let alone a rental apartment), a car, and, for many, a post-secondary education. Some struggle to pay for healthy groceries. Many are still living with, and being funded by, their parents, in some cases well into their thirties. We as parents hoped our kids would grow up confident, happy, and independent. For too many, the opposite has been the result.

Let's look at some of the Canadian statistics that reflect the environment in which our young people are seeking to get established:

- According to the Canadian Real Estate Association, the average Canadian house price increased from $142,091[10] in 1990 to $418,786[11] in 2014, an increase of 195%.

- Over that same time period, Statistics Canada reports that the median Canadian household income increased from $55,000[12] to $78,870,[13] just 43%.

- Statistics Canada also reports that the ratio of debt to disposable income was .89 in 1990 and had grown to 1.63 by 2013.[14] In other words, the average Canadian family carried $1.63 of debt for every $1 of disposable income.

- A 2014 *Globe and Mail* story on the cost of car insurance cites that a twenty-year-old male driver in Toronto could pay in excess of $7,000 per year. [15]

- A CBC News report points out that the average university tuition costs (when adjusted for inflation) were $2,243 annually in 1990, had tripled by 2013, and were expected to reach $6,482 annually by 2017.[16] (This is nothing compared to the escalating cost of housing and food.) Yet, a study published in 2014 by Workopolis, the online job search engine, showed 77% of those polled reported working in a job unrelated to their education.[17]

- In 2013, the Organisation for Economic Co-operation and Development reported that Canadians consumed 85 doses of antidepressants daily per 1,000 people. We ranked third highest in the world for antidepressant use.[18]

The world was a very different place for baby boomers than it is for their children today. But as baby boomers near their senior years, they will not be immune to the changes taking place.

Another change that has affected us greatly is that our society has become isolating and divisive. We believe that we must compete with each other to get ahead, to get our hands on what we believe to be rare and scarce resources. Even within our own families, we expect that once our children reach their early twenties, they will "strike out on their own," "leave the nest," and become self-reliant. We believe that they'll be able to support themselves so that we no longer need to. We also expect that our own parents will be self-reliant and not need to be physically or financially cared for by us. Statistics show that this ideal of "making it on your own," becoming totally self-sufficient, maybe isn't working out so well. The repercussions of this "failure" are a sense of shame, disappointment, and, often, strained relationships in families. Our isolating do-it-yourself attitude is screwing us up!

Yet so many believe it's a "good thing" for the next generation to scratch and claw their way out of a deep dark well on their own. Would it hurt to toss them a rope? Or even better, hand them a ladder? They still make the climb, they still build character and gain experience, but with much less anguish. The support and encouragement they are given through that lifeline significantly increases their chance of successfully finding their way.

And with the preceding generation—why do we believe it's okay to expect our parents to continue to go it alone? Why should they not need our assistance, financially and physically if not emotionally, just because they came before us? If the younger generation has more financial resources than the one that came before it, why not spend some of those resources on the elders, as they did for us many years earlier? Is it silly pride that prevents the generations from sharing the joy of money with each other?

On top of these stressors comes the fact that we aren't given a *Handbook for Loving, Supportive Family Relationships* to teach us how to be excellent parents, grandparents, and kids. We try to teach ourselves what we can and we learn from experience, but mostly we fumble through it with inconsistent results. Unlike a successful business that follows its business plan, we don't have a successful family plan. Unlike a thriving business that uses policies and procedures to reduce risk and maximize profitable results, families have to shoot from the hip. Unlike a sustainable business that expects you to treat fellow teammates with respect and to control your emotions to maintain professional integrity at all times, we dump all our crap on our family members because we can.

> 66 *Unlike a successful business that follows its business plan, we don't have a successful family plan.*

So what would happen if, instead, your family came together to agree on common values that gave you a clear identity of who you are and what you are about? What if you were unified as a family with a common mission and had a strategic plan outlining how you would each work to support one another to achieve the goals of that plan? What if, as a family, you found a structure and process that could pool your resources in such a way as to empower your results by magnifying your opportunities? What if you saw yourselves as a loving family—as well as a kick-ass team—that knows you are so much stronger and impactful together, if you realized that your own objectives could be met more easily if you also worked together to achieve a grander group objective?

The "business of family" would happen, that's what. Through the application of The Family Treasury model, your family could become a tool of empowerment for generations to come.

A Rope, a Ladder, or an Elevator?

Let's return to the deep dark well for a moment to better understand how the business of family best empowers. Without some help from those who went before, who now stand in the light at the top of the well (we hope), those at the bottom have little chance of climbing out on their own. So at the very least, we can throw them a rope (and a rope might be the only tool a family can afford at the time). Or, even better, we can hand them a ladder. In both cases, they must still find their own personal power, develop their own strengths and capabilities, take risks, set goals, and work one step at a time to get to the top. A rope will likely get them out of the well, but their climb will still be pretty extreme, their hands a little bloody, their spirits somewhat deflated. If we can hand them a ladder, they are more likely to get to the light faster and unhurt, grateful and energized to take on the next challenge life brings their way. It's up to you to decide what makes the difference between a rope and a ladder.

However, I do not advocate building them an elevator! No doubt they'd be lifted into the light with speed and comfort, but what have you done for them? You have taken away their personal power. They didn't have to exercise and discover their own muscle. They didn't learn to put one step in front of the other to reach a goal: it was just handed to them. They were robbed of the joy and satisfaction of a job well done. The adventure that self-discovery can bring was stolen from them. You eliminated opportunity for them to build their self-confidence. Plus you would have expended great resources to build that elevator—and for what? A moment of ease and happiness, perhaps, but you eliminated their opportunity to develop their abilities, talents, and knowledge.

To continue the analogy, you'll need to decide if the next generation's mobility will be supported by a bike, a used car, or a brand-new Mercedes–Benz. You'll need to decide if the educational opportunities will be funded by part-time jobs and student loans, part-time jobs and matching no-interest loans from you, or blank cheques and credit cards. You'll need to decide if the next generation will be asked to leave the house at eighteen and find their own way, invited to live at home while they save funds for their first apartment, or simply handed a house of their own.

For those with limited financial resources, such decisions might be easier to make. They become much more difficult if the family has ample financial resources and the kids know it! As a starting point in determining rope, ladder, or elevator, you may want to consider these guidelines:

- ✔ Our impact will be one of empowerment (not disempowerment).

- ✔ We seek to use our resources in a sustainable yet expanding way.

- ✔ Decisions will consider the well-being of the group as well as the individual.

- ✔ We will do no harm.

▲ ▼ ▲

The Family Treasury model is based upon the foundational understanding that a family already acts much the same as a business does, albeit all too often a dysfunctional one! Using best practices and proven processes, The Family Treasury enhances the power of the family team to achieve its objectives. It recognizes that with the proper tools, awareness, and attitude, and a network of supportive professional advisers, a family can be stronger and more impactful together than they can apart. By combining the principles and operating frameworks of successful strong businesses with those of successful strong families, *True* wealth can be created and sustained, enabling all family members to thrive.

If you're inspired to take the next step, let's apply what we've learned so far to discover how the "business of family" can be a profitable one when you adopt the best practices of The Family Treasury model. The remaining chapters outline in detail the three systems for *True* family wealth creation through The Family Treasury. They are STEWARDSHIP through a worthy mission, DEVELOPMENT through loving relationships, and a LEGACY of achievements through action. You can do this because each is an extension of the 3 Root Resources, which you already have within you. Let's take a look at those first.

The Family
Treasury Systems

The 3 Root Resources

▲ ▼ ▲

As you have by now deduced, *True Family Wealth* is not about families in business. It is about the business of family. It is about cultivating all the treasures of that family. If you could find a place to protect and preserve your treasures, would you consider it? What if this place also helped you and your family to grow those treasures? And what if you learned that this place doesn't exist somewhere "out there" but is right within your family? The Family Treasury is that place.

So how can The Family Treasury model make a family's future bigger, brighter, and better than its past? It renders what I call the 3 Root Resources—*will*, *relating*, and *action*—which we all have in abundance, into systems that The Family Treasury refers to as a worthy *mission*, loving *relationships*, and many *achievements*. How can we magnify the impact of these resources and allow the family to evolve to higher levels from a platform of balance and harmony? We do so through the power of triangles.

The Power of Triangles: A Primer

The equilateral triangle is the strongest geometric form known on Earth. It has been used since time immemorial to build stable structures such as buildings and bridges. Why is an equilateral triangle so strong? Because all three of its sides are of equal length, which means that its three angles are fixed at the same degree. The only way to weaken this type of triangle is to lengthen or shorten one of its sides. *But when in perfect balance, the triangle is powerful and enduring* (think of the pyramids).

> ❝ *When in perfect balance, the triangle is powerful and enduring.*

3 Primary Energy Forces

Triangles (trios, trinities, triads) are also significant symbols when comprehending the realms of the universe that influence our physical experience. According to esoteric psychology, the universe comprises three primary energy forces, or streams. Tibetan masters call these streams the three rays of *will*, *love*, and *intelligence*. Conventional scientists label them as energy, consciousness, and matter. My emphatic use of italics throughout the past two chapters might help you recall that I've referred to these same three energy forces in various ways. They manifest as *spirit, body,* and *mind; will, consciousness,* and *form; purpose, love,* and *intelligence; desire, choice,* and *action;* and *money, love,* and *freedom,* to name a few. These are all different expressions of the same thing and align with our 3 Root Resources described earlier (*will, relating,* and *action*), as well as the three systems within The Family Treasury (*mission, relationships,* and *achievements*).

These forces pervade everything and are everywhere. They all refer to, and form, the three corners (or points) of the triangle. You are living the universal triad in harmony when your will through a worthy mission is in balance with relationships that are loving and supportive, which in turn are in balance with your actions—and the result is achievements that are powerful and enduring.

Balance Equals Strength

For our purposes, Figure 3 illustrates a fundamental triangle for individuals, for businesses, and for The Family Treasury. When in perfect balance, or harmony, the triangle is very strong and can withstand a great deal of outside pressure. If any one of the angles is out of balance, or harmony, with the others, the triangle is weakened substantially when outside pressure is applied. And how do we know when we are in balance? Our spirit will tell us because we feel joy and

Figure 3: Fundamental triangle of energy forces for an individual, a business, and The Family Treasury

contentment. Our body will tell us because it feels energetic and lively. Our mind will tell us because it will be quiet, calm, and clear. And yes, I acknowledge that in the real world, this balance will be difficult to maintain, or we may only reach it for moments in time. But our goal is to continually strive to rebalance the triangle, no matter what the real world throws at us. It's how we evolve. Let's look at each triangle separately.

The Individual Triangle

The three primary universal energy forces of *will*, *relating*, and *action* are commonly referred to as the *spirit*, *body*, and *mind* when embodied in an individual. Will manifests in our spirit for life. Relating manifests in the interconnectedness of our body with itself and others. Action manifests first within our thoughts. You'll recall that in Chapter 1, Jack exemplified someone who applied his Life Energy Quotient (LEQ) wisely to achieve and maintain balance in his life. He exchanged a smaller percentage of his weekly available waking LEQ for money, which left him more LEQ for his sports/fitness activities and healthy eating habits, his family and friends. He also had time to enrich his mind with his woodworking, and time for lazing around enjoying nature in contemplation. His spirit, body, and mind received more balanced attention than did those of his counterpart, the overworked senior lawyer Jill. Jack remains contented, peaceful, and looking forward to tomorrow. He is alchemizing his LEQ into many resources, not just money, and through the harmonization of spirit, body, and mind, he supercharges that LEQ for greater results.

The Business Triangle

A common business model demonstrates *will*, *relating*, and *action* as the three Ps of success: passion, people, and profits. Passionate leaders create the vision, which fosters a positive culture in which people/employees thrive, which in turn transforms the collective intelligence into products and services that customers and clients buy. If owners lack passion and operate without a clear purpose, the business will have weak results. Similarly, when passionate owners haven't managed to attract positive people (rather, their employees are unmotivated, unskilled, hate coming to work, and don't like each other), the business will have weak results. Likewise, if passionate owners can't act to manifest their and their team's collective knowledge into a product or service that sells, the business will have weak, if not zero, results. However, when all three Ps are maximized, the business will thrive. In fact, the stronger the passion, people, and profits, the stronger the business grows, which in turn further reinforces the passion, people, and profits. As long as the triangle grows in balance and harmony, the results will spiral ever higher.

The Family Treasury Triangle

The *will* energy force is dynamic, direct, purposeful, strong, single-minded, focused, and can be ruthless. It's power and impulse. It's the drive to reach the goal. It can be experienced as an innate urge or a desire to achieve and evolve. It's the intention. It may be ferocious. The Family Treasury deploys *will* as System I: Stewardship through a Worthy *Mission*.

The *relating* energy uses the method of "gathering in," or "drawing into," as in love. It's the relating principle, and therefore the duality. There is a "you" and a "me," an "it" and a "that." It creates the illusion of separation so that we can perceive it. It's the knowing of something and the wisdom of gathered experiences and perceptions. It's also often known as the Law of Attraction. Being gentle and a line of least resistance, its magnetizing vibration, when set in motion, begins to resonate and draw like to like so that we may reach the goal. We experience it in the manifested world as relating to ourselves and to each other. It's the target of our wanting and desires, the impulse that begins to magnetize energy into a particular form. We either resonate well in creative flow or we do not, and are in "dis-ease" and destruction with ourselves and each other. The Family Treasury deploys *relating* as System II: Development through Loving *Relationships*.

The *action* energy carries forward the recognized plan to a goal intelligently determined. Its highest expression is education and evolution through experience. It's about mental illumination and the power to take action and produce results. It blends the will resource and relating resource to produce the forms of life, to manifest. The Family Treasury deploys *action* as System III: *Legacy of Achievements*. It is through taking action that we gain experience, which improves our next actions and experiences, until we become so refined we achieve the goal.

Bringing the Triad into Balance

If we all have this fundamental triad in our constitution as humans, why do so many of us have trouble manifesting what we want in life? If we all have the 3 Root Resources in endless supply, why does money, love, and freedom seem scarce? We might have a goal, perhaps some loving relationships, but our achievements seem lacking. We might have tons of money, but our relationships are suffering. We might have lots of freedom of, say, time, but no money. We might have loving relationships but can't make ends meet.

To live a whole, big life, we need to balance all three energy forces to achieve the strongest results. *Remember: Finding balance does not always require equal effort to each energy force but dynamic, responsive attention to all.* Most often, we spend all our time on one resource to the sacrifice of the other two.

Our triangle is not equilateral, but lopsided. Our three-legged stool is tippy. This is the biggest challenge we have, and it is pervasive in all cultures and societies the world over. A lack of understanding of these resources, their misuse and their misunderstood power, is what holds most of us back from achieving our biggest desires. This is where the work is.

> 66 *Finding balance does not always require equal effort to each energy force but dynamic, responsive attention to all.*

Everyone is born with the resources to evolve, which is our reason for being, our highest purpose. Every living thing on the planet is comprised of the 3 Root Resources in one form or another. We all have an evolving purpose, a way of relating (conscious or not), and an impact on something else. Everything has a job to do. Humans, however, are in the unique position of having self-consciousness and, therefore, the ability to self-direct how our resources will manifest in an intended, creative manner.

The rest of this book outlines the ways to manifest your energy resources into reality in a balanced, renewable, abundant way. This is what The Family Treasury is all about: a powerful, strong, energetic, and physical engine of amazing creative potential that allows a family to grow, evolve, and renew itself.

Are you and your family committed to do the work to create the results that you really, truly want? It will be a life-long process, so the decision to commit should not be taken lightly. The results are worth the investment, though. Without spirit, body, and mind, you don't exist. With a stable spirit, body, and mind, you exist with potential. But when you nourish your spirit by generating passionate will toward a worthy *mission*, your spirit rewards you with joy. When you *relate* to your body with the purest foods and to your *relationships* with the purest intentions, your body rewards you with bountiful energy. When you use your mind with the correct discipline of thought, emotion, and speech, your mind rewards you with clarity and peace. Working together as a trinity, these aspects spiral your potentials upward into a force for active creation, and the trinity rewards you with a life of many *achievements*. This is how *True* wealth is created. The Family Treasury systems support that.

The Family
Treasury System I
*Stewardship through
a Worthy Mission*

▲ ▼ ▲

What Makes a Good Wealth Steward?

Wealth stewardship is a developmental process promoting wealth preservation as opposed to wealth consumption. To be successful, The Family Treasury relies on its wealth stewards to be supportive, accepting, and willing to communicate openly and respectfully. This is necessary in order to create a safe place of equality for all persons where decisions are made and action is taken based on factual truths, not false interpretations based on self-created beliefs. The Family Treasury environment must be one of encouragement, not sabotage. Irrational beliefs created to support the status quo of a limited self-view and limited life will only destroy The Family Treasury and the unity of the family itself.

A wealth steward, then, is one whose actions and values embody a respect for the nurturing and sustainment of resources, whether financial or otherwise. The position calls for a level of competence, trust, and integrity that is both natural and learned. It requires an understanding of what it takes to create wealth and to keep it. It also requires a healthy attitude toward risk and reward as opposed to risky and wasteful behaviours. A wealth steward sees the care of resources as both a privilege and a responsibility, not as an entitlement. He or she understands that the resources passed into their care are not for their sole use but for the good of the family. To be an excellent wealth steward demands a fairly high level of self-confidence, acquired knowledge, and emotional maturity. If we are not wealth stewards, we are wealth consumers. Ideally, all members of The Family Treasury develop as wealth stewards. But this characteristic is imperative of the leadership: they are the keepers of the purpose, or mission, of The Family Treasury. They must have and hold the will, the passion—the 1st of the 3 Root Resources—and by example, commitment, and leadership, steward the family toward the accomplishment of that mission.

> **If we are not wealth stewards,
> we are wealth consumers.**

Those who inherit wealth resources, financial and otherwise, stand to thrive or be destroyed depending on their level of self-identity and their preparedness for the responsibility and privilege wealth brings. Self-confidence, acquired knowledge, and emotional maturity are not possible without strong self-awareness and self-worth. In other words, someone with low self-esteem will not likely be successful as a wealth steward for they aren't empowered by the inner strength and confidence to "do the right thing" for the good of the group, even if that might be unpopular with some. If they don't believe they have an ability to succeed, they won't take the risks of contributing their best. Strong self-esteem is, in turn, fostered by an understanding and expression of what makes each of us unique and useful. That individualization helps us identify healthy boundaries so that we can be both a unique and valued separate person and a valued member of a group. Therefore, identifying our own talents and our own particular purpose for this life is imperative to developing the life stability and emotional maturity of a good wealth steward. It is also imperative to the success of The Family Treasury, which relies upon wealth stewards to manage its resources for the good of the broader group in a sustainable way.

Your Personal Purpose

Knowing the purpose behind The Family Treasury leads to the definition of its mission. Inspiring the family to support the mission leads to its achievement. But before the mission of The Family Treasury can be defined, before the family will support the mission, and before great achievements can be realized, each wealth steward needs to find (or rediscover) their own personal purpose and have a plan for how to achieve it. A strong sense of self-worth is energized by having a personal purpose and mission that embraces your unique talents and leads you on a path of personal growth.

Discover Your Purpose

If you're reading this book, you've probably already found a purpose that got you to this point. You know how it feels, don't you? It gives you a feeling of belonging, of contribution, of being needed and even wanted. It gives you a reason to get out of bed in the morning. If you're lucky enough to have a purpose that can be expressed through your work, then you're very fortunate indeed to be spending most of your waking hours living your purpose. If you're using your natural-born talents to express that purpose, then you're probably achieving some success. You may even be well known for what you do and lead a large group of people who are part of delivering that purpose to the world. But, now, that can become a problem too.

Are you someone who, along the way, allowed your purpose to consume you? Has your will to achieve turned good stress into bad stress? With everyone dependent on you, are you working all the time, and are your relationships and health suffering? "There's just not enough time in the day," you say. You don't know how to get off the treadmill without losing everything you have built. Sound familiar? You have lots of money but freedom is scarce and your relationships suffer. Do you feel that you've stopped creating and are just maintaining? Trying to hold on to what has already been lived, what has already been done? How does that feel? Flat? Well, you need a new purpose.

And if you can't relate to any of this, is it possible that you've not found your purpose? Are you wandering from day to day, living in fits and starts, and, frankly, rather bored? This too causes great stress on the body and spirit. It can lead to despondency and malaise that is difficult to rise above. You have lots of free time, and maybe money, but your relationships are likely strained due to your unhappiness.

Having a purpose is an antidote in all of the above circumstances. Having a purpose empowers you to build upon your innate strengths, gain clarity of direction, and with self-confidence design a mission that directs you toward the achievement of a lofty and worthy life vision. That is a core element of creation. It is how evolution happens. It is the energy and commitment that transforms where we are today to where we wish to go in a conscious and catalyzing manner.

Formulating your personal purpose begins with looking back to your core values, unique talents, and passions. Your values should guide your priorities in life. By determining those values, you can identify your "calling" in life. In identifying your calling, you can discover, or rediscover, your purpose, which is to express your strengths and talents in some useful manner out there in the world.

When you focus on what is really important and set your priorities around that, you'll find that the universe organizes time and opportunities to help you reach your goals. *If you're spending time doing something you don't value to try to get something you do, your stress and negativity will likely prevent you from getting the very thing you want.* If you're miserable going to a job every day that isn't in keeping with your values just to get money, it will eat away at you emotionally and physically, eradicating your creativity and sapping your 1st Root Resource, your will. You will likely not get much of the money in the end either.

If The Family Treasury is something you want in your life, it cannot be created without your full, honest presence and contribution. Its unified mission comes from aggregating the purposes and talents of the underlying treasury membership—that includes you—in such a way that the sum of the parts equals a greater whole. Synergies are created that act as a catalyst to the creative potential of the group, thereby enhancing both individual and group ability to reach the stated goals and fulfill their purposes.

What's Your Calling?

Once you reach maturity and independence, it's up to you to define your calling in life. A calling is an inner drive to express yourself in a very specific way. It's your passion. It's discovered through awareness of your unique set of values that you have come to naturally identify yourself with. When you identify your calling, you'll notice that you have certain natural talents that support the expression of this calling. And you'll further discover that when incorporated into your life, expressing your calling brings you great joy. *You will know you have found your calling when you lose all track of time while doing it, when you are really good at it, and when you would do it whether or not you got paid.*

> **" You will know you have found your calling when you lose all track of time while doing it.**

Your calling may or may not be your career. If it is, great! You get to do what you love to do every day and make money doing it. We must not assume, however, that our calling will always be expressed through our job or career. For example, your passion may be to work with the rehabilitation of rescue animals. This is usually a volunteer or low-paying position, because it is a not-for-profit enterprise. It has no services or products to sell in exchange for other services, products, or money. So you may choose to get a job or develop a career that earns you enough to meet your lifestyle expectations but also allows you ample time to express your calling.

Your outer purpose is to perform your calling, or your special vocation, which may or may not also be your career, as part of your daily life. When you do that, you set in motion energy that brings more opportunities to grow within that vocation, continually creating higher levels of contribution to society and your own life. When we recognize our calling, it becomes our purpose to express it in the world, and it feels so natural and good that we become empowered to use our unique talents to create our current life mission.

Identify Your Calling by Determining Your Values

To help you identify your calling, I have designed the following simple process. Table 1 provides a list (albeit not an exhaustive one) of potential values. Values are words that express your deep sense of what is important in your life. They are more than a moral code. They are ingrained in you as qualities of expression that are so important to you that you feel physically unsettled if you don't live true to those qualities. They aren't "things" like family, nature, etc. And I didn't include money, love, or freedom because those are the results of the application of core values but not core values themselves. The society we live in certainly has its own set of values, but I'm not asking you for those either. I'm asking you to dig deep and determine those values you hold most dear *today*. Some you may like to have, and perhaps will have some day, but identify just those that are true for you now.

> *Values are words that express your deep sense of what is important in your life.*

In Table 1, circle the top twenty-five values that speak to you as the most important to you. You may relate to many of the values listed, but try to identify the twenty-five that are always at the forefront for you. It may feel like you wouldn't be you without them. They may occur more frequently than the others in your life, either in their continual application or constant testing. They may feel like your greatest strengths while at the same time aspects of your greatest weaknesses.

Look at Table 1 and note the column in which you circled the highest number of values. Then note the column in which you circled the second highest number of values. If you have a tie between two columns, break it. If you selected carefully,

Table 1: Your Core Values

1	2	3	4	5	6	7
Authority	Clarity	Accountability	Balance	Accuracy	Loyalty	Collaboration
Challenge	Compassion	Activity	Beauty	Credibility	Devotion	Competency
Competition	Comfort	Adaptability	Co-operation	Expertise	Faithfulness	Conservation
Commitment	Equality	Busy-ness	Compromise	Factuality	Honour	Efficiency
Courage	Fairness	Communication	Creativity	Innovation	Humility	Excellence
Decisiveness	Inclusiveness	Flexibility	Fame	Knowledge	Idealism	Finesse
Detachment	Kindness	Hard Work	Harmony	Objectivity	Inspiration	Orderliness
Independence	Love	Intellect	Honesty	Moderation	Meaning	Perfection
Leadership	Patience	Strategy	Humour	Practicality	Optimism	Planning
Liberation	Peace	Productivity	Imagination	Reliability	Sacrifice	Skillfulness
Vision	Respect	Professionalism	Pleasure	Scientific	Sincerity	Stability
Perseverance	Serenity	Reputation	Spontaneity	Intelligence	Enthusiasm	Timeliness
Power	Service	Risk Taking	Artistic	Methodology	Passion	Tradition
Strength	Volunteering	Status	Expressiveness	Discovery	Determination	Quality
Integrity	Wisdom	Variety	Calmness	Curiosity	Demonstration	Structure

and are being truthful with yourself, you will always have one column with more values circled than the others and a second column not far behind.

Know Your Calling, Establish Your Purpose

Generally, a life calling can be placed into seven broad categories, which correlate to seven broad categories of purpose. Those seven purposes can be, but need not be, expressed through certain careers. Table 2 summarizes these broad categories.

Table 2: The Seven Categories of Calling/Purpose

Category	1	2	3	4	5	6	7
Calling	To strengthen & liberate others	To understand & nurture others	To stimulate creative intellect, reasoning, & communications with others	To bring peace, harmony, & beauty to others	To experiment, investigate, & reveal that which is hidden for others	To aspire to achieve the highest values while inspiring the same in others	To organize & manifest for others
Purpose	To Lead, Empower & Evolve	To Illumine, Love & Include	To Think Comprehensively & Communicate	To Mediate, Beautify, & Unify	To Discover, Invent, & Solve Problems	To Inspire & Attain the Ideal Vision	To Design, Organize, & Perfect the Form
Career (examples)	Politician Executive Military Athlete Explorer	Teacher Scholar Social Worker Psychologist Healer	Entrepreneur* Philosopher Writer Salesperson Marketer	Mediator Artist Performer Ambassador Therapist	Scientist Technician Researcher Engineer Analyst	Coach Preacher Activist Orator Trainer	Builder/ Architect Farmer Administrator Environmentalist Lawyer

* You may wonder what entrepreneurialism has to do with Thinking and Communicating. An entrepreneur simply uses the practical platform of business to communicate and express into the world a vision for how things "should be" done. They create something new to communicate what they think the world needs.

Now let's evaluate your results:

✔ If you picked the majority of values in column (1) in Table 1, then your Purpose likely fits into category (1), in Table 2: *To Lead*.

✔ If you picked the majority of values in column (2) in Table 1, then your Purpose likely fits into category (2) in Table 2: *To Illumine*.

✔ If you picked the majority of values in column (3) in Table 1, then your Purpose likely fits into category (3) in Table 2: *To Think*.

✔ If you picked the majority of values in column (4) in Table 1, then your Purpose likely fits into category (4) in Table 2: *To Mediate*.

✔ If you picked the majority of values in column (5) in Table 1, then your Purpose likely fits into category (5) in Table 2: *To Discover*.

✔ If you picked the majority of values in column (6) in Table 1, then your Purpose likely fits into category (6) in Table 2: *To Inspire*.

✔ If you picked the majority of values in column (7) in Table 1, then your Purpose likely fits into category (7) in Table 2: *To Design*.

As an example, allow me to share the results of my family members, who were my guinea pigs in the development of this process.

My sons each picked the majority of their values in column 3 (with a second choice of column 7 for Son #1 and column 2 for Son #2). This hints to a calling in category 3: To Think. Their philosophy on life is communicated through their entre-preneurial endeavours. They are both entrepreneurs and are incredibly busy with a few businesses of their own at a very early age, yet they got there by slightly different routes. My eldest son inspired the business to express his life philoso-phies. My second son supports it with a flare for marketing and communications.

My husband and daughter each picked the majority of their values in column 1 (and secondly, column 3 for my husband and column 5 for my daughter). This hints to a calling for both of them in category 1: To Lead. I can confirm that my husband is a leader, in our business and in our home life, and that my daughter is executive material (but time will tell as she is still in school). Neither leads through extroversion and being the centre of attention but through a quiet strength, wisdom, support, and loyalty that provides an example for us all of power well used.

I picked the vast majority of my values in column 2, with the runner-up being column 3. Well, my greatest life expres-sion is my family and my family office business, and I work to nourish both with everything I have to offer. Those values listed describe how I "move" at the deepest levels (except for patience—I don't have much of that!). The Family Treasury model is a very column 2 manifestation.

In testing this process, I discovered that it gave me more information than I expected! I designed it to hint, very generally, to a calling to get you started. Then I noticed that the column with the second highest number of values accurately reflected the "flavor" or "manner" in which that calling would get expressed. I do my "illumining and nourishing" through my entrepreneurial business, and as a philosopher (and maybe even a writer?). This is all very column 3. For my eldest son, his entrepreneurial calling is best expressed when he is building structures and/or businesses (forms): very column 7. For my second son, his entrepreneurial calling is best expressed when he is using his unique talent with relationships to facilitate the best from his working team, including everyone and preserving "the peace," and wisely directing the group to the goal: column 2. For my husband, his leadership is best expressed in leading the operations of an entrepreneurial businesses, which is a column 3 expression. My daughter currently expects her leadership will ultimately be expressed in the finance business (time will tell): very column 5. It seems to me that the column with the most values is the "what" of the calling and the column with the second-most values is the "how" of the calling. It is as if the "what" column reflects your innermost self—your soul qualities, if you will—and the "how" column your outer, worldly expression of those qualities—your personality in action. I did not expect this, and I look forward to studying it further.

The model given here is, of course, only a starting point. It is by design very general in nature but intended to help you begin to design your personal mission from a place of your core values. If you already have a mission statement, then perhaps this exercise has given you fresh perspective. In reality, your actual mission or purpose will be unique to you. No one is quite like you. Your mission will be a function of where you are in your life cycle, your beliefs and level of self-awareness, your emotional and mental maturity, your current location in time and space, your current situation, and the state of development of your resources, including your 3 Root Resources of will, relating, and action. Even the values you are working from today may change and develop over time as you yourself evolve.

However, one thing is always true. You will know you have clarity about your purpose and mission when you feel passion for living ignited within you. You will be excited about the process of developing your mission toward its realization.

> *You will know you have clarity about your purpose and mission when you feel passion for living ignited within you.*

Other Personal Profile Tools

Given the unique nature of everyone's mission, there may be a need to dig even deeper than the basic models offered in

Tables 1 and 2. We have been given a number of tools, some ancient and some modern, to help us do just that. The ancient models are extremely comprehensive, but require expert interpretation, given that they are presented in a unique language all their own. To say any more on this would take us deep into the world of esoteric psychology, which is beyond the scope of this book.

I have found that the modern tools tend to be high level, but quick and efficient and somewhat do-it-yourself. If they have a weakness, it is that they are perhaps too simplistic. Most of these are now available online. I have found Kolbe A™ Index[19] and Prevue HR Systems[20] especially useful in the family setting. Others that are well respected but that I am less familiar with include Myers–Briggs Type Indicator, iPersonic, and DiSC tests and profiles. These tools ask a series of questions and then plot you into a generalized group of people with similar traits and preferences who enjoy or are suited to particular types of careers or manner of working. They look at your natural or preferred behaviour patterns and decision-making methods. They look at how you relate to others around you and how you prefer to be communicated with. To get to that point, they do ask questions that hint at your core values. However, they have no way of identifying your current circumstances and abilities and, therefore, cannot give you direction as to next steps to implement your mission statement. That is not to say they are not valuable. They are immensely valuable in bringing you awareness of your natural ways of expressing yourself and what will feel good versus what will be stressful and energy draining. Many people are self-aware enough to understand at some level what environments they feel most comfortable in. These tools take that understanding to a higher, conscious level to empower the individual not only to make better choices about their purpose and direction that will lead to better money, better relationships, and more freedom but also to create better flow and ease in their life.

Defining Your Personal Mission

With some clarity on our calling, our purpose, and even potentially a meaningful career, we can define our *personal* mission. *Another way to describe mission is the "how-to method" to realize our vision.*

Your mission should be very specific to using your talents and in keeping with your values, and should help you to grow and develop your purpose in a meaningful, evolutionary, and goal-oriented way. Keep in mind: *it is not about what you want to get; it is about what you want to give.* It is best expressed in a mission statement. A mission statement is a sentence or two simply describing your calling and what is for you the ultimate vision of its highest expression in your life and the world. It spells out the overall BIG goal and outlines the path to achieve it. It describes the what (the purpose), the how (the plan), and the why (the result).

A mission statement is important because, as life progresses, it helps you to direct your attention to what is important and to filter out that which is not. It keeps you focused, gives clarity of direction, and ensures right use of energy. It directs the pure energy of will in a concentrated, empowered, and passionate manner toward the creation of the desired result. It is the efficient, effective, and sustainable use of the 1st of the 3 Root Resources, will. It creates the needed momentum launching you from where you are today to where you wish to be in the future. Without it, you will be handicapped in your ability to create more money, more love, and more freedom in a harmonious way. Without a mission, you are not congregating all the forces together and moving them in the direction of your dreams, and fewer results will be the result.

> ❝ It is not about what you want to get; it is about what you want to give.

Here is my personal mission statement, which I share with you by way of illustration.

My mission is to empower the business of family to create *True* wealth. I do so by stimulating awareness, creating discussion, and using best practices to facilitate progress, thereby inspiring and nourishing the lives of all that I serve.

The Family Treasury is one of those best practices tools I use to fulfill my mission. This book is another.

In this example, I described the "what," the purpose, as "to empower the business of family to create *True* wealth." I live this, I witness this, and I am passionate about it. I wish everyone could see what I see. My "how" of achieving that is to stimulate people, through discussions and this book, to think outside the box, determine if they see some of the same patterns that I do, and look at themselves and both their outer and inner lives to see if True Family Wealth rings true for them. Then I hope for further discussion with anyone who wants to talk with me about it. I welcome those who wish to try The Family Treasury on for size. The "why" of it all, the reason I do this, is to nourish and inspire the lives of those I can reach to meet their greatest potentials. When that happens, we all win. It thrills me to see The Family Treasury in action and hopefully the people I've connected with enjoy the process too. This is my personal mission. It is the next step in my evolution and I hope also for those who are ready and willing to receive and share it.

I also suggest you summarize your mission statement in one word so that you can use it quickly to re-centre yourself when you get off course. My word is "Empower."

It Continues with the Family Group

When each member has discovered their own personal mission, they are well on their way to developing as people of excellent contribution and ever strengthening self-worth.

They exude a high-energy vibe and are interesting people to be with. They give and receive more love and are better able to love unconditionally and accept constructive criticism for self-improvement. They are also confident communicators and will say how they feel, which makes them better contributors to the group.

So imagine what a group of these people united by a common mission can do? A family so aligned is a powerful force indeed. With self-confidence and the support of each other, coupled with the discipline that comes with emotional maturity, they can truly be a force for creation. The unique talents expressed by each member of the group can be aligned to create something new and bigger than the individuals themselves could ever have created. The journey can be one of exploration, challenge, and growth. Family prosperity is enriched by the joy of challenges overcome and the satisfaction of resultant growth experienced together.

Your Group Identity

To have a true group identity—a family name—that you can be proud of requires emotional responsiveness, not reactiveness. It also requires honest and factual communication where family hierarchy has no place and every adult member of the group is an equal. After all, The Family Treasury is just like a business, a team effort where each participant's unique talents contribute to a much stronger whole. The key task in identifying the group identity is to uncover where individual talents and interests can complement each other and serve each other for the empowered success of each individual and the group as a whole. The result is achievement far beyond what the individuals alone could likely have accomplished. The group identity can also build a stronger financial foundation for the entire family so that wealth can be created more effectively.

What Is The Family Treasury Mission Statement?

The first stage in developing wealth stewardship was defining your personal mission statement. This same process should then be completed by those of your family members who are old enough to understand the task at hand. I suggest that typically someone under the age of eighteen will not have enough self-awareness to identify their values accurately. However, each person should be considered based upon their merit and ability, not their age. This step is important because The Family Treasury mission statement is empowered in direct relation to how self-aware each of its members is and how clear each is about what their current life mission looks like.

With your individual discoveries in hand, The Family Treasury mission statement will then identify, in a collaborative way, the values that all family members hold in common. There will be differences, of course—perhaps many of them— but there will also be a set of core values you all share. *By collating where the family members hold the same values, you will discover the purpose of the family as a unified whole.* Everyone has their own unique abilities, passions, and expertise. The trick is to find a mission that can use and celebrate them in a coherent way, such that each person understands the valuable contribution they can make individually as well as collectively. It should identify what makes the family unique and how that special ability can be fostered and developed. In other words, The Family Treasury is a manifestation that is separate and distinct from each family member but, at the same time, is part of each of you. It will have its own energetic profile, its own purpose for existence. It does not exist to serve you! It exists to serve the group expression.

With all that talent working together in an integrated and collaborative way, based on unified values and purpose, The Family Treasury becomes the business of family. It is a super power, more powerful than you alone could be, if it is managed successfully toward the achievement of its potentials. There is also a bonus! Each member contributing to The Family Treasury mission will find their own mission is also supercharged, empowered by the support systems provided by The Family Treasury they are contributing to.

> 66 *By collating where the family members hold the same values, you will discover the purpose of the family as a unified whole.*

A family mission statement becomes the template for all future decisions so that the family stays on track with their original purpose, in keeping with their family values. This is not much different than a business plan or mission statement that a company would use to align interests and focus activity for maximum results.

Discover Your Family Treasury's Purpose

As a wealth steward, before you can deploy the 1st of the 3 Root Resources (will and passion) in service of a mission, you first need to discover the primary purpose of your Family Treasury. To do that, collect the Table 1 list of values everyone circled earlier and, as a family, review them. At this point, you need not concern yourself with which values specifically coincide between you. Instead, using the format of Table 3, add up how many values were selected in column 1 by everyone in the group and put the number in the middle row under the purpose To Lead. Do the same for the values in column 2, column 3, and so on. Then, count how many people determined that their possible purpose was To Lead, To Illumine, To Think, and so on and put that number in

Table 3: A Purpose for Your Family Treasury

Purpose	To Lead	To Illumine	To Think	To Mediate	To Discover	To Inspire	To Design
Number of Value Hits	21	22	28	15	11	11	17
Number of Member Profiles	2	1	2	0	0	0	0

the bottom row of the appropriate column. As an example, I've used the tabulation from my family's questionnaires to complete Table 3.

The column with the highest number of value hits AND the most member profiles indicates the overriding purpose of your Family Treasury, but also pay attention to other columns that ranked close for they will hint to how that purpose will get expressed. In the example, my Family Treasury identifies most with the purpose To Think, followed closely by To Lead. The row entries in both the To Lead and To Illumine columns totalled 23, but this is a democracy, so the number in the bottom row takes precedence when we have a tie. For interest's sake, the one specific column 1 value that we all chose was "independence." We now have our overriding, uncompromising direction: column 3 indicates we are an entrepreneurial family, offering services driven by our vision and philosophies about how the world "should be." Column 1 reveals itself in how we *lead* those businesses and that we need to be independent. Our manifestations also fall into these categories. The business the boys developed is in the sports industry (columns 1 and 3). Our Family Office business is a column 2 and 3 business, and has provided the foundation for this book and the Family Treasury, which is all about unity, equality, loyalty, wisdom, and service. In truth, none of our values in any of the columns will be compromised, and each of us will express them in our own personal mission statement. But just as with the personal mission statement, a certain energy focus presented itself in this exercise that is, in essence, the energetic imprint, the unique purpose of our Family Treasury and what it is here to do.

Explore Ways to Express Your Purpose

Once the purpose has revealed itself, it is time to explore what your family can do together to express itself. In this exercise, the family is mining for ways to work together on this common purpose to create a common vision, and then a mission statement to support it. You might need to ask everyone to use their imaginations, do a little blue-sky thinking—imagination is the first step to manifestation. You may decide to create a family business, or express your purpose through philanthropic projects.

In addition, the family looks at ways to support each other to develop individual purposes and highest qualities. This might mean financing younger family members to start their own businesses or funding middle-aged members to undertake further education.

But please understand: to work with The Family Treasury does not mean you are expected to go into business together, or play in the same sandbox. Frankly, not all family members can work together because they just don't resonate that way. The key is to "work together" in a different way, where you understand and support each other in any way you can so that individually you can achieve great things, while collectively achieving growth as a family and contributing together to a better world.

▲ *Create Your Family Treasury Mission Statement*

As the next step in this process, create The Family Treasury mission statement that is unique to you as a group. By way of example, here is my family's:

> Our mission is to co-invest in entrepreneurial enterprise with leaders who are at the forefront of beneficial change. We will do so strategically, through financial, educational, and instructional support with a view to reasonable profit, that profit measured not only in money but also in human evolution.

It can be summarized in one word: "Lead." For my family, this word means, "to go before."

Can you see the themes running through this? The themes that are coherent with my stated personal mission and the purposes and choices that the rest of my family have made? Can you see the many ways that this mission can also serve to support each of us in our personal missions? The Family Treasury has taken the first step to enrich the 1st of its 3 Root Resources, will, through the energy of will/purpose (in this case cultivating entrepreneurial leadership both within ourselves and others). We have simply used the label "Lead" instead of "will" so that we can hold it and work with it. The potential for more money, more relationships, and more freedom for the entire group is put into play because we have a larger group will to manifest it.

A different family—with a different set of unique individuals, with their unique talents and interests, with a different collective set of values—could have a very different mission. Let's say, for example, there is a family with many of the values and individual purposes resonating with column 2. Their mission might be to do volunteer work with the financially and emotionally disenfranchised. A family that resonated with column 7 might choose to focus their energies and resources working together to change public policy for environmental protection. And even families that resonate with the same column find different expressions of their purpose. No one family purpose is greater or more important than another. All are equally valid and relevant, and when the collective family chooses to act upon it with passion, the benefits to the world can be magnificent.

The Family Treasury mission statement should reflect an overall purpose for the group. It may not be the only one, but it should be significant. It is not dissimilar from the mission a business would have and has the characteristics that a life mission should have, which include:

- It feels bigger than you and may or may not actually be fully achievable in your lifetime.
- If it is too easy to accomplish, it is not much of an evolutionary creation.
- It is not really about you and your team. It is a service of "good will" to the world.

- It expresses your group purpose (calling) and makes use of your talents but will still be very challenging to accomplish.
- It would be an evolutionary experience for you and the team.

> *"The Family Treasury mission statement should reflect an overall purpose for the group.*

So how is my family's Family Treasury mission statement bigger than we are? Because for us, trying to stay on top of three businesses is plenty enough challenge, never mind being influential and effective support for other young business leaders! To accomplish that will be a stretch for us: we will have to evolve our leadership skills, grow our network of like-minded entrepreneurs, and expand our resources of energy, knowledge, time, and money. We will have to overcome bad habits, doubt, and other limiting beliefs. And most important of all, we must not allow ourselves to be distracted and must remain focused on our mission. Believe me, at least once a week one of us in this household feels like giving it all up for the easy life of golf and martinis. But then we remember that we have a greater purpose, that talent is a terrible thing to waste, and that we have a responsibility to each other to keep growing. Anyway, none of us has ever been any good at sitting around!

Let's Look at Jack and Jill

After Jack and his family did their calling/purpose exercise, they found their collated results put them into column 7. So, in fact, did Jill's family results. However, they can have two very different Family Treasury mission statements.

Jack's family might be on a mission to work together on their family property to develop an organic farm, further refining state-of-the-art processes to enhance food quality and productivity, while remaining energy efficient. They may decide to do so by offering a co-op opportunity to young farmers in search of experience. Jack's family offers a corner of their land to them to farm for a couple years at no charge in exchange for their help in running Jack's farm. That way none of them has to give up their day job and Jack conserves costs which he can reinvest in additional land over time. This is a big vision, in line with their group values, which makes them all money, while allowing them to work together and grow together, evolving along the way. They could not do it without each other.

Jill's family might be on a mission to preserve the wetlands in the valley running through the centre of the city as well as other environmentally sensitive areas province-wide. Her family enjoys using the natural spaces for recreation and feels a sense of responsibility to share it with the animal and plant life that also call it home. Taking advantage of Jill's legal skills, they will band together to research the issues, petition for legal protection, fundraise for initiatives, and inform through media and other outlets in order to raise awareness and make long-term change. Does this make them money? No, but remember, not all Family Treasury mission statements need to do so. Do they grow as people while they grow their *True* family wealth? Absolutely!

It is important to note that the mission/purpose of The Family Treasury is not really about making money, although money has a presence. Money is one of the resources used to fulfill The Family Treasury's purpose. Money is also a resource that The Family Treasury needs to create to stay in existence so that it can fulfill its purpose. Lastly, money is one of the results of achieving that purpose.

Also be aware that it may take some time to set the mission statement for The Family Treasury. To be effective, everyone on the team must be clear about their own mission statement and also help develop, buy into, and fully support the mission statement of The Family Treasury. For some, this may be a simple process; for many, it can be a challenge. Much can get in the way and hold you back. Some family members may not want to co-operate, usually because of emotional issues. Some may have limiting beliefs about themselves and fears about the world can cause them to reach for mediocrity when setting their purpose and goals. Unexpressed emotions and traumas may need to be cleared. What forgiveness needs to happen? How well do you really know yourself to even be able to identify your values in the first place? Are you taking responsibility for your stuff, or are you blaming everyone else and playing the victim?

If these kinds of things arise and you want to keep moving forward, I have a suggestion. I believe it is often most appropriate to engage a life coach to work with any, if not all, family members as part of this process. It can be a challenge for some to define how their values can be expressed through a meaningful life purpose (often meaningful work of some kind). The Family Treasury focuses on identifying and developing each person's strengths. I hope I have shown that spending time and effort working on what you are weak at, and perhaps think you should do, but are not built to do, will not lead to big results. In fact, it is a waste of your natural talents. Using the example of a successful business: you certainly would not hire someone to do a job because they sucked at it! You want people to focus on what they do best, develop their potential still further, and delegate the rest. That way you have a high-performing team that gets maximum results.

Once you feel you have some clarity of direction in a Family Treasury mission statement, start to work with it. Don't wait until you think it is perfect. In moving forward with that first, best-effort mission statement, you will be better able to refine it and get it just right.

> 66 *The mission/purpose of The Family Treasury is not really about making money ... Money is one of the results of achieving that purpose.*

▲ ▼ ▲

We are building wealth stewards who see a group mission that is greater than their own. For The Family Treasury to succeed, everyone needs to contribute the absolute best of themselves to the process. It begins with personal mission statements that first contribute to and then are supported by the family mission statement. However, even with those in place, if the group does not know how to work together well, the The Family Treasury triangle will be weakened. The 2nd Root Resource relies on caring, if not loving, relationships with yourself and with others. That is the focus of our next step.

The Family
Treasury System II
Development through
Loving Relationships

The family environment is where we learn about love. We just don't always learn our lessons well. It is not that we don't all want to give love and be loved. We do. But we are distinctive individuals and, therefore, give and receive love in ways that are unique to us. That is where the problems lie. We often don't speak the same love language. *Love* is such a strange word. It has so many meanings in our culture. For example, "I love chocolate" and "I love you": do they mean the same thing? In this case, yes—we are talking about chocolate after all! But in most other cases, no. The word *love* means very different things to different people.

In my family of five, we have five different ways of loving. My husband gives love through his strength, commitment, and loyalty. He will lift you up onto his back to keep you out of the mud, and while carrying you on his back, build you a bridge over that mud, and then carry you over that bridge! He feels loved when we openly appreciate his efforts. My eldest son gives love by sharing his enthusiasm for the adventure of life. He is your coach. He wants to lift you up, inspire you to feel the same excitement and enthusiasm for life that he is feeling. He feels loved when you listen and understand. My second son gives love through his kindness and wisdom. He would never utter a word to hurt anyone and is able to mediate resolution between two people without offending either. He feels loved when given respect and space. Then there is my daughter. She is a natural-born leader—and lead you she will, whether or not you want it. That's how she gives love, helping you see through your blind spots and leading you to a new perspective. She feels loved when you embrace her as she is. Then there is me. I get my kicks nourishing others. I like to inspire, motivate, support, and empower them. That is how I give love. I feel loved when my loyalty is returned and when I feel needed and appreciated.

So in my little family alone, we have five different ways of giving love: we have the protector, the visionary, the sage, the leader, and the motivator. And we have five different ways of wanting to receive love: being appreciated, being understood, being left alone, being not alone, and being needed. How do I know this? As a family we have paid attention to it. We set as a goal long ago to strive to understand each other, be conscious of our patterns, and communicate our needs to each other. We used every tool we could find, including Kolbe and the Family Treasury Communication model discussed later in this chapter. With intention and right effort, we developed loving bonds. And from this platform of trust, belonging, and strength, we developed over time as better people through those loving relationships.

Developing empowered and loving relationships within The Family Treasury setting is not a one-time event. It is a lifelong process of committing to overcome the troubling times through collaboration instead of competition for position, of bringing light to the dark places with lots of celebration and good times together. It is working with what I call the 4 C's.

Creating a Family of High Esteem: The 4 Cs

I wrote earlier of self-identity and group identity. A flourishing Family Treasury understands the prime importance of its members developing resilient self-worth and emotional maturity. It is in that process of developing high self-esteem that you empower a family of "high esteem." The Family Treasury is built upon the foundation of a family with high esteem. The 4 Cs—consciousness, communication, collaboration, and celebration—are an easy way to remember the four tools that a family can use to develop high esteem, where all family team members feel they belong, are accepted, and are understood.

Consciousness

To have a good relationship with ourselves, and others, we begin by becoming conscious of the patterns and beliefs that limit our sense of self and therefore restrict our potentials. In her book *Family Business: United We Stand Divided We Fall*, author and psychotherapist Laurie Pick`ard talks about the negative impacts a low self-esteem family member has on a family business. She tells us that someone with chronic low self-esteem believes their happiness is in another's hands and continually needs to be validated by others. She describes how, "in an all-consuming desire to fill your hunger for recognition, [you] become stuck developmentally. In being led by your emotions rather than by facts and experiences, you become off-balance.[21]" She goes on to say that "a defective cognitive-emotional system is one that lacks clarity in awareness [consciousness] and judgement, with particular susceptibility to excessive sensitiveness in feelings ... faulty reasoning is labeled exaggeration. Likewise, you are also inclined to evaluate and re-label facts so your interpretation of them is disproportionate to the reality of the situation. This faulty reasoning is labeled distortion. Both exaggeration and distortion are based on an emotional, rather than on a rational, process."[22] Furthermore, "this self-interested performance level sabotages and undermines business-interest performance and team development."[23] Equally so, it sabotages The Family Treasury and the family itself.

Like any high-functioning business team, a family of high esteem is conscious of its patterns and those of its members, and with self-awareness identifies individual and group false beliefs and works together to remould behaviours from ones that divide into ones that unite and empower. And as in a high-functioning business, each team member takes responsibility for their own actions and seeks to improve their "professionalism" as opposed to blaming others for the consequences of their decisions and actions.

> *A family of high esteem is conscious of its patterns and those of its members.*

Communication

Laurie Pick`ard goes on to explain how the person of low self-esteem often withholds information that if expressed could have resolved their misassumptions long ago. She says, "when communications are withheld, when we conceal our emotional reactions to why we feel that we must withhold, we build barriers. Barriers of emotional distance and subsequent feelings of emotional isolation create tension within the organization climate and anxiety within one's own physical being. Disillusionment sets in … one becomes emotionally tired, frustrated, and angry, not necessarily just with others, but with self as well. One engages in negative self-talk, disordered thinking, misperceptions, conversations within that focus on one's expectations, fault-finding, and 'if-only' reasoning. This lack of inner-peace is marked by caution, fear, and discomfort. In spite of any technical skills achieved or validation thereof, one feels that he or she has not gained mastery over his or her environment. This is evidenced by the fact that one does not see oneself as emotionally strong enough or competent enough to speak up and to maturely express what is on one's mind or deal with the consequences."[24]

So self and group reflection, awareness, and communication is critical to a family of high esteem, just as it is in a successful business setting. *The family team (just like a business) should formalize methods of communication that are democratic, kind and respectful, and value equally the need for each person to express themselves fully and honestly.* The Family Treasury Communication model can help you achieve this (as discussed later in this chapter).

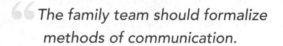

> **The family team should formalize methods of communication.**

Collaboration

As with a successful and profitable business, the family of high esteem understands that each person is uniquely talented and has something to contribute to the whole in a collaborative as opposed to competitive manner. They do not have to work with each other but they do work for each other. For example, some members of The Family Treasury may decide to form an operating business together because they work easily together and their particular talents and mission mesh well with the objective of that business. Others may strike out on their own to work in careers separate from any family business. However, they all are members of The Family Treasury working collaboratively to build the family resources of (worthy) mission, (loving) relationships, and (many) achievements.

> *They do not have to work with each other, but they do work for each other.*

Celebration

Again, as with a successful business, celebrating the milestones and accomplishments is part of the fun of being together. A family of high esteem relishes time together to celebrate each other's accomplishments and that of the family as a whole. It is so important to celebrate how far each of you has come and collectively what you have achieved. We can get so focused on our goals that we miss the journey along the way. Celebrating those milestones keeps you in the long game.

It is a lifelong process not a one-time event.

▲ ▼ ▲

You might be thinking that you're at a disadvantage: you like the idea of a family of high esteem that enjoys being together, but your current family relationships aren't all that good and you don't know where to start. First, understand that all families have their challenges, that some times are more difficult than others. But if you can accept that family is a major means by which our 2nd Root Resource (relating) is meant to evolve and are willing to give the 4 Cs a shot, then you can begin to heal those relationships. How? Better relationships begin with you.

Better Relationships Begin with You

Most of us have okay relationships with some family members, crummy relationships with others, and even worse relationships with ourselves. Why is that? I believe a leading cause of these circumstances is that we misunderstand love. So how can we improve our love and relating with ourselves and others so that our family can be a healthy and dynamic team? To have great love in the physical world, we need to understand it in the energetic world. Yup, we are going again to the world of philosophy to understand the underlying issue.

Because of *duality*, we perceive ourselves to be separate from each other and everything. There is an "us and them" or an "us and it." Yet, in reality, this is not actually true. It is only our minds, our perceptions through our five senses that make it appear so, and therefore, for us, it is. There is a you and a me. There is a this and a that. There is a here and a there. There is a then and a now. There is yes and no, black and white, light and dark, happy and sad, fun and boring, life and death … well, you get the point. Ours is a dualistic world, where there is a flip side to everything. This is absolutely true, and absolutely untrue (oops, there it is again!).

Science has proven that duality is an illusion. We are energy that cannot be created or destroyed and, therefore, has always been. All forms are simply permutations and variations of the same vibrating energy soup from which everything arises and to which everything returns. Brain scientist Jill Bolte Taylor suffered a massive stroke in the left hemisphere of her brain but remained conscious throughout and in the aftermath. In her book *My Stroke of Insight*, she describes her perception of the world and other people when only the right side of her brain was working. "I was consciously alert and my perception was that I was in the flow. Everything in my visual world blended together, and with every pixel radiating energy we all flowed *en masse*, together as *one*. It was impossible for me to distinguish the physical boundaries between objects because everything radiated with similar energy … I could not perceive three-dimensionally … If there was a person standing in the doorway, I could not distinguish their presence until they moved. It took activity for me to know that I should pay special attention to any particular patch of molecules."[25] It is only when the left side of our brains turn on that we see other people as separate from us. Even though technically this is not true, we can forgive ourselves for believing it since we live through our outer senses usually eighteen out of twenty-four hours a day. Given that we see ourselves as separate from each other, we automatically go to a place of judgment when relating with that "separate" person. We either like or don't like the way we are with them, or the way they are with us. Just because it's a family member doesn't mean we like the way they behave or how they treat us. This perception sets us up to *love conditionally*. We give them our heart, our grace, our trust and loyalty when we like them, and as long as they serve our needs.

So what is wrong with duality? Nothing and everything (yup, yet again!). Without it, we would never know ourselves, for there would be no subject and no object. We would never know each other. I can think of all sorts of things that would be a lot less fun without two of us! Yet, because of it, we feel separate from each other.

It is from the illusion that we are separate that we judge each other as good or bad, smart or stupid, ugly or beautiful, etc. From this belief comes unhealthy competition, greed, and aggression. It tells us everything is separate from us, so if we want it, we must grab it and hold it tightly. Alternatively, if we don't like it, we must repulse it in any way possible.

> 66 It is from the illusion that we are
> separate that we judge each other.

This is how the 2nd Root Resource, love (or relating, as I called it in Chapter 3), is misunderstood. Most approach relating and love from a place of separation. We unconsciously ask: "Do I love that other, or not?" Remember, the truth is that we are One, made of the same stuff. And that illusion of the other is a gift, for they are a mirror of us. *In other words, what we like or don't like in the other is recognizable to us in the first place only because we already know it: it is in us, and we have judged it as something we like or don't like within ourselves.* We can see our "stuff" in them. They mirror (respond) back to us with what we put out there. When you understand this, you can begin to upward spiral the love (relating) principle toward its highest expression. The highest expression of love is unconditional universal love: when we have learned to love ourselves and others, warts and all. We also realize that how well we love others, warts and all, is a direct reflection of how well we've learned to love ourselves. We love universally, no longer "separatively," and are appreciative and grateful for all of it.

> *The highest expression of love is unconditional universal love: when we have learned to love ourselves and others, warts and all.*

I know that this is a huge stretch for most of us, and for many not likely to be accomplished in this lifetime. So how about we aim for something a little more achievable but very powerful: loving ourselves and our family members unconditionally. Key word: unconditionally.

The Family Treasury can help your family work with this, which I will get to later in this chapter. However, there is also likely a great deal of work that must be done by you on your own (and each member of the family on their own as well). *To be able to fully give and receive love unconditionally, you must first become more self-aware as you journey to loving yourself unconditionally.* Remember, it all starts and stops with you. You are solely responsible for the life you are experiencing.

There are three tools that I would suggest—homework, if you will—to help you on the journey of self-awareness:

1. Develop an attitude of gratitude.

2. Figure out your own shit.

3. Decrease your emotionality: turn reaction into response.

Develop an Attitude of Gratitude

Start with yourself: gratitude (or appreciation) for who and how you are, for your strengths and talents, for the love you give. Appreciation for the fact that you have free choice. Even if you are in jail, you still have choice as to how you feel each moment. Nelson Mandela describes this very experience during his time in prison and is a testament to that truth. Gratitude does not mean everything in life is rosy. Sometimes

life is tragic. We all feel pain; it is part of the human condition. We will all eventually die, too. But in the meantime, you
can always find something you are grateful for, something
to appreciate. When you live in appreciation, it feels good.
And when you do so, the real magic happens. *Gratitude is
the antidote to life-limiting fear. It shuts off that part of your brain
that lives in fear.*

> *Gratitude is the antidote
> to life-limiting fear.*

Fear and love cannot be in your mind and body at the same
time. You simply cannot feel both at once. Don't believe me?
Try it yourself. Sit quietly with your eyes closed. Relax your
body while you take three long, slow, deep breaths. Notice
how you are feeling. Now think of something you are afraid
of. Notice that tightness in your throat, maybe in your belly?
Feel how your heart clenches? Now think of something or
someone you love, and while you do that, smile. I mean *really*
smile! A show-your-teeth kind of smile, with a sparkle in your
eyes behind those closed lids. Did you feel how the tightness
in your body eases, how the heart space opens? The fear is
instantly gone—just like that.

It is pretty cool that a daily practice of living in gratitude
can override the fear in our lives. But what does the practice
of gratitude have to do with love and relating? Because fear
is ruining our relationships, with ourselves and each other.

It brings anger, anxiety, guilt, jealousy, and distrust into our relationships and our lives.

But we did come by fear honestly. It is hard-wired into our biology. In his book *What Happy People Know*, Dr. Dan Baker says that "this biological circuitry of fear is the greatest enemy of happiness."[26] He goes on to say that "what once saved us now slowly kills us."[27] When fear rules us, we don't do the things that lead to wonder, excitement, and a BIG Life. Instead, we live a small life. Dr. Baker describes "the many faces of fear … [often being disguised as] anger, perfectionism, pessimism, low-level anxiety, depression and feelings of isolation."[28] Throughout his book, Dr. Baker adds to this list: control and domination, obsession, insecurity, shyness, and guilt. What fun—we often feel fear, and can't find a reason for it, so we call it other things! The truth is, it is just there, at our core. Unless we consciously override fear with an attitude of gratitude, it will rule us, our relationships, and our lives.

> 66 *Unless we consciously override fear with an attitude of gratitude, it will rule us, our relationships, and our lives.*

How many people do you know, even in your own family, who are ruled by fear? Are there unusually controlling people who irritate you? Angry people who offend you and steal your energy? Depressed or nervous people who aren't much fun to be with? Could any of those be descriptions of you?

Just to be clear, I am talking here about what most of us suffer from: irrational fear—the kind we make up to worry about (not the kind of rational fear we feel in a dangerous situation). What then is the antidote to fear? Thankfully, there are many remedies for irrational fear. These are some of the top recommendations.

1. Express love and gratitude. As Dr. Baker suggests, this action destroys fear.

2. Realize that there are always two sides. As much as possible, in every occurrence or event, look for and choose to focus on the light (the silver lining) not the darkness.

3. Practice detachment. Nothing is permanent; this too shall pass.

4. Put fear in its place. In a difficult situation, acknowledge the reality—including how bad it is and how fearful you may be—but do not allow fear to compound by creating a projection of something worse that is not real and, in fact, may never happen.

5. Give without expecting a return.

6. Play like a kid.

7. Fake it until you make it. If you behave as though you're *not* afraid, your mind accepts that as reality and will not encourage or dwell on thoughts about fear.

You could even consider being grateful for your irrational fear. You can always choose to work with it, learn from it, and appreciate the life lesson gained in it as you evolve the 2nd Root Resource, relating/love.

Figure Out Your Own Shit

Remembering how it all starts and stops with you: Are you truly aware of the many ways in which "your shit" has impacted your relationships and your life?

Historically, the most common way to heal relationships was through visits to a psychotherapist. But that can only go so far. I am not speaking here of major trauma: you absolutely need clinical help in this regard. But when it comes to our behaviour in family relationships—frankly, a therapist can't solve the problem for you; he or she can only assist you. The therapist, while no doubt an expert in their field, is limited by three main factors: (1) they can't be with you every moment of every day, (2) they can only work with what you are willing to give them, and (3) what you usually tell them is a pile of hooey. Your therapist must sort fact from fiction, wading through your relative reality, your perceptions, and the stories you have told yourself over the years. The stories you tell are often not based on fact but on your interpretation of the facts, and the opposing parties are seldom invited into the room to give balance and colour to your perspective. Unfortunately, your perspective is most likely that your family, or someone in your family, is to blame, but seldom do you see the truth about yourself. Trained therapists are specialists we can turn to when our spirit is broken and we need major mental, emotional, and even physical healing. But the day-to-day stuff we impose on relationships can be healed by growing our self-awareness, with or without the assistance of a professional therapist.

A more powerful way to do that on your own, or while working with a therapist, is through mindfulness training and meditation. In fact, many therapists will recommend meditation as a complementary therapy tool. It has many other benefits, too, although these are not the subject of this book. Meditation empowers us to develop emotional maturity by teaching us how to stay centred and move away from emotional reactivity toward intelligent, compassionate, and respectful response. Meditation, coupled with journaling your experiences, is a key method to achieve this maturity and also helps you get in touch with your patterns, behaviours, and beliefs. This gives you clarity through higher perspective in your relationships with others.

Meditation and Mindfulness

Ultimately, meditation allows you to have control over your mind and thoughts such that your mind no longer controls you. The practice helps you develop space between thoughts and emotions to give you time to choose a healthy *response* versus a potentially harmful *reaction*. It helps you discover a joy and bliss (that is always within you) that no amount of money can ever buy. With practice, you can carry that joy and bliss with you off the meditation cushion into your daily life. Meditation harmonizes the energies within the cells, organs, and nervous system of your body, enhancing your energy and health like nothing else. It can play a major role in curing disease, and certainly cures "dis-ease." It improves your relationships, helping you to be truly present and in the moment when someone needs you.

Meditation helps "self-interested you" get out of the way so you can see just what is needed in the moment to be the right support in your relating situation. You become a better listener. Meditation helps you let go of attachments as well as fears that can hold you back from becoming who you were meant to be. This helps you to be of better service to others. It gives you emotional stability during the storms that inevitably come. It connects you with your intuition, your higher knowledge that seems to have all the right answers, thereby helping you make decisions that will always be in everyone's best interests. Meditation puts you in touch with your highest creative power, allowing you to unfold potential into realities you could never have imagined. Meditation opens the doors to wisdom beyond simple brain intelligence. That is where the real fun begins. I believe meditation is the greatest tool humanity has available to it to grow in joy, peace, and abundance. Yup. It's not a new sports car or luxury holiday—it's meditation. It is the greatest key to unlocking our highest potentials. Everyone and anyone can do it. No amount of education, counselling, or money can beat its power to transform a life. To quote one of my meditation coaches, Donna Mitchell-Moniak, "Meditation changes everything."

> *Meditation helps you let go of attachments as well as fears that can hold you back from becoming who you were meant to be.*

I am a committed meditation enthusiast (in case you haven't noticed). I admit that it was very difficult to fit meditation into my jam-packed life, so I worked with it in fits and starts for many years. Over fifteen years later, it is part of my daily nourishment and has brought transformational changes to both my outer and inner life. It is the changes in the inner life, which others may not see, that are the most profound. For those of you who are seasoned meditators, I am sure you will agree that meditation training is a lifelong and, at times, difficult-seeming process. I have not met anyone who could just sit down for the first time, or even the first fifty times, and experience a truly meditative state. Perhaps deep relaxation, but not true meditation. However, do not be discouraged, for even the first sitting will reap benefits. There is never a meditation that does not enhance your day and your life in some way.

The good news is that it is becoming trendy in modern western culture to meditate, and more and more of us are jumping on the bandwagon. We even say "I will meditate on it," meaning I will contemplate it. Yet true meditation is not well understood in western society. People will say, for example, "I like to walk in the woods. It is so meditative." Or "I went to yoga, and we meditated at the end of class." Or "I meditate when I run." While those experiences are beneficial, for sure, I suggest that these are examples of only deep mental and physical relaxation at best. That is not true meditation. Meditation is when you are in deep inner and outer stillness: you do nothing at all, you become nothing at all, and you enter into nothingness. To have to be "doing" something to be meditative actually misses the point.

I believe meditation is so central to improved relationships with yourself and others that I decided to include a brief discussion about technique here. You should always learn meditation from a properly trained practitioner. It is so powerful a process that it can do harm if not introduced and practiced properly. However, even though I'm not qualified to instruct, to give you a sense, a taste, of meditation, I will "high level" some aspects of it, using language that unfortunately is very limited, to help you understand the benefits. There really aren't the words to express a non-worldly experience, but I will give it a try. For those who are already well-practiced meditators, I believe you will relate to this sample process, and please forgive me for my oversimplification. For those who are not meditators, I hope this will pique your interest enough to give it a try, and then never stop.

The first key to a meditation sitting is just that: SIT. Preferably in lotus position, but even in a chair if you can't cross your legs. Sit erect, with shoulders back, tummy muscles taut, chin parallel to the floor. You will likely find it easiest to have your eyes softly closed. Place your hands in your lap, left hand resting in the right with thumbs touching at the tips. This hand "mudra" creates a closed circuit of your body's energy flow. To find the stillness within, you need to start with assuming stillness without. Your body should feel alert, enlivened, and strong.

Then start to notice your breath as you breathe slowly, softly, deeply, and rhythmically. Follow your breath in and "up," then "down" and out. Sense how velvety it feels. Imagine that breath as light, which it is, coming into your body from the outer expanse, enlivening you but bringing you peace and tranquility at the same time.

When you feel "settled," calm and comfortable, you can go to the next level. Imagine roots of light spreading beneath your seat down into the earth, giving you an anchor and making you feel "grounded." This posture, which you will hold during the entire meditation, is called "good asana."

Then smile. A real, heartfelt smile! (If you need help, think of something you love and smile.) Don't forget this part. When you smile, it opens your heart and instantly puts you into an attitude of gratitude. It softens your hard edges and opens you to receptivity. A smile transforms the moment. It is accepting of the moment without projection, without grasping, but with gratitude for what is.

Now, as Donna would say, "with eyes bright and sparkly behind closed lids," place your focus softly at the third eye (the ajna centre), just above and between your eyes. It is like you are looking through the middle of your forehead at a point just in front of it. Another way is to gaze through your eyes outwardly, but from behind your eyes. The gaze is soft and is not forced. It may seem or feel like the point of focus is dark or light—it does not matter. Be with that a few moments, gently—don't force it—and keep breathing. As you do this, sense yourself softening, opening. This is very important. Despite sitting in an active and erect posture, you are at the same time softening and opening your receptivity.

Now gently return your attention back to the point of focus at the third eye and HOLD IT THERE. I laugh to myself as I use capitals letters here, because it is very difficult to do, but so central to achieving a deep meditative state. You must not "think" about it at all! You must not "try" at all. That is the meditative paradox. You can't think your way into meditation. The practice requires a soft, gentle, yet laser-like, keen, interested, unwavering focus from your ajna centre straight out into nothing. Stay soft, stay open.

As you gently feel your way to this focus point, or the "point of tension" as Donna calls it, you will begin to notice your mind is thinking stuff. All kinds of stuff: the grocery list, the kids, the to-do list at work … The practice—and this is the really tricky part at first—is to notice yourself thinking. Become the "observer" in there, the second you, that notices, "ah, that is a thought" and then lets it float away. Refocus on your breathing. When the next thought comes, notice it, and let it go, bringing yourself back to the point of tension. *This separation of you from your thoughts is the first step to realizing that you are not your thoughts; you are the one watching them. They are separate things from you.*

> **You are not your thoughts;
> you are the one watching them.**

Meditation has no required timeline to deliver benefits. If you are starting out, even a five-minute sitting is beneficial. That will extend to perhaps twenty minutes quite easily as you practice. Before long, you may find that you can sit in meditation for an hour and not notice the time has passed.

As you practice meditation, you will get to know the many different variations and experiences and will begin to know what is needed in each moment by listening to what is going on inside you. With each sitting, you may also notice certain phenomena occur. You might have visions or see colours or shapes. Other times you may feel your mind space quite suddenly move from a contracted to expansive space, as if you have leapt into a river of energy. The key here is to not be distracted by these phenomena. Yes, they are interesting, but the key is to let them come and go as with your thoughts.

The other thing to keep in mind is that there are many different meditative practices and techniques the world over, and it may take some time, and experimenting with different practices and different practitioners, to find the one that resonates best with you. The good news is that, thanks to the Internet, you can meditate with groups and practitioners located just about anywhere in the world.

Even after years of practice, you will notice those thoughts in your mind still come and go. So don't be hard on yourself if you still have a head full of them after only a few months of meditative practice. It is just your mind doing what it was made to do: think. You are already successful with the first important stage of your practice: you now know that you are not your thoughts, and therefore, they need not control you.

The next step in the practice is to extend the time between thoughts, and discover the empty space between thoughts. Donna suggests an effective tool to her students to sense what this feels like before they can successfully hold it for longer periods of time. She says when you breathe in, pause for a moment at "the top of the breath" and sense that space of both "nothing" and yet "anticipation of something." It is the pause where potential-for-what-can-come-next resides. You will find yourself keenly interested in that moment.

As you develop this part of the practice, the space between thoughts gets longer and longer, and you go deeper and deeper into meditation. Then you will feel or sense (not think) a place that Donna calls "peaceful abiding." I think that phrase describes the feeling of that place more than adequately. As you sit in peaceful abiding, you begin to go deeper still, where you become aware of thought coming and going, but it is so very far in the background that it is only an echo. It does not grab your attention. It can, in fact, disappear altogether for the most trained meditative practitioners (of which I am not one!).

The other you in there, the observer, is transitioning into the real you: awareness itself. As awareness detaches from the current of thoughts, you detach from emotions and memories, too, because they no longer seem to be you at all. You just don't notice them and, frankly, just don't care. Then your awareness of time disappears. As you continue to penetrate deeper into awareness, you no longer sense your physical body. While you are aware of it, you can't feel its edges unless you refocus on it. Where you end and the outside world begins becomes blurred. Now, you might have a sense of floating, but notice what kind of "floating." If you are dreamy and unfocused, you are actually heading off to sleep, so refocus on your breath, and place your focus back at the point of tension. However, if you remain totally aware, acutely interested and focused, but soft, open, and floating, that is good stuff. You have discovered the place of complete emptiness. It feels blissful and deeply peaceful. It is vibrant, alive, and black. It is nothing but everything at the same time. You will know what I mean when you visit there yourself. Over thousands of years, the great sages and mystics call this "The Ground of Being." It is the primordial soup from which all manifestation arises and to which it returns. It is the core energetic fabric of the universe. It is pure consciousness: that which never dies, but only changes form. It is what you really are underneath that made-up personality of yours. And when you find it, you won't want to leave it. Ever!

Notice I said, YOU won't want to leave it. That is the really cool part. Even though you have detached from the world—everyone and everything in it, your thoughts, your emotions, your physical sensations, your wants and desires, your beliefs and personality—and found what lies deep within to be the empty stream of pure consciousness, somehow, you are still there. You still exist. Dare I say: you are consciousness itself. It is the rest of you that is all made up.

The highest purpose of meditation is to show you through first-hand experience who you really are. When you have experienced it for yourself, it will no longer be theory to you, no longer a belief or a hope or a wish. You will KNOW it as the truth. If at your core you are really empty space, pure consciousness, out of which all things are created, then can you not create anything you want? Absolutely. But you have to get out of your own way first—and that is even harder than learning to meditate.

> " The highest purpose of medita-
> tion is to show you through first-hand
> experience who you really are.

If you have not already experienced this state of being for yourself, with a lot of practice, you someday will. The masters of the world are able to live their lives in that state on and off the meditation cushion. I myself, after fifteen years of practice, can hold that state for maybe a few seconds, but, when I notice it, I am out of it again. Maybe I am a slow learner! The good news is that I can get back there pretty quickly even if I can't yet hold it. But at least I get the privilege of tasting it every day, which keeps me hooked. So I will keep practicing for the rest of my life. Meditation teachers down through the ages also tell us that we won't be able to hold that space for long until our physical bodies evolve to a point where they can safely hold that vibration. Going into the inner space and leaving the physical world behind feels very different. That is how you know it is not all in your mind. Your body tingles and feels like it could float right off the cushion. The reality is you are vibrating at a much higher resonance than before you sat down. Our physical bodies need to adapt and slowly change to be able to hold that higher vibration without blowing our spark plugs. Even so, I promise you it is worth the long arduous effort to evolve your meditative practice. It will change your life, because, as Donna would say, "meditation changes everything."

This brings me to another point. If there is anything that some may see as a negative about meditation, it is that you will become a much more sensitive person. The more you meditate, the more sensitive you will become. You will physically react with discomfort to harshness in the world. You will no longer be able to tolerate violent movies and TV shows.

You will find bad language toxic, not because of the words themselves, but when they are carried on harsh energy. You will no longer be able to physically tolerate junk food, chemical-based products, or noisy shopping malls without experiencing a drop in your energy. That is because as you work with meditation over the longer term, everything about you lightens and brightens. You gain new strengths and are no longer as compressed as you once were.

We use meditation to develop mindfulness, objectivity, and awareness so that we can see our patterns and begin to fix our own shit. When you learn to reach that place of pure consciousness, that place of primordial emptiness from which everything arises, you will want to stay there forever. But you won't be able to, unless perhaps you live in a monastery. The job won't let you, the kids won't let you, life won't let you. So I think the trick is to live *there and here* at the same time. The Tao Te Ching talks about The Middle Way. As I understand it, the Middle Way encourages us to be able to go to "our happy place" daily and carry that sense of love, peace, and mindfulness into our daily lives. One foot in both worlds at all times. The greatest meditation masters of our world, such as the Dalai Lama, are examples of those who meditate many times daily but then come into the world to shine their bright light and to lead and educate the rest of us about living here and now. We can do our little part too. Our experience with the Ground of Being gives us the strength, courage, and control over our minds to be the best contributors we can be.

If all we had to do was learn to meditate, and then with mindfulness respond only compassionately and kindly in our relationships, then why doesn't everyone do it? Because our egos hold on for dear life! Our personality (ego) is a collection of our teachings; our judgments and beliefs; our experiences, emotions and traumas; our memories and stories; and our families and cultures. That ego is powerful. It is demanding, fearful, and selfish. It has good reason to be. In order to survive, we are hard-wired firstly to be fearful. The world today is still violent, tragic, painful, and seemingly chaotic. Mother Nature herself can behave this way.

Scientists propose that the universe is 14 billion years old. Since the beginning, survival has been a violent struggle for most species, including us. In order for humanity to survive, we needed to fight against predators of all kinds, and kill. But mountain lions are no longer chasing most of us. We are all grown up now, are we not? We are no longer children learning about boundaries, and how to share and be kind, and how to think for ourselves.

All of humanity is the first species on this planet to know itself, to be conscious of itself. As we leave babyhood and become toddlers, we begin to see ourselves as separate from Mommy and Daddy. As we became adults, this "separate-self" awareness often leads us to seize possessions so that we and our families survive, believing no one else will help us. Our personalities still live this way today, more so in some countries and cultures than others. Our legacy is still fear and separation. Some cultures live more from unbridled emotion than others; I suggest they are the more reactive, violent ones. Other cultures, usually the more developed nations, live from a place of unbridled mentality, but often with a lack of emotional maturity or compassion.

Yet, with time and practice, meditation can change all that. As the meditation experience brings us back to our selves of pure power (will), love (relating), and intelligence (action), those 3 Root Resources start to infuse our psyche like a teabag in hot water. Once experienced, there is no going back. You begin to move with more grace, more deliberately, unhurriedly. You begin to appreciate the little things in life again, and regain childhood wonder at the simple moments. You are more compassionate. You become aware that, like your thoughts, your emotions are not you either. They are things that come and go after a thought. We hold on to them either by creating stories around them that often judge others or by shoving them deep into our cells where they turn on us. Meditation helps us hold composure while we feel them, express them, and let them go. And yes, that goes for the happy emotions too. You just won't be so emotionally reactive anymore, either way. This is the single biggest factor to stronger, happier family relationships supported by unconditional love.

Meditation sets us up to begin to unravel our personality. We see emotions as separate from us; therefore, we conclude that the stories we told about them were just that, made-up stories of blame and judgment. So we can let them go. We see that when we treat someone harshly, we feel awful, and therefore, we do it less and less. We can no longer hold anger in our bodies because, as our vibration increases, anger is too heavy and toxic and makes us feel ill and tired. So we just don't go there anymore. We tend to let go of relationships that hurt us or no longer help us as we recognize what is their junk and what is ours; we no longer feel the need to save others as we respect everyone's personal responsibility to travel their evolutionary path. As we become more open to accessing a higher place of wisdom through a heart and mind now working together, we question everything from that place. We recognize our bad habits and let them go. We let go of cultural beliefs and traditions that are false, judgmental, or "separative." Slowly we heal, we forgive ourselves and others, and the personality begins to purify. When you meditate regularly, you are not only increasing your own vibrations but also pulling up everyone else along with you, because again, we are all One, all part of the same energy field.

You're in the process of letting go of all your shit, so where does that leave you and your relationships with self and others? It should bring you to a place of contentment and joy. Joy is a more permanent state of stability, peace, and gratitude, no matter what life brings, no matter what tragedy you experience. It becomes a joyous state of being, separate and distinct from a fearful state of being. From a platform of joy, we can express passion, fearlessness, courage, and inspired livingness. Dwelling in joy, you realize that you have the power to choose (in the space of the moment) how you respond to anything life throws at you. You no longer default to patterns, emotional drama and stories, blame, and anger. You can offer unconditional love.

> 66 *Joy is the permanent state*
> *of peace and appreciation.*

Heart over Brain

A key to understanding the power of mediation and why it works lies in the heart. Your heart is smarter than your brain. It will tell you how to fix your shit and will lead the way to a better you in a manner your brain never could. Yes, the heart is about love. But it is also the transmitter of wisdom in your body!

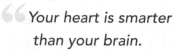

> 66 *Your heart is smarter*
> *than your brain.*

The brain transmits thoughts, but they are usually recycled knowledge that already exists out there. The heart accesses the wisdom from the intuitive spaces, where new things come into being. I know how this sounds—but science has recently proven that the heart is actually a second brain in the body.

HeartMath Institute (HMI) is on the leading edge of scientific research around the huge capabilities of the heart both physically and energetically. When one blends heart and mind, miracles happen. Since 1991, HMI scientists have been researching heart-brain communication, exploring "the electro-physiology of intuition and how all things are interconnected … and how the heart's magnetic field radiates outside the body and can affect other people." I am not a scientist and cannot attest to their testing methodology. But I can tell you they have concluded that when the heart rhythms are in coherence, it creates dramatic positive shifts, including heightened perception, stress reduction, and more effective handling of challenging circumstances. I have used some of their technology and have confirmed their findings for myself from my own experience.

> We observed that the heart was acting as though it had a mind of its own and was profoundly influencing the way we perceive and respond to the world. In essence, it appeared that the heart was affecting intelligence and awareness.
>
> The answers to many of our original questions now provide a scientific basis to explain how and why the heart affects mental clarity, creativity, emotional balance and personal effectiveness. Our research and that of others indicate that the heart is far more than a simple pump. The heart is, in fact, a highly complex, self-organized information processing center with its own functional "brain" that communicates with and influences the cranial brain via the nervous system, hormonal system and other pathways.[29]

The energetic field emitted by the heart is much stronger and reaches out from the body much further than that emitted from the brain. You can physically feel it in meditation. You can feel it "talk to you" in everyday life. Phrases like "her heart burst with joy at the sight of him" describes well the feeling of your heart space suddenly expanding outward in a moment of love. Or "his heart contracted with fear" describes well the shrouded, shrivelled-up heart space those who live in fear experience. Fearful people are often referred to as "cold-hearted." Loving people are often seen as "warm-hearted."

The heart talks to us in feelings. The brain talks to us in thoughts. I think most people now agree that intuition (i.e., the ability to understand something immediately, without the need for conscious reasoning) is centred in the heart, not the brain. The brain, while a valuable centre for deductive reasoning, is at risk of making destructive decisions when the heart is absent. The brain on its own is separative. The brain infused with the heart is inclusive and collaborative. Yet at the end of the day, if you want to make any decision, or take any action that you hope will be for your highest good, as well as the highest good of others, let the heart ultimately decide. Thinking "correctly" happens in the heart space. Between the brain and the heart, the latter has the more powerful energy connection to universal wisdom. So I would be listening to it.

*"Between the brain and the
heart, the latter has the more
powerful energy connection
to universal wisdom.*

Decrease Your Emotionality

The Universal Law of Perpetual Transmutation of Energy tells us that all persons have within them the power to change the conditions of their lives. Lower vibrations get consumed by, and become, higher vibrations; thus, each of us can change the energies in our lives by understanding the Universal Laws and applying the principles in such a way as to effect this change. Most emotions are lower-density vibrations and require transmutation.

Emotions are energy fields that will turn inward if not outwardly expressed. Locked up inside of us, they will cause "dis-ease" mentally and, ultimately, physically. But they can be processed and expressed outwardly in a healthy, non-destructive way by making the choice to do so. It is that simple—and at the same time, so very difficult. You have less than a split second to turn a reaction to a response, but the time is there. And meditation will help you "extend" that split second by deflating common everyday reactivity and transforming it through mindfulness.

Emotions are things—forces of energy—moving through us. But we don't realize that they just want to come and go.

We grab on to them, and alarmed and reactive, we begin to tell ourselves a story about why they are there. Usually it is to blame someone else.

The key to reducing emotionality is to take advantage of the half-second before the emotion becomes a story and "step back." This may mean taking a few deep breaths, or even leaning back a little to physically separate from the scene. Then notice how you actually feel. Embrace the emotion instead of flipping it up into your head. By its nature, your mind will want to jump to a judgment, but instead, keep it busy noticing how the emotion feels in your body. Let it be felt and it will eventually dissipate. You might rightly be thinking: "Wait a minute. If tragedy happens, you are not going to just notice it and then it will dissolve. Grief can stay with you for years." That is true. But grief is not an emotion. Before you get your knickers in a twist, let me explain.

> **The key to reducing emotionality is to take advantage of the half-second before the emotion becomes a story and 'step back.'**

An emotion is a quality such as anger, jealously, boredom, sloth, happiness, excitement or pleasure. Core feelings are different. They are deep-rooted, always soft and kind, and actually a reflection of the essence of love. They come from the heart. Grief and sorrow, for example, are feelings since they are long lasting and come out of love. So too is joy, which is a state of peace and bliss that comes out of love. Happiness is fleeting and usually based in transient pleasures independent of love.

So, going back to that half second, by focusing on experiencing the emotion fully and in that moment choosing not to react and jump to a story, we are retaining neutrality. We are in equipoise. As my meditation coach would say, you have to let "awareness take its seat." Again, meditation offers us a tool: it is hands down the best way to train yourself to be less emotionally reactive. It trains you to create space in the moment, to hold just enough space to not chase or repulse what is happening, but to intelligently respond to it.

I remember the first day I noticed the significant change meditation had made in my inner world and outer expression. My husband brought it to my attention. We were driving to the office, and he was feeling very angry about something—I can't recall what exactly, but it had something to do with a situation that was also impacting me. He was expressing his anger and frustration as he discussed the situation. He was clearly agitated as he spoke. I listened. Then he stopped mid-rant and said, "Why aren't you mad! Doesn't this piss you off? Don't you ever sometimes just want to get mad?" Right then, I realized that no, I don't. I don't like the emotion of anger. I had chosen, without being aware of it, to listen and observe from a place of detachment. The issue affected me negatively, too, but somehow at that moment, I was present in the "space in between." I had the space to choose to respond rather than react. This is what compassion can feel like.

Creating space in the moment helps you recognize, before it is too late, that what you are usually reacting to is not the situation itself, but to the disturbance it has caused in you. You can then ask: Why am I reacting this way? What does this tell me about me? You can use the "point of tension" from your meditative practice, that I spoke of earlier, to consciously focus on the "point" of the moment, what is really happening, so that you can get a broader perspective and perceive the truth of the moment. It creates a stillness within you, a centralization of power, so that when you choose to respond, from a depersonalized space, you are empowered. You also empower others by learning not to try to fix their stuff for them. They are responsible for their own emotions, as they are cues to disturbances within them that are asking to be looked at and healed.

Emotional Maturity

Emotional maturity is so very important to living a successful life, and yet so few people display it. Frankly, without emotional maturity, you have troubled relationships. And your most troubled relationship is likely the one with yourself, although you probably won't see that at first. Without emotional maturity, your ability to deploy the 2nd Root Resource, relating (which is the attracting principle), is weakened. Emotional maturity is most seen in those who have a healthy sense of themselves and their contribution to others. A good level of self-esteem allows them to react to adversity with a level head, stable emotions, confidence, clarity, and without resorting to drama. People without strong self-esteem overreact, become defensive, and are incapable of seeing any other point of view. They are often stubborn and unable to listen to another's perspective. All of us have moments like this, but as a modus operandi, it can be the cause of most family dysfunction. Recognizing this danger, The Family Treasury systems nurtures the self-esteem and emotional maturity of each family member.

> *Without emotional maturity,*
> *you have troubled relationships.*

The Law of Attraction

Decreasing our emotionality enables us to listen to our intuitive feelings about ourselves and others, which nourishes our relationships. But the bonus is: it also enhances our ability to create what we most want in our lives. It is our feelings that first engage the Universal Law of Attraction. This law shows something that might seem counterintuitive at first: We actually create the things, events, and people that come into our lives. Our feelings lead to thoughts, words, and actions that produce energies, which in turn attract like energies. Positive energies attract positive energies and negative energies attract negative energies. What you experience on the outside is a direct reflection of what is going on inside of you. By paying attention to what is going on inside, you can transform it to what you want for the outside. Yup, this takes steadfast effort. And yup, this is not a job for a lazy person.

> 66 *Decreasing our emotionality enables us to listen to our intuitive feelings about ourselves and others, which nourishes our relationships.*

Have you noticed that the Law of Attraction is just another expression of the 2nd Root Resource, relating? In fact, I would suggest that it IS the second resource in its highest, purest form. The law is the ultimate relating, attracting principle. It is the attraction of love, drawing a beloved toward you. It is magnetic attraction. When you have done your homework— are living with an attitude of gratitude; have released a lot of your shit and forgiven yourself and others; and have learned to control your emotional reactivity—you have super charged the Law of Attraction. Energy is infinite. Your light (consciousness) is vibrating at a much higher level. Whatever you focus your light on, give your attention to, will now attract the vibrational match, just like a magnet. The wonderful thing is that, since energy is infinite, you having more does not mean someone else has less. You are not depriving anyone. They, too, can manifest abundance in their life by taking charge of their 3 Root Resources (will, relating, and action).

Something to bear in mind, though, when using the Law of Attraction: manipulating to get what you want is not the same thing as inviting what you want. The first is to control and take. The second is to invite and let go. To maximize your chance of attracting your desired outcome, set the goal, perhaps even loosely develop a plan to get there, and then LET IT GO. To over-strategize actually causes a contraction of energy, a forced manipulation of it. This creates small-minded human boundaries and limitations on what the all-knowing universe could otherwise provide. Instead, put it out there, then follow your intuition and let the creativity free flow. This is when true evolution takes place, when something entirely new and beyond your imagination can be created. This is the true difference between control and mastery. Control is a dense, constraining force, usually bringing a sense of dis-ease. Mastery is an open force that flows with ease, bringing a sense of "being above," of altitude, with a feeling of both detachment and the heart being fully engaged.

Money provides examples of how control plays out in many lives. Those who manipulate money toward them-selves through greed or selfishness may symptomatically hoard it as a result. They feel like they never have enough. It can cause congestion in them, if not congestive heart fail-ure. Other hang-ups about money include: I'm not smart enough. I don't deserve it. Money is bad. It would cost me too much in other ways to make more money. These people are exercising their control by repulsing money. Instead, they should simply choose to receive it with gratitude, which will attract more.

What parent would tell their child they want them to have "just a little" abundance. Would we not want unlimited abundance for our children? Why should we expect anything less for ourselves? Also, abundance isn't just about money. Gifts of love, intelligence, learning, opportunities, experiences, friends, sunshine, warm baths, and so on are equally valuable and need to be recognized and appreciated in order to attract more.

▲ ▼ ▲

It is time to figure out *our* shit. For those of us living in the developed nations, it is our responsibility. In his book *Evolutionary Enlightenment*, Andrew Cohen puts it like this: "those of us at the very leading edge of cultural development today are in a different position … we are the luckiest people that have ever been born in the history of our species … The problem is, most of us don't seem to know it. We don't act as if it is true. The luckiest people in the world don't seem to be aware of how lucky they are."[30] He describes how we are the lucky few who have the privilege of higher education, material wealth, comfort, security, and leisure time. We have personal, political, philosophical, and religious freedom. He says "there have never been human beings who have had the extraordinary liberty we have to experiment with our own lives,—to think in whatever way we want, to do almost anything we want, to say anything we want, to go anywhere we want, to be whatever we want."[31] He suggests that if you were observing humanity during a conversation with God, it might go like this: "And what are they [humanity] doing? They are lost in their separate, privileged personal worlds, with little or no sense of who they really are, oblivious to the grandeur and the majesty of what it could mean to live your glory as themselves."[32] "Surely it [the ego] was never intended to be merely a vehicle for self-absorption and self-infatuation."[33]

It's time to figure out *your* shit. It's also time to discover who you really are and who others are in relation to you. Work to drop false beliefs and separative, judgmental negative behaviours. Evolution requires that we all move forward toward a more conscious self. Practice relating to people and situations more through the heart and less through the mind. Meditation is a key, if not the most important, tool for all of us to get there. It is a powerful tool to strengthen your family relationships and the relationship you have with yourself. Over time, it will bring you to a place of compassion and unconditional love that will result in both peace and power like you have never before experienced. It will seriously increase the love quotient in your life. As my friend Donna would say, whenever you feel yourself drift away from this centred place during the day, "Stop, Drop, and Meditate!"

▲ ▼ ▲

Your homework will be a lifelong but very rewarding endeavour. You only need to begin it, not complete it, to start to grow your 3 Root Resources and manifest your dreams using The Family Treasury systems. We used systems to develop your purpose, the 1st Root Resource of will, and the mission of The Family Treasury. As with any good and successful business, we now need to use systems to ensure our implementation team is harmonized, motivated, and inspired to see The Family Treasury mission realized. We need to develop our family team culture to amplify the power of our relationships—the 2nd Root Resource, relating or unconditional love—for each other and for ourselves. We hope each member of the team is working at their highest potential, developing their unique abilities and talents, and in so doing, enhancing the overall success of the team. If we are all on the same page, the Law of Attraction dictates that our ability to obtain results is magnified.

Tools to Manage Your Family Relationships

As with your homework above, the systems that follow are an ongoing process. As you practice with them and gain experience for what works best for you and your family, you will achieve ever more refined results.

△ *The Family Documentary*

Celebrate! Celebrate who you are individually and what you as a family collectively stand for. Every year, look back at what you have accomplished, where you have been together, and what you hope to achieve going forward.

When my children were growing up—this is going back twenty-five years—we were very fortunate to have a video camera at a time when many families did not. I was the documentary filmmaker in the family. And I filmed everything! In fact, looking back at the videos taken, it is a wonder my children know I exist. Not only am I not in most of the footage, because I am behind the camera, but I am sure my babies all thought my face was a big black lens with a red blinking light.

But now that my kids are in their twenties, there is nothing that we like doing together more than watching those home videos. Okay, maybe that is not entirely true—we like ski vacations better. But home videos come a close second. Even the girlfriends love to watch them and think the kids were hysterical. In fact, I have often caught the "kids" on the couch with a beer in hand laughing by themselves as they watch the hilarity that was our life. The really interesting thing about those videos, though, is seeing how each of us has progressed, grown, and changed. It somehow gives perspective to what you have become while reminding you of who you were. The videos (now in multiple copies and some stored off-site) are one of the greatest assets of our Family Treasury. What I love most about them is that when I miss my little children—my sweet angel of a daughter and my adorable little boys—I grab a glass of wine, turn on a video, and am right there with them again. Just like it was yesterday.

In the early years of your Family Treasury, may I suggest you video record a family documentary that celebrates your family and everyone in it. This can be an ongoing tradition as well, which I discuss later. I suggest you start with a history of your family, where it came from, how it came to be what and who it is today. Tell as many stories as you can: and remember, it is often the challenging stuff, the difficult relationships that make us who we are today. There is light and dark in everything, including every relationship, and when they both weigh in together, you will find they are what forms our unique characters. Talk about things like your life lessons, your experiences, and the discoveries you have made about living along the way. Magic can happen in this process. When you share yourself out loud, you often see things differently. The recording process can be very healing, so try not to make it too fluffy or too formal. Make it real. The generations that follow will thank you for your insights. Yes, someday they will be watching it!

> " *When you share yourself out loud,*
> *you often see things differently.*

If you are not comfortable in front of a camera, another option is to write it all down and then put together a coffee table book. It can describe your family history, great loves and challenges, individual and collective successes and what it took to create those successes. It can reflect your philosophies and the important lessons you wish to pass on. And it can be full of wonderful memorable photos. These types of family documentaries are often professionally written, compiled, and published.

Complete the documentary by stating what you as a family have determined is The Family Treasury mission and why. What glorious vision are each of you individually and together working toward? What kind of a future are you aiming for? Putting it on video is the first powerful step in manifesting it, for you have now put it out into the universe on the wings of love, mutual support, and enthusiasm.

By way of preparation, it might help to write out a list of questions or discussion points ahead of time so people can mull them over before their recording day. But try not to share what you wish to say with each other beforehand. Firstly, so that the recording is as spontaneous and natural as can be—which makes the finished product a lot more fun to watch. And secondly, so no one has the chance to talk you out of doing it.

And a last prompt: take videos of more than just the people. Film the pets. Film the cottage. Film the house, the backyard, and the new lawn tractor. Anything and everything that you think is part of the story. Have fun with it—it is a celebration!

My son did our first documentary. He directed, produced, shot, narrated, and edited the project. He interviewed family members, inserted clips and photos from previous family videos and added music to round it out. In our media-driven world, unless you live under a rock, it is not hard to find video and photo material. It is best if someone in the family can take this on. But if no one in your family has that artistic flair, then I suggest that at least for the first family documentary, you find someone who can film and produce a quality production for you. Often their editing ability, including adding music and other effects to enhance the story, can make the video so much more memorable.

▲ *The Family Treasury Roundtable*

The Family Treasury relies on co-operation and collaboration when managing the family resources and making decisions that affect all family members. This is most effectively achieved through the use of some form of family council. This is not a new concept. Many of the wealthiest and most influential families of our time successfully use the family council as a platform to assist with the complex process of managing family wealth and keeping families united over multiple generations. The council is a group of senior family members whose job it is to create opportunities to grow a strong family culture and to deal with challenges to it in a healthy and respectful manner. In multi-generational families, council membership grows to ensure that a representative from each family "arm" is in attendance. How these councils function is a topic for another book, but an important point to understand at the outset is that this can be very challenging work when you are dealing with many different people with varying attitudes about what it means to have financial wealth. I have great respect and admiration for the work done at Pitcairn Trust Co. in this regard. Dirk Junge, chairman of the company and a fourth-generation Pitcairn family member now working with the fifth and sixth generations, generously offered a perspective on this and has permitted me to share it with you. Dirk points out that "wealth is an amplifier ... NOT the input." He goes on to say that "love, power, and money makes for a volatile cocktail." Dirk provides the following outline (edited for these purposes) to demonstrate the benefits and challenges wealth brings.

Benefits of Wealth	Challenges of Wealth
Career/volunteer options	Isolation/resentment
Education opportunities	External expectations
Charitable participation	Lack of respect/"rich-bashing"
Lifestyle enhancement	Abuse of friendship
Intergenerational wealth sharing	Lack of initiative/motivation
Travel/multi-cultural experiences	Dependency
Recreation/hobbies	Addictions/abuse
Pride/heritage	Unequal wealth in relationships[34]

As you review this list, consider how either a positive or negative experience with wealth can be significantly amplified depending on the "inputs" (i.e., beliefs, maturity, effort, motivation, ethics, intentions, values, etc.) and the focus of attention on the benefits or challenges in isolation of each other.

Regularly Scheduled Meetings

The Family Treasury Roundtable is a best practices family council tool capable of managing this relating process in a relatively productive and much less volatile manner. Just as every successful business would hold regular strategic group meetings to monitor and refine the strategic business plan, The Family Treasury Roundtable is a meeting format that can keep the team engaged and on the same page.

> 66 *The Family Treasury Roundtable is a meeting format that can keep the team engaged and on the same page.*

Quarterly meetings are best, if you can swing it, but at the very least, they should be held semi-annually. It can be a challenge for large family groups from different regions with busy schedules to get together. But with proper planning and commitment, it can be done. Try to hold the meeting at the same time every year so that everyone can build it into their routine.

If held quarterly, the meeting is usually over a weekend, beginning Friday night and ending Sunday afternoon. The sessions usually start at 8:30 a.m. and end at 3 p.m. with catered meals. No more than two three-hour sessions per day is recommended, with two to four sessions in total over the weekend, depending on the agenda items. Each meeting should have a different leader whose responsibilities include canvassing family members for agenda items, sending out the agenda ahead of time, making arrangements with the venue, preparing materials, and booking speakers. They, of course, should have assistants. A new leader is chosen for each meeting, which nurtures leadership skills in every family member while sharing the burden.

Location

Where you hold the annual meeting is important. Remember, it is a celebration! If affordable, some or all of the meetings should be away from anyone's day-to-day home turf. Someplace where the family can be at play and leave behind their busy work lives is ideal. The more neutral the location, the better, so that everyone present is on equal footing. If possible, the annual meeting could be longer and incorporate a family holiday. A resort with meeting facilities offers a good option. Days are added before and after to create fun family memories. If there are younger children, babysitting arrangements should be made so the adults can enjoy the meeting times uninterrupted. In some instances, those times with the babysitter can also be productive for the youngsters with activities related to The Family Treasury on offer. For example, let's say that part of The Family Treasury mission statement is to perpetuate a healthy respect for the natural environment. A guided nature walk to learn about plants and insects could be arranged for the kids, or even sailing lessons.

Purpose

The Family Treasury Roundtable is like a strategic business meeting, keeping the family focused on its priorities and making maximum use of their resources. It provides a forum to resolve relationship issues before they fester and seeks opportunities to grow the unique abilities, potentials, and interests of each member. It gives everyone a sense of belonging, reminds them how important they are, and reinforces that each has a role to play and something to contribute to the group. They matter and are valued just for being who they are. The Roundtable heals hurts and replaces falsehoods and misunderstandings with truths. It gives each person healthy substance to work with. It helps dig up opportunity while providing a sense of grounding, foundation, and security. It lets each person know they are enough, and provides "the wind beneath their wings." That one might be corny, but nevertheless, it is true. The Roundtable brings minds and hearts together in a group, in an integrated way that celebrates their togetherness and their individuality. It keeps their heads in the game, their fingers on the pulse of the action, and—you guessed it—super charges the Law of Attraction. *Interesting how the resource we want, more love, is also the resource that we already have, and that when attended to, gives us more of it.*

> *The Roundtable brings minds and hearts together in a group, in an integrated way that celebrates their togetherness and their individuality.*

As mentioned previously, in most families, there are issues creating dysfunction. They need to be dealt with—and will be—but not right away. The Family Treasury needs time to assert itself, display its benefits, and nurture a sense of belonging in every member of the family. Once everyone feels the benefits and the commitment to continue is established, then the really difficult stuff can be tabled. No one needs to hide the issues or pretend they are not there. However, as mature adults, there can be an agreement to focus initially on what unites the family and leave the issues that are bubbling just below the surface until such time as a good foundation for healthy discussion has been formed (such as in the Charter described below).

Attendance

One question I often get is: how do you get everyone to the table? Most twenty-year-olds would not think a weekend with Mom and Dad the highlight of their social calendar. Most forty-year-olds will be hard pressed to find one afternoon to meet, never mind two to three days. Most family members are still coming from a place of self-interest, isolative (go-it-alone) attitudes, and lifestyle overwhelm. They have not had the benefit of reading this book like you have and may look at you as if you have sprouted two heads when you suggest a "Family Roundtable Meeting."

The answer to the question is: you get them to the table by bribing them! For example, Jack might coerce his family to their first round-table meeting with a weekend trip to a local cottage resort, offering everyone free beer, wine, and food—significant others welcome (but not necessarily in the meeting). Full disclosure would include that he wants four hours of their time to explain this new thing called The Family Treasury, which he has learned about and thinks could benefit everyone in the family. Jill might entice her family with a trip to the Bahamas. You get the idea. Once you get them there, however, the trick is to capture their attention and imagination by following a meeting plan.

Before we discuss the meeting format, I think a few words are warranted about family dysfunction. All families have some dysfunctionality as it is a symptom of being human. However, depending on that level of dysfunction, it may take some time to get the entire family at the table. For some it may take months to years of each of you *figuring out your own shit*, before you are able to come together as a functional group. Yet you, the one holding this book in your hands, can lead this process by example, allowing yourself the vulnerability to share what you learn with your other family members. In doing so you are showing how important it is to you that they be in your life in good relationship. You will know when the time is right to introduce the first Family Roundtable Meeting and you need not have full attendance. To paraphrase the 1989 movie *Field of Dreams*, "build it and they will come."

Meeting Format

In the first year, whether you hold two, three, or four meetings, most of your time will be spent outlining what you have learned about The Family Treasury and its many potential benefits, and exploring how it might benefit each member of the family and the family as a whole over time.

At the first meeting, to solidify The Family Treasury's value and capture the interest of those in attendance, I suggest you arrange for a Kolbe or Prevue analysis (see Chapter 4) of each family member ahead of time, and then have the results presented to the group. A guaranteed great conversation starter! And good for some laughs too, no doubt. You can also spend that first meeting exploring and defining each person's personal mission and purpose using the exercises offered in Chapter 4. It may be an opportunity to help the younger generation analyze and make some of those tough life decisions to get them on their way. You may not get the answers after one meeting, but the process will have begun. No one will commit their time and energy to identifying a group mission until they have clarity about their own, so the idea is to impress upon everyone the benefits of coming to the next meeting, and those after that.

To be successful, The Family Treasury Roundtable meetings should follow a set format. The topics of discussion can evolve over time, but the meeting format should stay true. Below is a sample format or agenda that can be used once family members are used to coming to weekend meetings and investing appropriate time. Of course, your family will and should design its own format. For all of the sessions, have someone record or take notes. These will become the minutes of the meeting for future reference. It will also become a basis for the script for—you guessed it!—your next video.

> ❝ *To be successful, The Family Treasury Roundtable meetings should follow a set format.*

The following outlines a sample agenda for a Family Roundtable weekend meeting where the individual and Family Treasury mission statements have already been established.

Friday Night
We want a positive tone of unification and collaboration for the weekend, so this initial meeting is meant to "set the mood." It is intended to be intimate and personal, and non-confrontational. It is also meant to be light on agenda items as family members have often travelled during the day to be there after a busy week.

Agenda

1. Watch last year's documentary, if this is your annual meeting.

2. Do some team-building exercises. These should be fun but meaningful. The aim is to enliven everyone and get them working together as a team on the little stuff before asking them to be a team for the big stuff. Plenty of exercises or games are easily sourced on the Internet.

3. Review the agenda for the rest of the weekend and make any amendments needed. If anyone in the group has a potentially emotional issue or conflict with anyone else, now is not the time to discuss it, although it can be respectfully raised within context.

Saturday

It is time to dive into the main agenda items of the meeting. They should always relate to the advancement of The Family Treasury mission. By its nature, this will include the development of every member of the family, the harmonization of the family relationships, re-igniting the fire of passion and purpose for your group goals, and putting plans in place to achieve them while celebrating your past achievements. The weekend will be working with the three Family Treasury Systems (founded in the 3 Root Resources of will, relating, and action). Saturday will focus on Stewardship through a Worthy

Mission (will) and Development through Loving Relationships (relating). Sunday will focus on Legacy of Achievements (action).

If some of the issues to be addressed are difficult or likely to be highly emotional, consider if it is appropriate to engage a trained family facilitator to help the family navigate to a peaceful resolution that all can accept. The facilitator should know the family well while retaining absolute objectivity at all times. They should have had the opportunity to speak privately with each of the affected parties to gain their perspectives. The goal of any good facilitator, and the family too, would be to come to a win-win resolution where no one affected feels that they have "lost."

The Family Treasury charter (as described below) also plays a significant role in this situation. It helps families to resolve conflict in a respectful, rational manner without resorting to reactions learned in childhood. More about this in later sections.

Agenda

1. Use the personal Mission Statements to set the stage. Everyone has a chance to speak and share their experiences since the last meeting related to The Family Treasury and each of their own missions. Everyone should strive to share as much as they can—their triumphs and accomplishments, and their trials and tribulations. The intention is to discuss happenings, both

happy and sad, and describe how they have impacted the family member physically, emotionally, and mentally. Everyone should be encouraged to include the successes they are grateful for, even if they have had a rough few months. At the end of the meeting, if you have shared the real you, those in attendance will have received the real you. The more homework they have done (see the earlier section in this chapter), the more they will make you feel loved, supported, and valued. Even if you are such a close family that you think you already know all this, the formal approach will always give the opportunity for depth and some surprises. What are you most grateful for? How is each member of the family progressing with their own personal mission? What, if any, changes might be needed?

2. Review The Family Treasury mission statement and any amendments needed.

3. Address any areas of interfamily conflict. There should be no "you" discussions—only "I" discussions. See Conflict Resolution in the following sections for more on this.

4. Review the family charter (discussed below) and any amendments needed.

5. Run an educational session. As discussed later in this chapter, an educational curriculum can become a central part of your Family Treasury Roundtable meetings.

You can review a book or books on themes pertinent to your group mission, or perhaps have a speaker come in for a one-hour presentation followed by a discussion. This could feature presentations by the younger crowd on topics of interest to them. The focus of these sessions often includes wealth management issues, philanthropy, world events, health and welfare, etc.

Sunday

Saturday dealt with the worthy mission and loving relationships. If there are leftover issues from the day, they should be thoroughly addressed before moving to Sunday's agenda about the legacy of achievements. In fact, if by the end of Sunday, the previous agenda items remain unresolved, a new meeting should be set to address them. This may occur because the team culture is either too unfocused to achieve a worthy mission or too emotionally misaligned to develop their potentials together. Harmony is needed within these two systems before the third, legacy of achievements, can manifest. Assuming we can get to the achievements section of the weekend, the following outlines processes to quantify and measure our progress and further refine our go-forward plans.

Agenda

1. Review the results of The Family Treasury financial plan (discussed in Chapter 6).

2. Plan and document next steps for The Family Treasury financial plan.

3. Review the results and plan and document next steps for The Family Treasury strategic plan (see Chapter 6).

4. Review The Family Treasury balance sheet (also in Chapter 6) for progress.

As discussed at the end of this chapter, both the family and community can be well served by the Family Foundation. If the family has a charitable foundation, review of its achievement of initiatives should be on the agenda as well, if not quarterly, then at least annually.

Meeting Wrap-Up

At the end of the meeting, we suggest you video record comments from each person about how the weekend went and what their takeaway is. In fact, the filmmaker may be "on duty" the entire time you are together (during leisure time, not meeting time) so that you end up with a Family Treasury of wonderful memories from your times together. And a personal request from one who always ends up behind the camera: *please share that duty!* Either that or, if you're comfortable with it, hire someone to discreetly film in the background. One beautiful advantage is that they can record the kids in action while you are in sessions. You can also appoint someone as interviewer, if you have a family member who is comfortable with that role. The aim is to interview each family member about their learnings and realizations, goals and objectives as they come out of the meeting and also capture what they are excited about going forward. This will not happen after all meetings, of course; some agenda items may be too heavy or private, and thus inappropriate.

▲ ▼ ▲

It is unlikely that all of these suggested agenda items could be addressed in one weekend. The good news is you have complete flexibility to decide how many sessions you want to hold on a meeting weekend, how many times in a year you will meet and for how long, and what the priorities are for each meeting.

It is also important to be flexible when setting the agenda. Some Family Treasury Roundtable meetings may deal with difficult emotional issues. Not all meetings are going to end with everyone singing "Kumbaya" by the campfire. Time may run out before issues can be fully addressed, and there may be participants feeling tired at best, or angry at worse. The important thing is to ensure a follow-up meeting is arranged in short order with affected parties to resolve those issues before they fester. A family facilitator can play a key role to move these difficult conversations and issues to resolution.

The Roundtable Charter

The Family Treasury Roundtable charter is a document that the family puts together (often with the help of a facilitator) to outline agreed-upon policies and procedures. This may not be developed right away, but should be on the agenda by the third or fourth meeting into the process. Three very common elements of a charter include conflict resolution, rules of participation, and expectations of behaviour.

> 66 *The Family Treasury Roundtable charter is a document that the family puts together to outline agreed-upon policies and procedures.*

Conflict Resolution

Conflict resolution is best achieved by following a procedure the entire family has agreed to before there is actual conflict. The charter outlines what this procedure is. Conflict is something most people are uncomfortable with and will do just about anything to avoid. In fact, there are often issues so deeply disturbing that they have become taboo and are just not discussed. However, the result is that negativity only festers and relationships worsen. But there is a silver lining to conflict. Innovations and improvements seldom occur without some friction or discomfort causing enough conflict to attract attention to the areas needing to evolve.

A good Family Roundtable charter documents the following elements:

1. A safe, non-judgmental environment will be provided to all parties so they can feel free to express their grievances without being rejected. Individuals must feel supported rather than criticized or they will not open up. Personal attacks are not tolerated.

2. There is no leader, no boss as the Roundtable is just that: round! All at the table are equals. All titles of parent, child, boss, employee, elder, younger, etc. are left at the door. Each individual is respected as a powerful being with much to contribute.

3. Basic rules about speaking and listening are listed, and expanded upon, as and if needed. For example, when someone is speaking, no one can interrupt until the speaker states they are finished sharing. When someone is listening, they will do just that: listen fully, with attention and without interruption, unless that interruption is to gain clarity. When the speaker is finished, the listeners will reframe what was said to ensure they heard the facts (and did not misjudge or make assumptions about what was being said). This also serves to let the speaker know that they were heard. Speakers also will be encouraged to be succinct and not "hog" the floor, and to self-reference always, using "I" statements to express how they feel about a

situation, not "You" statements that blame someone else for something that was done.

4. A process is established to resolve conflicts. A flip chart can come in handy for this. One such process looks like this:

- Record the issue and each person's concern about the issue.
- Identify what each person believes will happen if the issue is unresolved.
- Explore the facts surrounding the issue and try to sort fact from projection.
- List every option or solution possible: brainstorm.
- Agree on an ideal outcome that looks like a win-win for all.

Rules of Participation

The rules of participation include who can and should attend the Roundtable meetings, what to do if people don't or won't show up, and what the process and content of the meetings should be.

For example, your family may decide that all family members over a certain age should be invited to attend the meetings. This is a delicate but important decision. For example, if you decide that everyone over the age of sixteen should be invited, be aware of their levels of maturity and ability to associate with and understand the adult issues that will inevitably be discussed. They must be mature enough to both respect and retain confidentiality. In addition, during these meetings, discussions about family money will be part of the agenda. If you have been able to build financial assets into your Family Treasury, you as a family will need to decide what is an appropriate age for your young people to receive full disclosure of those financial assets. Of course, there is always the option of splitting the meeting into two groups with appropriate agendas for each group session. For example, perhaps financial business is not discussed until Sunday morning, while all the under-21s get to sleep in! I recommend that spouses of blood family members always be invited, not only to honour the relationship but also to provide full integration of issues needing to be addressed.

Rules of participation might address what happens if people don't or won't show up. Items to consider might include required quorum before meetings can go ahead, protocols around taking and issuing meeting minutes for those who could not attend, RSVP deadlines and penalties for non-attendance—not unlike what would happen in a business if key team members continually fail to come to important meetings. Rules about permissible meeting content is important to ensure team members know what are appropriate meeting topics and what are not. This depends on the family culture, values, and, of course, the mission of The Family Treasury.

Rules about decision-making are helpful to ensure everyone has a democratic vote and that the final decision is accepted, even if not preferred. Will decisions be made by majority vote or by consensus (where a solution that everyone feels they can support is found through negotiation and discussion)?

Expectations of Behaviour

The expectation of behaviour element conveys how the family members have agreed to represent themselves out in the community. It reiterates the values that the family holds dear, a creed that they aim to live by. It can set out how individual family members are expected to act, hopefully with kindness and respect toward others. Perhaps it can also confirm that members are to be responsible for themselves and for developing their own potentials. They are expected to keep family matters confidential. The group's views on education should be discussed and hopefully unified. For example, if the view is that education is important, are members expected to gain an education at university or college and/or through internships? Are all paths equally respected and valuable, or does the family favour one over the other, and why? It might describe how all family members are expected to display a strong work ethic and make healthy lifestyle choices, and so on. Views on drugs and alcohol can be outlined.

▲ ▼ ▲

By way of example, The Family Treasury Roundtable in my family designed its charter around Miguel Ruiz's book *The*

Four Agreements: A Practical Guide to Personal Freedom. Ruiz relays the four agreements to us as:

1. Be impeccable with your word.

2. Don't take anything personally.

3. Don't make assumptions.

4. Always do your best.[35]

By extension, our Roundtable charter holds to the following principles:

- Words are a powerful force of attractive energy, so use them wisely.

- It's almost never about you.

- Ask for the facts.

- Embrace it as if you asked for it.

For those of you who have read Ruiz's book, you will note that each of these agreements has a great deal of depth. Having said that, we think that on the surface they also provide an excellent system of behaviour that all Roundtable participants can strive to model.

The Family Treasury Communication Model

It is one thing to agree to methods of conflict resolution, rules of participation, and expectations of behaviour; it is quite another to stick to them when things heat up. Matters get worse when we don't speak the same language. Each of us has very different ways of receiving and processing information. Firstly, of course, we process it through our filters— another way to describe our values, beliefs, and biases. But you are doing your homework now and working to understand those filters and eliminate those that are detrimental to your relationships, right? Secondly, we receive and respond to information in a manner unique to us. Some people have a natural ability to perceive the manner in which another person would best receive information. Others need some help with this. The Family Treasury Communication model seeks to identify for each member of the team how they wish to receive information and how best they work with it. It then creates a framework that the team can follow to ensure a more balanced approach to communication and decision-making so that everyone can participate to their full potential.

Let me demonstrate with an example modelled on a family we worked with recently. The most notable point of tension was between mother and son. Mom is by nature very detail oriented and rather conservative. She likes to research the pros and cons of every decision before it is made, with a bent toward choosing the conservative option. She will use past experiences of her own as well as others to evaluate the decision at hand. Mom likes to do this analysis on her own, processing her thoughts without interference; prepare her position; and then return to the group with facts and figures to support her decision. This past-based perspective is absolutely a gift to the group because it helps prevent mistakes that can be avoided by retrospection. However, it can also cause a challenge: because she has put so much work into coming to that decision, Mom is very resistant to changing her mind once it is made up. Now, Son is by nature more of a risk taker. He makes decisions more from intuition and feel than from mental reasoning. He is more forward-thinking and cares little for what happened in the past. He is a visionary who thrives on change and is confident that his creative intelligence can overcome any obstacle that he may face. Son enjoys the uncertainty of the outcome and is adventurous in his approach. This, too, is absolutely a gift to the group for it is how evolution happens. Yet it can also cause friction when caution is thrown to the wind and excessive risk is taken.

What is needed is a respectful and appreciative validation of both of these communication styles. On one hand, Son might be incredibly frustrated and energetically drained by sharing information with Mom when she does not respond with immediate enthusiasm and excitement for his ideas. Son thinks she is resisting, when, in fact, she is listening intently and absorbing what he is saying so that she can take it away and process it at her own speed. On the other hand, Mom might feel stressed and anxious with all that information and energy blasting at her and want to put up a block to protect herself from the onslaught and pressure she feels to respond when she is not ready. She thinks Son is pressuring her to agree and act immediately, when, in fact, he is simply opening his heart to her, trusting her with his precious dreams, and freely sharing with her his joy in the act of creation.

If they could understand how the other needs to give and receive information and respect the gift that each style brings to the group as a whole, they are better equipped to find a place of balance and harmony with these polar-opposite tendencies. Having a model that outlines each other's tendencies provides a framework for communicating that can meet the needs of both, while getting the absolute best out of each of their creative potentials. You can access some of these tools online as previously discussed in Chapter 4.

> 66 Each of us has very
> different ways of receiving and
> processing information

The Family Treasury Curriculum

You will recall in the sample Roundtable meeting agendas previously discussed that an educational curriculum was encouraged. The family can put together a long-term educational plan, complete with resources and presenters, that addresses the family's development needs and interests. How successful would a business be if no one who worked there developed their professional skills? The world is constantly changing and evolving. As new information comes to light, opportunities exist to grow our knowledge base, not just to stay ahead of the competition and improve our products but also to enhance right relations with each other, with ourselves, and our planetary home. Knowledge is power. Yet we all stumble into knowledge at different times, often in an ad-hoc circumstantial manner. A successful business tries to empower the access to and assimilation of knowledge by encouraging its staff to follow a particular path of professional development that is of interest to them and in keeping with the further development and evolution of their unique abilities. The Family Treasury does the same thing.

After each family member has identified their personal mission and once the Family Treasury mission statement is developed, The Family Treasury is in a position to design a customized educational curriculum that empowers the experience and creativity of each person and the collective group. Education helps eliminate false beliefs and superstitions. It develops mental faculties of reasoning and logic and reduces emotional reactions. It helps us to lead a healthier lifestyle and take better care of our bodies. After first teaching us what is and is not the controllable, it gives us control over the controllable. It is a catalyst to creativity. It brings economic independence and possibly the tools to create great financial wealth. Education builds a strong sense of self-worth and the grounding power that comes from knowing you are doing the right and ethical thing.

" The Family Treasury is in a position to design a customized educational curriculum that empowers the experience and creativity of each person and the collective group.

Yet unlike general schooling, The Family Treasury curriculum is designed by the family members, based on their interests and their strategic plans as well as the strategic plan of The Family Treasury itself. The curriculum evolves over time as the family identifies where it needs to gain additional knowledge, but it always holds a central place both inside and outside of The Family Treasury Roundtable. Responsibility for executing The Family Treasury curriculum should rotate so that everyone has the opportunity to take the lead in designing the program, tools, and speakers for the upcoming year.

There is no limit to themes for The Family Treasury curriculum, which can include:

- health and wellness

- culture and travel

- philanthropy

- ethics and tolerance

- investment management

- business management

- financial planning

- environmental protection

- science and technology

▲ Mediation and Facilitation

Processes have been offered to help a family and the members of The Family Treasury to develop empowered and loving relationships with each other as well as with themselves. These tools and practices foster improved levels of the 4 Cs (consciousness, communication, collaboration, and celebration) to build family esteem. They foster self-awareness and mindfulness in the family members and develop a strong team culture of supportive loving relationships. This is done with the knowledge that we are stronger together than we are apart, and that harmony is needed within the team to manifest the mission into great achievements. However, there may be occasions when you need some outside help.

Depending on where you are starting from, you or your family as a whole may benefit from professional counselling, mediation, or facilitation if past behaviours have caused deep-rooted "unspeakables" that you are having trouble moving past. These situations are often resolvable over time when respect, tolerance, and love are part of the picture.

That said, while very sad, in extreme cases, you may conclude that some adult family members just are not emotionally mature enough to be part of The Family Treasury team at this time. Remember, The Family Treasury functions with best practices similar to those employed by successful and sustainable businesses. While the profits sought by The Family Treasury are not only financial but also emotional and spiritual (in the sense of belonging and experiencing the joys of creating something wonderful together while sharing life's adventures with each other), the business analogy holds. If you have an employee in your business who, despite your best efforts, continually brings negativity and intolerance to the workplace, sabotages the team "vibe," and obstructs forward movement through discouragement and lack of commitment to the group—would they be your employee for long? Does someone who, despite your best efforts, behaves this way within the family deserve a seat in The Family Treasury? While they will always be a family member by blood and by familial love, they would be a destructive force to The Family Treasury and, therefore, should not be part of it *until* such time as they can contribute. The Family Treasury can be a great gift to all the others in the group, so don't let the one bad apple spoil the barrel. And unlike a business, this person can be invited back to the group when they are prepared to commit to group consciousness, communication, collaboration, and celebration.

> *The Family Treasury functions with best practices similar to those employed by successful and sustainable businesses.*

While these are extreme examples of dysfunction, you will probably agree with me that all families have a certain level of dysfunction. That is because family is where our buttons get pushed. Rightly or wrongly, we often feel safe enough among family to express the "ugliest" sides of ourselves, thinking that they should take it because they love us. If you think there might be issues, or just want to ensure that none flare up, a trained family facilitator can help a family form healthy communication and interpersonal habits at The Family Treasury Roundtable. They can help family members sort through the often-unintended consequences of past conflicts and destructive behaviours and guide communications so that going forward they can be kind, respectful, and constructive. The facilitator also has the extremely important role of converting the normal family hierarchy (parent, child, sibling, etc.) into a democracy of equals within The Family Treasury environment. This is something that can be extremely difficult for some—most often the "power parent." The family facilitator brings tools and techniques that create breakthroughs in conflict situations and helps ensure that all view the resolution as a win-win solution. They bring impartial and objective perspectives that can resolve impasses. They can teach the family members rules of conduct for a more constructive and responsive (as opposed to emotionally reactive) way to communicate so that the family can move forward on their own with new skills and understanding. A family facilitator should be trained in this service role and be independent of the family relationships to better help families calmly discuss troublesome issues, ensure each family member feels heard and understood, and snuff out future spiralling conflict. Family members may resist engaging a family facilitator—frankly, because they are afraid or embarrassed to air their dirty laundry. It might help to think of the facilitator as a doctor: they have seen it all before and nothing much is a shock to them. Remember, however, that a family facilitator is NOT a therapist and should never play that role. They are a communications coach, a facilitator, and, at most, a mediator. But in some cases, if your family situation warrants it, the facilitator should, in fact, refer you to a professional therapist.

▲   ▼   ▲

Bottom line: one size does not fit all. The previous section modelled a template for the operation of the Family Treasury Roundtable. In reality, your version will evolve as it needs to, responding to the needs of your group and the individuals within it.

Someone asked me why a family with lots of financial resources would bother to go to "all this work" when financial wealth creation was no longer a concern. As I said earlier, I did not invent the family council (which the Family Treasury Roundtable is modelled after). It is used by wealthy multi-generational families to nurture young wealth stewards to preserve the *True* wealth that has been created. They recognize the importance of empowering the next generation of wealth creators in the family to continue to grow the capital over time as the number of family members also grows. They also use it because they realize True wealth is not sustainable by simply growing and spending the money under the assumption that love/relationship will just take care of itself. Anyone who says family relationships do not require at least the same attention and governance that money management takes is wasting their family's human capital. As I said previously: *Money without love is shallow. Love without money is wasted potential.*

Love at its highest level, in its most powerful form, is unconditional group love. The Family Foundation takes our love/relationship resource to that whole new level and calls us to live the idea daily. It can be a very useful tool to keep family members coming back to The Family Treasury table time and again.

⚠ The Family Foundation

The next level in development through loving relationships is establishing a family foundation, or in other words, a charitable foundation. It can be an important step to building strong working family relationships while fostering great teamwork and financial acumen among family members. At the same time, through the foundation, your family can make the world a better place. It can also help more self-centred family members realize they are not, after all, the centre of the universe.

Do you have to be financially wealthy to have a foundation? No. And with that often-first question out of the way, let's look at what a family charitable foundation is and the role it plays within The Family Treasury.

Funding Charities

A foundation is a legal non-profit organization that has tax-exempt status as long as certain requirements are met. It has a fixed or regular form of funding (usually from a family or a small group of known individuals) and will make grants to charities of its choosing from those funds. Unlike a charity, it does not need to engage in fundraising activities and, therefore, does not have to contend with the related costs of those fundraising activities.

At the time the money goes into the foundation, the donor receives a tax deductible donation receipt. Money that goes out to the selected charities in the form of a grant is not entitled to a second level of charitable tax deduction. A foundation can be directed by one person or a group of people in the family who ensure the money is disbursed according to the family's mission statement, values, and strategic plan. The foundation provides the funds to the charities and they administer the charitable programs, usually without any further involvement from the foundation.

Rather than simply making a gift to a charity fundraiser, setting up a foundation gives you much more control over how your charitable donations are managed and disbursed. Even if you are very committed to a specific charitable cause, individual charities can change over time, and so may your interests or priorities. With a foundation, you can manage how your grant-giving process can create a legacy of charitable giving into the next generations. If you want philanthropy to be part of your family's legacy, you can accommodate different choices from other family members and consolidate your giving together through a foundation.

> " Setting up a foundation gives you much more control over how your charitable donations are managed and disbursed.

Types of Foundations

There are two main types of foundations: private and public. In many instances, a family will set up their own private family foundation. There are generally three types of public foundations: (1) community foundations, (2) financial services firm foundations, and (3) independent foundations. It is becoming more and more common these days for families to set up a "donor-advised" fund within a public foundation. There are pros and cons to each structure, which are highlighted in the table below.

Table 4: A Comparison of Foundation Vehicles

	Public Foundations Offering Donor-Advised Funds (DAF)			Private Foundations
	Community Foundations	*Financial Services Firm Foundations*	*Independent Foundations*	
Set-up	One day No legal fees	One day No legal fees	One day No legal fees	6 to 9 months for registration Legal fees from $10,000 to $15,000 to completion
Minimum Gift	Usually $10,000 (can be contributed in instalments)	Usually $10,000, set by firm (can be contributed in instalments)	Usually $10,000 (can be contributed in instalments)	$5 million or more recommended
Reporting	Donor receives reports	Donor receives reports	Donor receives reports	Donor holds board meetings and creates and maintains accurate records and reports
Charity Selection	Donor selects, but limited to local community focus	Donor selects from broad national focus	Donor selects from national focus with some ability to reach out internationally	Donor selects from national focus with some ability to reach out internationally
Control over Investment of Endowment Funds	Foundation Board/ Trustees select investment managers	Captive with financial services firm (in-house)	Donor works with foundation Board/ Trustees to select independent investment managers	Board hires and fires investment managers, monitors investments, and has fiduciary obligations for capital preservation
Annual Tax Compliance	DAF administers	DAF administers	DAF administers	Donor must file annual returns, including financial statements, with tax authorities
Annual Expenses as Percentage of Endowment Asset Value (average)	2% to 4%, including investment management	1.75% to 4%, including investment management	0.5% to 1.25%, plus investment management (independently selected)	Trustee, legal, tax, audit, insurance, bookkeeping, investment management, and staff costs
Privacy	Financials are confidential	Financials are confidential	Financials are confidential	All financial and contact information publicly listed with tax authorities and broadly in the not-for-profit sector

* Prepared in partnership with Canada Gives.

The foundation can be established by a family, a company, or a trust. My team has chosen over these past many years to work with an independent public foundation through our own company donor-advised fund. We were able to get up and running immediately with no set-up costs. All of the foundation administration has been downloaded to the experienced administrative support at the public foundation while we retain decision-making control over which charities get funded. The folks administering the public foundation write and distribute the charitable grant cheques, prepare tax receipts, and manage all administrative, reporting, and fiduciary responsibilities. We are free to apply our time and energy to the important decisions of choosing the charities, the grant amounts, and whether we want our name disclosed or kept private when the grant is made.

The Foundation and The Family Treasury

Before looking at the role a foundation can play in The Family Treasury, it is important to understand three key terms.

First, what is the difference between philanthropy and charity? The word "charity" represents writing cheques or giving your time to worthy causes on an annual or "as it comes up" basis. Philanthropy is much more strategic. Some would say charity aims to relieve the suffering caused by social or environmental problems, while philanthropy seeks to solve the causes of that suffering. Philanthropy is a way of life. It describes a person or family that has an altruistic concern for the welfare of humanity, the planet, and all its beings, and acts to support and develop fundamental change that has a longer-term positive impact on the lives of many. I use the term "philanthropy" to describe an individual or family that thinks of their charitable giving in a strategic way and that puts time and effort into ensuring they have a significant positive impact. These folks have a strong sense of social responsibility to "pay it forward." Philanthropy is the aim of the Family Foundation.

> *Philanthropy is the aim*
> *of the Family Foundation.*

Second, what is an endowment? Although not a necessity, strategic philanthropy is very often accomplished by setting up a long-term endowment within a public or private foundation. An endowment fund is a permanent gift of money established with a charitable organization as a pool of capital that is to be invested such that the capital is preserved over the long term and the income generated through its investment provides the cash flow for grants. This is often called "forever funding." Rules prescribed by the jurisdiction where the foundation resides set out how much of the income must be granted each year and how much of the capital can be gifted.

So how does a family foundation fit into The Family Treasury and support The Family Treasury System II focus:

development of loving relationships? It is often the platform used to bring families together and nurture their relationships in a non-threatening manner. *What better way to heal wounds, forgive past wrongs, and communicate positively and respectfully with each other than to get your head out of your own butt!*

The Family Foundation becomes one of the brightest jewels in The Family Treasury by bringing people together in a purposeful way to make positive change as a group. You need not be financially wealthy to invest a little money, time, and passion into philanthropy. It provides the motivation to learn and create together in support of worthy causes based on shared vision, beliefs, and values that are, in turn, based on The Family Treasury mission statement. Identifying that those beliefs and values are shared gives a sense of belonging that is empowering. It shifts the focus from selfish petty concerns to broader family and community issues worthy of attention and care. To set strategic philanthropic goals and then to support and implement those goals through disciplined decision-making while diligently monitoring and assessing results gives the family a reason to come together, work together, and be together in a manner that can really make a difference. Multiple generations can be involved, thereby creating a legacy of charitable giving for generations to come. Learning that you can be together and enjoy it sets the groundwork for addressing tougher interpersonal relationship issues that are not yet ready to be acknowledged.

> *The Family Foundation becomes one of the brightest jewels in The Family Treasury by bringing people together in a purposeful way to make positive change as a group.*

The Foundation Makes Financial Sense

There are many reasons why we give, including:

- ✔ Duty: it is expected.

- ✔ Generosity: it feels good to give back.

- ✔ To share the wealth: it helps others "rise up."

- ✔ To build strong communities: we are a part of where we live and work.

- ✔ To support specific causes special to us: it makes the giving personal and meaningful.

- ✔ To be a benefactor: good things can continue despite reduction or lack of government funding.

- ✔ Tax savings: it keeps money in your pocket for other endeavours.

Having said that, if making the world a better place is not enough incentive to start a family foundation, and if improving family relationships is also not enough reason to start a family foundation, then would saving more taxes cause you to give it serious thought?

Forewarning: this section gets a little heavy on the math. It is also written for families that have the ability to make large donations or can park significant capital into an endowment (like Jill's). If this is not where you find yourself right now, feel free to skip to The Family Foundation Mission Statement section (page 222). However, I recommend you give the next few pages a go since learning is always time well spent and you will see that even families like Jack's can make a significant charitable contribution.

Lifetime Instalment Giving

The vast majority of people contemplating major donations plan to make them through their wills, after they and/or their spouse have passed away, as opposed to during their lifetimes. While these gifts can be very generous, they may be ineffective for tax purposes.

An example we created with Canada Gives shows how. Basic donation tax rules certainly encourage charitable bequests in wills. As of 2016, an individual can claim a tax credit for a donation of up to 75% of net income in the year the donation is made. However, that limit is increased to 100% of net income in the year of death and the year preceding death. With a financial planning approach to major gifting, in some instances, an individual can see a larger tax benefit by making major gifts in annual instalments during their lifetime rather than making

Table 5: Tax Liability with a $600,000 Charitable Bequest in a Will

	Year 1	Year 2	Year 3	Year 4	Total
Net Income	$ 250,000	$ 250,000	$ 250,000	$ 250,000	$ 1,000,000
Income Tax before Donation	$ 97,600	$ 97,600	$ 97,600	$ 97,600	$ 390,400
Donation Applied to Tax Credit	0	0	$ 202,000	$ 202,000	$ 404,000
Net Income Tax Paid	$ 97,600	$ 97,600	$ 3,154	$ 3,154	$ 201,508

Table 6: Tax Liability with a Lifetime Giving Plan for a Donation of $600,000

	Year 1	Year 2	Year 3	Year 4	Total
Net Income	$ 250,000	$ 250,000	$ 250,000	$ 250,000	$ 1,000,000
Income Tax before Donation	$ 97,600	$ 97,600	$ 97,600	$ 97,600	$ 390,400
Donation Applied to Tax Credit	$ 150,000	$ 150,000	$ 150,000	$ 150,000	$ 600,000
Net Income Tax Paid	$ 25,993	$ 25,993	$ 25,993	$ 25,993	$ 103,972

* Prepared in partnership with Canada Gives.

one large donation upon death. The simplified example shown in the tables above compares the tax benefits associated with a $600,000 cash donation upon death (in the fourth year) to a lifetime giving plan of $600,000 spread over four years using 2015 tax rates for an Ontario resident. Please note that it assumes the donation is being made from capital and not the income earned in the year otherwise needed to fund lifestyle expenses. It also ignores Ontario health care premiums, etc.

In Table 5, the donor made a $600,000 donation through his will to a charity that was important to him. However, only $404,000 of the $600,000 donation was required to eliminate the federal tax liabilities and most of the provincial tax for the third and fourth years. As a result, the tax benefit was lost on the remaining $196,000 of donation made. Also, by doing it this way, he had to pay $201,508 of income tax over the years. If he had given away the same amount of $600,000 during the past four years, as shown in Table 6, he would have reduced his final tax bill to $103,972. His net worth and, therefore, his estate would be wealthier by $97,536 if he had donated during his lifetime as opposed to waiting to do it through his will.

Capital Replacement Plan

Often, a family would like to create the bonding experience of developing and working together on a Family Foundation but they don't move forward due to a belief that the children's inheritance should come first and should, therefore, be protected and conserved. Unsure of what might be left for the next generation, they forego giving today. There is a solution for this too. We call it the Capital Replacement Plan. In essence, you can create a major gifting strategy through a Family Foundation from assets that are available in an existing investment portfolio but replace those donations back into the estate with a new insurance policy, either at today's value or at the future value of the donated capital. This assumes that the investment portfolio is not required to fund lifestyle expenses. Essentially, you will be guaranteeing your children their inheritance while together developing a legacy of philanthropy at significantly reduced cost to the estate. Jack and Jill provide a case study example.

Let's Look at Jack and Jill

In this scenario, Jack and Jill are a married couple. He is fifty-five years old and she is fifty. Both are in good health and have substantial financial assets. They are at the highest marginal tax rate and are seeking advice on the most effective way to create a Family Foundation. They decided they could make major donations now while they can participate in philanthropic giving with their children and then buy insurance to preserve the estate.

The Strategy

- Donate $3 million to their Family Foundation.

- Purchase a $3 million 20-year premium, whole life dividend participating policy on Jack and Jill's lives on a last-to-die basis (annual premium of $71,355 for 20 years).

The Philanthropic Plan

- Donate $3 million in 10 equal annual instalments of $300,000 over the next 10 years with the participation of the children.

- Tax savings are $151,142 annually for 10 years totalling $1,511,420—which more than covers the total cost of the annual insurance premium over the 20 years of $1,427,100.

- Death benefit proceeds are paid directly to beneficiaries tax free and without probate fees.

- Death benefit if paid out in 10 years is expected to be $3,968,562. If paid out in 25 years, it is expected to be $4,902,694. If paid out in 35 years, death benefit is expected to be $5,226,270.[36]

This capital replacement plan illustrates how insurance can mitigate, if not eliminate, the cost of donating capital today at the expense of the inheritance to the estate. The tax savings pay for the insurance premiums. Also, the death benefit would return value to the estate in excess of what a conservatively invested portfolio earning 4% (2% after tax) would earn for the first twenty-five years. After that, the death benefit reduces to be worth gradually less than an investment portfolio due to escalating cost of insurance charged to the policy. Of course, this is an illustration and many variables over the years, such as dividend scales, investment returns, costs, and expenses, can affect the outcome. Each situation is unique and should be evaluated as such.

Government Matching Program

Another fairly simple way to build an endowment fund within a foundation rapidly is to use what I call the "Government Matching Program." This requires that you have annual taxable income at the highest marginal tax rates since this produces a donation tax credit that reduces your taxes by approximately 50% of the donation, often producing a refund. As an example, let's say you wish to build a $500,000 endowment fund within your Family Foundation and you have $50,000 in cash available per year that you can donate to build this fund. You will get a full tax credit for this donation. For illustration purposes, let's say you get a $25,000 refund from the tax credit (it will not be exactly this). If you spend the refund elsewhere, it will take you 10 years to build the endowment fund. Instead, let's assume that you also donate the $25,000 refund with the next year's donation of $50,000 previously committed, for a total donation in the second year of $75,000. That year, you will get a refund of up to $37,500. When you add that refund to the third year's donation of $50,000 you add a further $87,500 to the endowment fund. By continuing this strategy, you will reach your target of the $500,000 endowment in only 6 years.

You can speed up this process still further if you have a line of credit available to you. If you match the $50,000 donation from your cash with a further $50,000 drawn on your line of credit, and assuming you have the income to fully deduct this donation, you will get a refund of approximately $50,000. You use that $50,000 refund to pay off the line of credit, and you now have $100,000 sitting in the endowment fund. Do the same in subsequent years, and you will reach your target of $500,000 in 5 years.

▲ ▼ ▲

You do not need to earn this kind of money or have this level of wealth to have a philanthropic strategy. Tax savings are only one of many reasons why a family would wish to incorporate philanthropy into their Family Treasury experience. The process of philanthropy—whether you give money or time, a little or a lot—has numerous rewards.

> *" The process of philanthropy— whether you give money or time, a little or a lot—has numerous rewards.*

The Mission Statement

I spoke previously of The Family Treasury mission statement and Roundtable. Those tools are a good place from which to develop the philanthropic strategic plan for your Family Foundation, based on its own mission statement, which is a reflection of your family's values and goals. Ask yourselves, if you do not already know: What areas of humanity and/or the environment are a good reflection of your group purpose?

Which areas could benefit most from the unique talents, interests, and abilities of the family members? For example, you might find that if the purpose of The Family Treasury according to Table 2 on page 109 is column 2 (To illumine, love, and include) and your family has a passion for education, then improving accessibility to post-secondary education could be an excellent philanthropic focus. This can translate into concern and focus toward those who are unable to access appropriate education for themselves due to financial or social reasons.

Discuss and document these values and concerns to narrow down an overriding purpose and vision for your Family Foundation. It does not necessarily need to follow the same calling and purpose reflected in The Family Treasury mission statement. However, it will have a higher chance of being impactful and successful if it focuses on an area that family members are familiar with, passionate about, and committed to. To avoid becoming too scattered and ineffective, try to limit the focus to no more than three broad areas of concern where you feel you can have the biggest impact. Then, just as was done for The Family Treasury, write a mission statement for the Family Foundation.

Selecting Charities

To begin the process of fulfilling your Family Foundation mission, ask family members to put forward charities that might be of interest. That compiled list should be considered independently by each member before the group comes together for discussion and to make the final selection. This process should not be rushed, and decisions should not be made without careful deliberation. Remember, the purpose of strategic philanthropy is to make lasting change and contribute to the elimination of that which causes suffering in the world. This is not decided in a few minutes. Research into the charities should be done by each family member old enough to work independently or, for those too young or inexperienced, in concert with older family members.

> *The purpose of strategic philanthropy is to make lasting change and contribute to the elimination of that which causes suffering in the world.*

When researching a charity, some of the areas requiring due diligence include:

- What is the mission of the charity and how does it go about accomplishing its goals? Watch out for vague or over-ambitious comments like "end world hunger." You want to understand very specifically how the charity intends to go about reaching its objectives, what its past results have been, what has worked and what has not worked, and what its future needs are. This is accomplished by reading its annual reports and reviewing its ranking on various rating websites, but this cannot replace the benefits of an in-person interview. You are looking to evaluate how effective the charity has been and/or will be through clarity of mission, and you can use data sources to objectively evaluate progress.

- How specifically will the money you give the charity be spent? Over what time frame are those results expected and what performance benchmarks are there to assess if the results were achieved? There is a general rule of thumb that a charity should not be spending more than 25% of its funds on administration and fundraising. However, if the budget is too tight, the charity may only be capable of making a ripple of change, when what we want is a tidal wave of change whenever possible. Sometimes they need to make major capital improvements in order to grow and be impactful. If we expect them to be too lean, they may not be able to attract talented staff and we may be handcuffing them. It is more important that you assess that expenditures are worthwhile and reasonable given the goal at hand and then monitor that spending for results. Review their historical financial statements to see patterns of healthy, productive spending. If no independently audited financial statements are available, you still may wish to go ahead, but really consider the risks of giving your money to a charity that does not provide independent financial accountability.

- How are decisions made? Is there a board of advisers with diversification of expertise to guide the charity? What kind of political support does it have or political roadblocks does it encounter? What is its expertise, motivation, and ability to influence change? The right people, passionate about the charity's work, are as important as the right program.

As a group, decide on the charities to be funded using a democratic decision-making process such as majority vote, consensus, or some other pre-defined method. If the Foundation is managed under The Family Treasury charter, you will have a process in place that can be applied consistently. This need not be a permanent decision as the Family Foundation can select different charities at anytime when new information inspires a change of direction. The Family Treasury Roundtable is a good place to table potential projects for discussion and perhaps implementation. However, this can be difficult for the charities that have come to rely on your support, so a decision to change or reduce funding should not be taken lightly. It is best to keep the number of charities you fund to a reasonable level so you can effectively monitor them. Also, the more charities you choose, the less funding each receives. To reinforce continuing involvement, it is important that each member of the family involved in the foundation should either have at least one of their favourite charities chosen or agree to support those that have been chosen. Over the years, as the generations of family members involved grows, it will be especially important to reinforce the overall mission of the foundation so as not to water down its impact. The younger generations, however, can be inspired to commit to the process by allocating a portion of the annual giving, even if in a minor way, to charities important to them.

The next step is to actually set up and fund the foundation, if you have not already done so. The table on page 211 reflects that this can be done in a day if you work with a public foundation or six to nine months if you prefer to set up a private foundation. The biggest step will be to decide if you wish to fund the foundation with annual donations that will be immediately re-gifted in grants (flow-through funds) or an endowment fund, or a combination of both. This depends on the current resources of the family. A good financial planner can help you assess the most appropriate amount of funding that will not threaten the family's cash flow or financial security. In our family office, we determine what is called the philanthropic capital threshold, which is the amount of capital we have determined through careful analysis that the family can donate without threatening their lifestyle security or their children's inheritance. Maximizing the tax benefits is also an important consideration and is part of this process. Both a current giving strategy and a long-term plan of sustainable giving is essential to any strategic plan for enduring impact. Keep in mind that you can be a philanthropist whether you are giving a few hundred dollars or a few hundred thousand dollars. The charities appreciate anything you can do, and regardless of the size of the donation, the benefits to the family of working together on the philanthropic plan are most important of all.

Subsequent family meetings can entail each family member providing a progress report on their chosen charity—celebrating the impact the family's efforts have made, or are in the process of making, and reviewing performance and progress to benchmarks—and can include discussion of any new charities for next year. All the while, the family is coming together in a positive way, making positive change together, and reminding each other that together they are stronger and more impactful than they are apart.

▲　▼　▲

A Family Foundation can be formal as described above, or informal, and you don't have to be wealthy to enjoy its benefits. If money is tight, perhaps you won't go the formal foundation route, but within The Family Treasury you can still follow the processes and develop a family philanthropic strategy. You don't even have to give money. You can give your time or wise counsel to someone in need. Either way, you will receive benefits far greater than what you have given. From ancient times we have known that giving invokes the Law of Attraction. What you put out, you get back. Putting a twist on a Brendan Bouchard quote: If you don't seem to be getting much of what you want lately, then *ask not what you are NOT getting—ask what you are NOT giving.*

When proper attention is paid to developing a strong foundation of self-identification and self-worth within a family, founded in love and appreciation for each other, you truly have a powerful 2nd Root Resource to work with. *We are truly happiest when our entire family prospers due to the contributions and successes of each of its members. When each member of our family thrives, we can come together to create the future we envision. That is* True *family wealth.*

The Family
Treasury System III
Legacy of Achievements

▲ ▼ ▲

How Do You *Want* to Be Remembered?

Family Treasury System I: Stewardship through a Worthy Mission (will) and Family Treasury System II: Development through Loving Relationships (relating) are the first two critical aspects in building The Family Treasury. The systems are a recognition, development, and hopefully evolution of our 1st and 2nd Root Resources. They bring clarity of purpose for the Treasury and its members individually and collectively. They bring supportive relationships, education, and development of skills and teamwork as a foundation of strength from which to move forward. These systems must be continually reviewed, nurtured, and refreshed if they are to grow in power and be a greater catalyst to the achievement of the agreed-upon mission.

Now it is time to introduce the last element, The Family Treasury System III: Legacy of Achievements (action). This is the activity principle, the 3rd Root Resource, where the vision is manifested through the step-by-step efforts of the motivated team. In acting on, and not just talking or dreaming about the vision, each family member moves closer to a life full of a variety of achievements—both expected and unexpected. When The Family Treasury supports the talents and unique abilities of family members so that each thrives, the resulting accomplishments benefit everyone directly and indirectly as it inspires the same creative force for generations to come.

Most think a legacy is defined in their estate planning documents such as wills and powers of attorney. Some think of it as the money that their children and/or grandchildren will inherit. Will documents are often interpreted by families as "how much we were loved." Do you really want lawyers, accountants, and investment advisers to tell that story for you? Your legacy is so much more, your achievements include so much more, than your financial estate. You can pass on your values, wisdom, traditions and stories, your network and support systems, your reputation, and your accomplishments. A lifetime of hard-earned wealth and wisdom is wasted if it is not shared *both before and after your time on Earth.*

> 66 *A lifetime of hard-earned*
> *wealth and wisdom is wasted if*
> *it is not shared both before and*
> *after your time on Earth.*

What exactly is meant by achievements? That depends on the value system of The Family Treasury, which is a direct reflection of the value system of its members. This was discussed in Chapter 4. For example, one family may find that building a successful profitable business together is a great achievement. Another family might find it a greater achievement to have influenced their local community and politicians to enact municipal law that protects the family-owned farm against large, massive-scale corporate farming. The family values will determine whether or not it is an achievement to be celebrated. But if one does not act at all, nothing will happen. How do you want to be remembered? Can your Family Treasury become a legacy of achievements you and your family can be proud of? Remember, manifestation is a *co-creative* effort. Yes, the family working together will engender more powerful results. But I'm referring to something bigger: by co-creative, I mean the universe has your back.

The Laws that Support You

Before we discuss some practical tools The Family Treasury can use to manifest its goals, we should also consider the energetic tools we have available. We have already touched on some of them in previous chapters. Chapter 3 spoke of the energy soup from which all things manifest and of how, to create well, we must harness the 3 Root Resources of will, relating, and action in harmony, like a perfectly balanced and powerful equilateral triangle. We also spoke of some of the Universal Laws that support us. Whether or not you are aware of it, you use them all the time in the act of creation, so knowing more about them is to your benefit.

Manifestation is a physical phenomenon that occurs through *right* effort. There is a frequently quoted saying by Napoleon Hill: "Whatever the mind can conceive and believe, it can achieve." What you are passionate about, can visualize in your mind, you can manifest. You might be thinking, "Sounds great, but how can I really believe anything I really want can be mine when the world seems so random and circumstances are so out of my control?" You can come to believe it by doing some homework: (1) understand the Universal Laws, (2) study them, and (3) experiment with them until you can work with them with ease. You will need to work with the Universal Laws to manifest your mission, so you had better get along! The laws are known and passed down throughout the ancient wisdom of many cultures and religions. Some are now even supported scientifically. Let's look at those that initially will be most relevant to your legacy achievements within The Family Treasury.

> *Manifestation is a physical*
> *phenomenon that occurs*
> *through right effort.*

The Law of Attraction

I think of this as the head honcho. All the other laws really describe how this one works. It sums up how creation works, how life works, how the physical world works, how you work. It is about vibration and the scientifically proven fact that "like energy attracts like energy." It is the magnetic principle that holds us and everything else together. To understand how to use it requires, I believe, an understanding of how it works through a look at the other supporting laws.

The Law of One

We spoke of this earlier when describing how, from the wisdom of ancient times to the explorations of modern-day science, there is reference to the one omnipresent Universal Mind from which all else arises. Although using different names—the energy field, God, universal consciousness—scientific, religious, and esoteric psychological teachings tell us that each human mind (of which the brain is only a part) is part of the Universal Mind, just functioning at a different level of awareness. The more aware you are, the more conscious you become, the more information from the Universal Mind you have access to—and therefore, the more awesome your creations and manifestations! The energetic realm is the source of your creation; your thoughts are the process of that creation; and the physical object is the result. *Understand this unlimited potential as your starting point.*

> *The energetic realm is the source of your creation; your thoughts are the process of that creation; and the physical object is the result.*

I want to take a moment to note that I do not see the scientific, religious, or esoteric psychological views of this law as being any different. They are describing the same thing but in different ways. When I say "the more aware you are, the more conscious you become, the more information from the Universal Mind you have access to," all of these disciplines say this too, do they not? It is not my idea. All three teach that the more you study the texts, the more you learn. In science, those texts are research publications and journals. In religion, those texts are the sacred scriptures of the particular religious practice. In esoteric psychology, those texts are the writings of the ancient wisdom as well as religious scriptures in combination with modern research papers. These are all paths of enhanced awareness. The key is what you do with what you have read in those materials. An aware individual does not stop there and simply follow the dogma laid out before them. They read more, they discuss and debate their faith and beliefs with others and their mentors, they ask questions about what they learn, and they experiment with the answers they have been given to determine what resonates as Truth for them at their place in time. It is this process of asking questions and observing results that makes us more aware. Science will say that the more you study and experiment, the more factual information you will get, and the closer you will come to discovery of the Truth, which allows you to create evolutionary solutions to human challenges. Modern religion will say that the more you study and practice the faith, the closer you come to God and the more you are in resonance with the Divine energy, which makes you more capable of great creations (if not miracles). Esoteric psychology will say that the more you study yourself and others and the more you meditate, the higher your vibration will become, which heightens your intuition and access to the Universal Mind stream. From all three perspectives, your creations become more magnificent, impactful, and beneficial as your ego and false beliefs get out of the way, and you open up to unlimited potential.

The Law of Correspondence

This law (and science) tells us that the principles of physics, which explain the physical, material world we live in (i.e., thoughts, sounds, and things), have their corresponding principles in the "un-manifest" energy field. Religion might call this the spiritual field. Esoterics might refer to it as the mental field (of universal consciousness). Hermes Trismegistus said it first: "as above, so below and as below, so above." This places an enormous responsibility upon us to be impeccable with what we think, feel, and say because the universe is listening. What is formed physically must first be formed energetically, that is, in our mind. As within, so correspondingly without. The correspondences are not always exact—in fact, they are often distorted as in a warped mirror—but they are there. What is formed physically ultimately returns to its energy form. Once you have thought it, it is already made real on the mental plane. If you un-think it, or change your thought about it, you will have instantaneously changed it again on that plane. You will get a mixed-up soup of nothing as a result. Gaining clarity of your vision, and then sticking to it no matter what, is important because that gives it time to manifest on the physical plane. *Understand that to manifest your vision, you must master your mind.*

66 **What is formed physically must first be formed energetically, that is, in our mind.**

The Law of Cause and Effect

I like to think of this one as "Fake it till you make it." This law must be employed in order for us to manifest things on Earth. Every thought, word, or action creates an energy wave that will ultimately manifest that which you thought, spoke, or acted upon most often. This law is really about the consequences of our actions. The Law of Correspondence tells us

that as soon as we think or speak, even before we act physically, there is an instantaneous effect in the unseen energy
field. Concentrated and focused thought electrically charged
by creative action will eventually materialize in the physical
world *although you are not in control of the time and space of that*
occurrence. Every action (including thought) causes a reaction
or consequence. *Understand, therefore, that you must engage in*
actions that support your thoughts, dreams, emotions, and words,
even if today you take only baby steps.

> 66 *Every action (including thought)*
> *causes a reaction or consequence.*

▲ ▼ ▲

Holding steady to your vision with clarity and taking action
step by step creates a wave of vibration that the Law of Attraction assures us will bring into manifestation that same quality
of vibration. If it was that easy—and knowing that we have
unlimited potential—why wouldn't we all master this "white
magic" and create just about anything we want? The reason is
that our human senses in the physical world perceive through
time and space, and there is usually a time lag. We often quit
before we realize the results of our efforts for one of two
reasons: (1) it feels like it is taking too long or (2) we do not
recognize its creation in the physical world. Why? Because
of our ignorance of two other laws.

The Law of Polarity

There are always two sides to the same coin. Manifestation is dual. Everything is one in the field of un-manifest spirit, but as it takes physical form, it will have two sides. This duality is absolutely necessary if we are to experience life. You won't know what happiness is without sadness to compare it to. You won't know what wealth is without poverty. You won't understand health without illness. The pattern continues: hot and cold, love and hate, light and dark, yes and no. And always, the "negative" side has a lower vibration than the "positive" side. There is no judgment here. At times cold can be better than hot, no better than yes, and vice versa. Both aspects are always there, so on the spectrum of the polarities, do you wish to focus your attention on the lower or the higher vibration side? It depends on what you wish to create. The choice and responsibility is yours alone.

Due to vibrational resonance, the Law of Attraction will bring you more of what you focus on most, just as a magnet attracts metal filings. For example, let's say you are experiencing financial difficulties. It is very natural to focus on this with frustration and even anger. Yet this very resistance, this act of putting all your energy, thoughts, and words toward the low vibration, negative aspect of the situation, will only bring more financial difficulties to you. Giving you more to be angry and resistant about. Instead, work at focusing with an attitude of gratitude on that part of your financial circumstance that you do feel good about, and the resulting vibrations you put out there will attract more of the same. You may not get the results you want right away. But if you are aware, you will notice that financial events and circumstances begin to occur more and more frequently around you. Remember, these will still contain the full spectrum of dark to light, so you will need to keep choosing how you will experience them on the polarity spectrum. But your response will continue to attract more and more of the similar vibration. That is how evolution happens, how we move through difficulties to a better place. *Understand that it is always your choice to perceive the glass as "half full or half empty."*

> Due to vibrational resonance, the Law of Attraction will bring you more of what you focus on most, just as a magnet attracts metal filings.

The Law of Cycles

Everything in nature has its time. All things move in cycles, rise and fall, are born and die. Your own life moves in cycles with time for work and time for rest, time for achievement and success and time for recalibration before the next climb. At times, you may find your progress toward your vision thwarted, or even moving backward. The good news is that while you are not in charge of this and cannot change this, you can ease the effects by remembering the Law of Polarity. Staying focused on the positive outcome of your goals keeps your personal vibration high during the down cycles. This causes the entire cycle to speed up (as higher vibration speeds up) and also spiral up to an elevated place. Your declines are shorter and weaker; your growth stronger and brighter. This is evolution! This can create an outcome bigger than your vision ever dreamed. *Understand that if you don't give up, your time will come.*

> 66 *Staying focused on the positive outcome of your goals keeps your vibration high during the down cycles (that can move you away from your goals).*

▲ ▼ ▲

Now that you have an understanding of the Universal Laws, you can work with them. You don't have to believe in them at the outset, but at the very least experiment with them and watch for them. You will see them everywhere and in everything. This homework will serve to empower and equip you and your Family Treasury team to create like you may never have before and to trust that your efforts will ultimately manifest into your life. *So be careful what you wish for!*

Effortless Effort

We are taught in our society that creative imagination is for kids. That is such a shame, for it is completely untrue and that belief has robbed many of us of our potentials. Have you heard the phrase, "Act as if"? In doing so, you are using your creative imagination to actually visualize what you want, and then by acting as though you have it, your mind accepts it as reality although you have not yet physically manifested it. That is why it works so beautifully: the mind is tricked into thinking it is already real, so it doesn't put out any repulsing energy. This puts the Law of Attraction in action as your creative imagination elicits response from the Ground of Being, the energy field of pure potential.

However, to really change your reality, you need to go to the "space" I talked about in the meditation section in Chapter 5. You can still create without going there, but it will be a lesser creation. It will be something that already exists in manifestation, something that perhaps you can reframe. But something truly new, something transformative, is found in the space. Trust in the natural Universal Laws and use them to your advantage. Interestingly, the Laws state that the most effort we need to put in to creation is mastering our mind, staying focused on our vision, and acting on opportunities as they arise. That is no easy feat, but the laws indicate they will take care of the rest! Is it therefore possible that most of us have been creating our lives and working to achieve our desires in entirely the wrong way?

The Universal Laws make right effort sound quite effortless! Yet we have been taught just the opposite. Since the Industrial Revolution, we have been taught that we must work very hard to achieve our goals. "No pain, no gain" is our mantra. Oops, I guess we get what we ask for because of the laws of Attraction, Correspondence, and Cause and Effect. The more we put out long hours, lots of stress, and sacrifice, the more the universe gives us back long hours, lots of stress, and sacrifice! Nothing else in nature operates with such strain. A seed grows into a magnificent flower effortlessly. Both the lion, king of the African plains, and your house cat sit around sunning themselves and sleeping most of the day, working to feed themselves in only short bursts of activity.

The key ingredient to nature's effortless creation is its use of the Universal Laws with balance and harmony. If nature gets out of balance, there is trouble, but it fairly quickly (in Earth time that is) corrects itself, moving back to its effortless point of balance. On the other hand, most of us humans are out of balance. We focus on one thing, like money, at the expense of our health, relationships, and peace of mind: this is not right effort. We struggle; we think fearful, negative, contracting thoughts; and the Universal Laws give us exactly what we put out. If, instead, we understand the prime importance of mastering our mind (our thoughts)—keeping it focused on the vision without confusion, fear, and doubt—and living a life of balance (good health, loving relationships, play, work, and rest), our vibration will be higher, and the Universal Laws will give us that in return. We have catalyzed our Life Energy Quotient (LEQ). This is right effort. The Universal Laws are true for everyone and everything, so why would they not be true for you?

> *We focus on one thing, like money, at the expense of our health, relationships, and peace of mind: this is not right effort.*

▲ ▼ ▲

While you are doing your homework—practising with the Universal Laws at your command and working "effortlessly" to master your mind and increase your own vibration through living in gratitude and service—we can take the next actionable steps in building The Family Treasury.

Tools to Build Your Legacy

You have defined your Family Treasury mission and each family member has done the same. You continue to build a strong foundation of teamwork and knowledge. You have put processes in place to ensure each team member is doing their part and expressing their unique talents toward the achievement of the mission and in their relationships with each other. Now we need to take action to build the systems that will house and protect the mission and its people now and into the future.

Not unlike a family business, you need to take The Family Treasury from the place of ideas and build it step by step. As with any business, some will take longer than others to build and bring to a place of profitable operations, but everyone will have a point from which to start. How long it takes and how big The Family Treasury becomes depends on the amount of resources it is intended to hold and for how long.

We have spoken of the 3 Root Resources, the energetic resources within each of us. The only variation between us is the extent to which we have developed them. We have also spoken of the processes to more fully develop the 1st and 2nd Root Resources. Now we turn our attention to the steps required to develop the 3rd Root Resource, action, in order to create our legacy of achievements. You will note that money is not the area of focus. It is the result. Education, leadership, and strategic planning are the steps toward getting that result. Along the way you will also pick up knowledge, experience, and hopefully an excellent reputation, which are worthy results to seek, preserve, and pass on. These results, in turn, become the resources for still further growth toward your individual and group potentials in this lifetime and those of the generations that follow. They grow and expand as long as they are attended to in a balanced, harmonious manner.

It is now time to put the following tools to work in order to sustain The Family Treasury achievements well into the future.

⚠ *The Strategic Plan*

The Family Treasury mission statement was established in System I, as explained in Chapter 4. In order for it to be realized, you need to take action. To direct that action in a focused and efficient way, setting goals and objectives helps immensely. In the world of business mission, goals, and objectives each mean something a little different. Another business word for mission is "vision." It is the "big dream" that the group seeks to achieve through service of some kind, which, when realized, could make the world a better place. We have already discussed defining the mission/vision in Chapter 4. Goals set benchmarks that define what our mission will look like when we achieve it so that we know when we have arrived at our destination. Successful businesses use this process all the time, or at least they should. Objectives are the action steps you will take along the way to get there.

> *Goals set benchmarks that define what our mission will look like when we achieve it so that we know when we have arrived at our destination.*

Setting goals is the process of visualizing the realization of your mission. They will look a little different for The Family Treasury than those set personally. When setting Family Treasury goals, ask yourselves questions such as:

- What will it look like for us and how will our lives change—experientially, financially, operationally, socially—when we realize our collective mission?

- What would be the benefits to the team?

- What will the benefits to the world look like?

Goals should be inspiring and exciting to you and your team, whether in business or within The Family Treasury. They should fulfill each of your personal and group life desires, especially around money, love, and freedom. You have a much better chance of achieving your goals if they serve you, the family, and the world at large. They must also be specific. You need to have a very clear vision for what the result will look like, both the sum and its parts, for it to have a greater chance of manifesting. As described in Chapter 1, bubble charts can be used to model the goals. Figure 4 shows bubble chart examples for an individual, The Family Treasury, and a business and reflects the similarity of categories that should normally be considered when setting goals. For example, the spiritual goals of a person, the cultural goals of a business, and the experiential goals of The Family Treasury are very similar in nature. A personal spiritual goal, for example, could be to become a content and positive person. A cultural goal of a business may be to become a workplace that is energetically positive and develops the leader in each team member. An experiential

Figure 4: Similarity of categories for an individual, a business, and The Family Treasury when setting goals

goal for The Family Treasury might be that the family enjoy being together and do so often.

> 66 *You have a much better chance of achieving your goals if they serve you, the family, and the world at large.*

Try to keep your goals to no more than three per category to enhance your ability to achieve them through more efficient and focused effort with less distraction. To try to accomplish too much can water down your results. After all, we are aiming for one or two magnificent creations not many mediocre ones. It is best to prioritize those goals too, focusing on the most important first and adding others as momentum comes into play with the previous. A longer-term goal can still be a priority goal. Later in this chapter, I write about the importance of a succession plan. To achieve succession, goals such as developing a strong culture and growing capable leaders are important and should begin to be addressed early on.

Another important aspect of goals is that they be measurable. When setting financial goals, this is easy to do because money is mathematically based. Relationship, social, and even experiential goals can be less easy to measure for they are not normally mathematically based. However, we can overcome this challenge using The Family Treasury Balance Sheet discussed at the end of this chapter.

Also note the importance of each member of The Family Treasury sharing their personal goals with the other members. One of the key roles of The Family Treasury is to support each of its members in any way it can to achieve their personal potentials as well.

Again, you must also really, really want what you visualize. You should feel excited and passionate about it. Imagine how you will feel, look, and behave when your group goals are achieved. Imagine how the group will get along, what they can experience together, and how impactful they will be.

Let's Look at Jack and Jill

In order to know he has realized his personal mission, Jack visualizes his personal financial goals. They might be: (1) I am debt free, (2) I earn $200,000 per year, and (3) I give 10% annually to charity. Notice that wording reflects how you will BE when your unique mission is achieved.

On the other hand, The Family Treasury will have different financial goals since it has a group focus. In Jill's family, for example, they might be: (1) a pool of capital sufficient to educate three generations of family members, (2) investments in socially responsible companies making change and (3) a "family bank" paying 3% dividends to family shareholders.

Unlike many folks, I do not believe goals should be timeline specific. We are not in charge of when we will achieve our goals since there is no doubt that life will throw us curve balls along the way. It reminds me of a famous quote attributed originally to Allen Saunders, who worked in the 1950s as a writer and cartoonist for Publishers Syndicate, but made popular in the early 1980s by John Lennon: "Life is what happens to us while we are making other plans." To set up specific deadlines for goals as big as I am suggesting is setting yourself up for frustration, loss of confidence, and a high chance you will abandon the mountain path before you climb the first hill. Remember the Law of Polarity and the Law of Cycles? Goals need time and you will need patience. But if you pay attention, you will see activity and results begin to manifest. And don't be fooled if the result comes in disguise.

Hopefully, each of your goals will feel like the subpeaks on your way to the summit of a huge, beautiful, majestic mountain. To stand at the bottom and imagine what it will be like at the summit top is absolutely necessary, as is the importance of envisioning reaching all the subpeaks along the way. To reach those goals, however, you must begin by climbing the very first subpeak. This is your first objective. As I pointed out in Chapter 1, you are not going to climb that mountain any other way than step by step by step. (That is, of course, unless someone builds you a mountain elevator and robs you of the joy of great achievement!)

The team needs to assess as best they can what those chronological steps along the way—the objectives—look like. It sets those as short- and long-term targets that need to be met in order to achieve your collective goals, and then ultimately—you hope—your purpose and your mission. *In documenting the steps you are creating a strategic plan.*

Objectives are what you (as part of the team) will "do" next, the action steps you will take in collaboration with the group. As with goals, they too must be measurable; but unlike goals, I recommend that objectives be timeline specific. Specifically, set your objectives weekly, monthly for three months out, and yearly. I suggest you do not set timelines for objectives related to your group goals more than one year out; they will likely have to change anyway as life happens and timelines for shorter-term objectives alter. However, you can see the objectives and their likely time targets over the next three months more clearly, and then, of course, those for this week can be quite accurately scheduled. You will want to be flexible with your time to respond to daily-life priorities as they arise without feeling like you failed to meet your plan objectives or let your team down. Setting your objectives in the way described is a great benefit in helping you and the team see what steps you need to take next to move you closer to your group goals. Once those steps have been taken, pause a moment, catch your breath, celebrate how far you have all come up the path, and then step out again toward the next level you wish to reach. The timeline also allows you to step off the path, or take a detour, but find your way back by using your trail markers: your objectives.

> *Set your objectives weekly, monthly, for three months out, and yearly.*

Again, you might use a bubble chart to map out your objective categories and then create a list for the specific objectives related to each. Figure 5 compares samplings of some annual objective categories for a personal mission to those for The Family Treasury mission.

Figure 5: Comparison of categories of annual objectives for a personal mission and The Family Treasury mission

By way of example, here are a couple of simple timelines based on The Family Treasury objectives in Figure 5. To support Social Goals, a specific philanthropic objective for this year might be to select a charity that supports child health. The one-month objective may be to visit one associated charity. The one-week objective may be to book the appointment. In the category of Networks, a specific objective might be to introduce the young adult members to the family's professional advisers. The one-month objective may be to meet with one of those advisers. The one-week objective may be to discuss with one of the young adults the role that adviser plays for the family so they understand the importance of this relationship.

Once your specific objectives are outlined for the week, quarter, and year, you have your dynamic strategic plan in place. To be effective, the strategic plan must be flexible and modifiable. New information will come along that may cause you to take a detour. The strategic plan is a working document that gets updated regularly with amendments, while noting and celebrating achievements along the way. Of course, to manifest it takes more than drawing it on a piece of paper. It takes action. Once a year, updating of the strategic plan will bring into short-term action those objectives that, just a year ago, were too far out to address more specifically. As you move forward, you will be closer to seeing what exactly needs to be done to meet the goal given the information and objective outcomes that have come before.

Remember in Chapter 5 we talked about the Law of Attraction and inviting rather than manipulating it? Your strategic plan needs to invite flexibility. Plan your route but ultimately *let it go*. Go with the flow. Respond to detours, don't resist them. Follow your intuition along the way and give your creativity free reign.

> *To be effective, the strategic plan must be flexible and modifiable.*

So, keep your strategic plans front and centre, stay focused, minimize distractions, and apply the 3 Root Resources of will (your mission), relating (your relationships), and action (your achievements) in a balanced and harmonious way. And remember to celebrate the accomplishments along the way.

And a final reminder: The Family Treasury strategic plan should work together with each member's personal strategic plan (outlined in Chapter 1). In order to have harmony and balance the objectives outlined in both must be synergistic and not compete with each other. Timelines and boundaries can be better established when the picture is viewed as an integrated whole. You will have better commitment toward the achievement of Family Treasury objectives if individuals feel their personal objectives are also being met.

Now, it is time to dig a little deeper and outline some of the additional processes that can support the accomplishment of the strategic plan.

⚠ *The Personal Financial Plan*

Let's face it, money makes the world go around and that is not about to change anytime soon. Second to personal relationships, the world of money is probably the most complex aspect of our lives. The complexities of wealth management can be daunting even to the most financially astute. Guidance is required from many advisers (i.e., legal, insurance, financial, tax), but it often lacks strategic integration. Marketing and media hype makes it difficult to sort fact from fiction. You may be left confused and wondering if you are getting the best, truly unbiased advice. How can you combat this?

A financial plan is the most impactful document you can have to help streamline your focus, get you results, and achieve your goals. It is one of the first objectives every adult person or couple should aim for, and it certainly plays a central role in The Family Treasury. No success-minded business would ever dream of operating without a financial plan to manage their financial resources efficiently and safely, so why would you and your family?

> ❝ *A financial plan is the most impactful document you can have to help streamline your focus, get you results, and achieve your goals.*

Figure 6, from our website, illustrates that before anyone is likely to think about their greater family legacy (in this case, as expressed through The Family Treasury), they must first feel in control of their own finances. They will benefit from a *personal* financial plan—at my firm we call it The Family Prosperity Plan™. Individual members of the group will want to know that some of their immediate needs and desires are being met, and their financial independence secured, before The Family Treasury can help them build their future dreams. Then and only then will they look to longer-range, broader family security, cultivating the finest life possible for every family member and seeking to empower a long-term legacy. Even those folks of significant financial wealth, out of fear that they just won't have enough capital to support their needs throughout life, will want to see evidence that they are financially secure before moving forward.

Figure 6: Hierarchy of priorities toward financial freedom

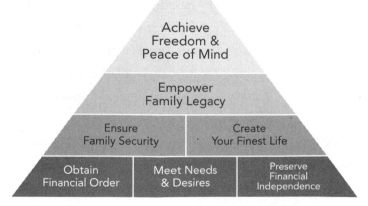

Source: Your Family Prosperity Plan™ © First Affiliated Holdings Inc., 2011. By permission.

The family needs a financial plan to ensure they will be able to meet their lifestyle needs, as well as a few wants and luxuries, before they will contemplate contributing to a larger Family Treasury financial plan. There is most likely a very good financial planner in your area that can work with you to prepare a personal financial plan, but be diligent about who you choose. Personally, I believe the best financial planner is a Registered Financial Planner (R.F.P.), but I am biased, as I am one; I am also a member of the Institute of Advanced Financial Planners. According to their website, the R.F.P.® (Registered Financial Planner™) is a professional financial planning designation. It has been the hallmark of the professional financial planner in Canada since 1987. The Institute grants the R.F.P.® designation to financial planners who demonstrate competence in the practice of personal financial planning. Some of these competencies include demonstrating they have the knowledge required to complete a comprehensive financial plan through experience, by passing an examination, by submitting financial plans for peer review, and by complying with a code of ethics and meeting annual professional development requirements.[37] Most financial planners will belong to an association that encourages professional standards are met, so do your homework.

I believe that comprehensive financial planning advice should be objective and independent of the sale of an investment or insurance product. That is often not the case. That is not to say that there are not honest and ethical investment advisers and insurance brokers out there who would put your best interests first. I merely suggest that I think it best practice that the financial planner and the investment broker and insurance agent work collaboratively but remain at arm's length from each other. That way you can be assured not only that the advice received is truly for your benefit but also that the advice will probably be best in class with three professionals working together, instead of one trying to deliver it all.

As a first step, the personal financial plan should take a full inventory of all of your current resources. Your financial planner should also understand clearly your values, your mission, your goals, and your objectives. Share with them your strategic plan so they can plan for the monies needed to meet those objectives.

The financial planner's assignment is to create an orderly and well-defined road map of how to get you financially from where you are today to where you want to be, given your short-term objectives and long-term financial goals.

Of course, a financial plan is not worth the paper it is written on if it remains unimplemented. Input and coordination from your professional advisers ensures the financial plan is of the highest calibre and gets implemented in a thoughtful and integrated way. Be sure your investment advisers, tax advisers, insurance advisers, and estate advisers work off your plan so that their advice is collaborative, integrated, and complete. Your financial plan will benefit if implemented with regular monitoring and updates allowing you and your advisory team to assess current strategies and remain on track proactively in the pursuit of your goals and objectives. As a result, your relationship with your planner should be ongoing.

> 66 *A financial plan is not*
> *worth the paper it is written on*
> *if it remains unimplemented.*

▲ *The Family Treasury Financial Plan*

The Family Treasury may be serving one small "nuclear" family or it may be serving multiple generations of multiple family groups who have agreed to participate in the larger group mission. If serving just one nuclear family, the personal financial plan will suffice to get you on your way to achieving your goals. But if The Family Treasury has evolved to the point that it is serving multiple generations and their families, it remains important that each of those family groups has their own mission, strategic plan, and financial plan. It is no different than in a business. The employees will individually have personal financial and lifestyle goals and, hopefully, strategic and financial plans to help achieve them. But for the business not only to exist but also to succeed, it needs its own plan for financial growth and sustainability. So, too, for The Family Treasury when dealing with multiple family generations. At my firm, we call this document The Family Treasury Financial Plan. Not a very creative name, but it certainly identifies its purpose.

The personal financial plan is about wealth security. The Family Treasury financial plan is about True family wealth creation.

Regardless of whether your Family Treasury is starting out with significant capital funding or none at all, you need to begin with the mission statement. Then address what are the goals and what are the short-term and long-term objectives you wish to achieve as laid out in The Family Treasury strategic plan. Then it is time to put some numbers to those goals, to give them a price tag. What is the cost to build and manage that new community recreation centre? What is the cost to buy and farm that property in the country? How much money is needed to hold a Family Treasury meeting at a resort next year? What will your dream cost in terms of financial resources? In order to get started, we need a founder.

The Founder's Capital Threshold

All Family Treasuries will have a founder. The founder, or founders, will be the folks who commit to bringing The Family Treasury into existence for the benefit of themselves, those around them, and those who come after. Not unlike a business, the founder is the one who sacrifices time, energy, and money for a dream/vision that is bigger and more important than them. If The Family Treasury mission statement is just that—bigger and more important than them—the founder (or founders) will willingly make that initial gift.

Therefore, the first step in development of The Family Treasury financial plan is to identify what the founders are willing to contribute to get it up and running but with the proviso to also demonstrate preservation of their personal financial security. At my firm, we do that by calculating the founder's financial independence capital threshold. We do that as part of their Family Prosperity Plan, or personal financial plan, spoken of previously.

To illustrate this, let's look again at Jack and Jill. Each wishes to found their own Family Treasury. They understand the many benefits of founding The Family Treasury but are not sure they have enough capital to commit to it at this point in their lives, so they are considering deferring it to later years. We would hate to see that happen. The earlier The Family Treasury starts, the more effective and powerful it can become. So we perform a series of financial calculations that take into consideration the founder's income and lifestyle expenses, risk mitigation needs, tax minimization opportunities, and financial independence and other personal goals. We define financial independence as occurring when your existing financially productive assets, plus your future passive sources of income (pension, annuity, or investment income) are sufficient to meet your expected future spending needs. This financial security allows you to devote more of your LEQ to areas of life other than earning an income. We break out the future goals into separate cash flow streams to assess the current capital required to meet each of them, based on certain assumptions such as inflation rates and asset returns. These are referred to as capital thresholds (I introduced this concept first in Chapter 1).

Figure 7: Model of Jack's and Jill's ability as founders to fund The Family Treasury

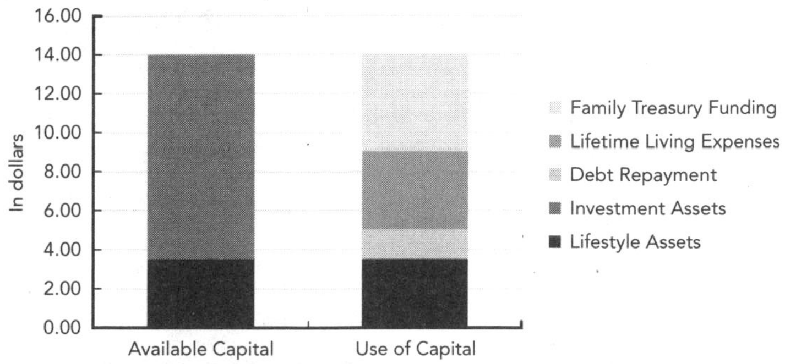

Source: Model designed by Brent Barrie, Family Office Director, First Affiliated Holdings Inc. By permission.

Figure 7 models Jack and Jill's ability as founders to fund The Family Treasury by defining its capital threshold requirement and comparing it to other capital thresholds needed to meet their other goals. We then compare the results to the resources available to meet all those goals.

Let's Look at Jack and Jill

As illustrated in Figure 7, Jack and his wife have available financial capital of $1,400,000, with $350,000 of this being the value of the log home, which Jack wishes to keep for life. They have accumulated investment assets of $1,050,000. Remember that Jack's wife is guaranteed a healthy teacher's pension when she retires. This analysis shows them that they can keep their home, pay off their debt, and set aside a financial independence capital threshold (i.e., Lifetime Living Expenses) of $400,000 to supplement the pension and meet lifetime living costs. They have room left over to fund their Family Treasury with $500,000.

Jill and her family can do the same. However, their income bracket is significantly higher, so the categories all have an additional zero. Jill's potential is to fund The Family Treasury with $5,000,000.

Would either of them transfer this much to The Family Treasury from the outset? Not likely. But they can start with appropriate amounts to get the investment in The Family Treasury mission rolling and then decide, as things evolve, whether more investment is warranted. This is, after all, how a business would do it. The Family Treasury balance sheet (spoken of at the end of the chapter) is a great tool to help measure this return on investment.

The decision to fund The Family Treasury is often made easier when one puts their estate in perspective. If you intend to leave an inheritance, why wait until you are dead and can't witness the joy these "extra" funds can bring to you and your family as you co-create together? Figure out your "just in case you might need it" capital threshold, put that in reserve, and invest the rest into The Family Treasury mission.

What if Jack or Jill has not yet met their financial independence capital threshold? What if they have other personal goals they want to achieve separate and distinct from the group mission? I have spoken with folks who feel because they have not yet met their own financial security needs that they have no scope to be a Family Treasury founder. Remember Jill's Family Treasury Mission? That did not require any money at all, just a group passion for environmental change and her legal expertise.

In addition, there are small ways to start. For example, financing the group meetings—they wouldn't happen without you. Leading The Family Treasury Roundtable—again, it wouldn't happen without you. Sharing what you do have, even if it isn't money. Remember Jack? He offered the unused corners of his land to other student farmers in exchange for their labour to help him build a family organic farm. It couldn't happen without him. My own family is an example of how we contribute non-monetary value to our Family Treasury. In addition to being a pilot, my husband has a background in building, carpentry, and civil engineering. I have experience in marketing, psychology, finance, and accounting. These are of great value to the young budding entrepreneurs in the family starting their own businesses. We share what we know, and they listen. We have their back. The money to fund The Family Treasury can come in over time; it need not happen all at once.

> 66 *The money to fund The Family Treasury can come in over time; it need not happen all at once.*

This process of determining capital thresholds allows the family to see what they have available to spend on setting up The Family Treasury without sacrificing their own financial security. If they do not have the capital available yet, then the question becomes: how much of their individual and collective LEQ are they prepared to convert to money for The Family Treasury? This is a function of balancing the personal mission statements of the individual with the group mission statement of The Family Treasury. How much money can they get for your collective LEQ efforts? This is a function of catalyzing the conversion of LEQ to higher and higher amounts of money, most often accomplished through education, leadership, entrepreneurialism, and savings (paying yourself first). More about this later in the chapter.

Net Financial Wealth Accumulation Targets

The next few sections of this book will be most helpful to families that have accumulated financial capital beyond that needed to meet their own financial independence needs. In particular, this next section deals with financial management concepts that can be technical in nature. If you are not yet ready to learn this material, feel free to skip to The Family Treasury Succession Plan (page 303). However, having said that, as outlined in the Introduction, I encourage you to read on whether or not these concepts have immediate applicability. We all have a responsibility to manage our own financial affairs and to be educated about best practices to do so. Money is a form of energy to be used in the joy of creation. If you don't know how to work with it, your creations will be limited.

After the capital needs are assessed, the capital thresholds defined, and the capital either available, or still needed, for the funding of The Family Treasury mission identified, it is now time to plot the course. One of the goals of The Family Treasury is often, but not always, to build and preserve financial wealth for the family over time. The Family Treasury financial plan should model how this is expected to unfold, based on the founder's capital (in the form of asset transfer or cash investment) as a starting point and cash management going forward. In order to sustainably build financial wealth, it is most helpful to set net wealth accumulation targets along the way so as to achieve the goal step by step. We are putting numbers to the annual objectives. In order to do this well, one aims to match the cash flow requirements to the objectives set out in The Family Treasury strategic plan. This is no different than any business would do. A business doesn't just think about bringing in enough income to pay for its expenses. It is in business in the first place to build wealth, which can in turn be reinvested to grow the business further and diversify its interests beyond that business alone. Likewise in The Family Treasury: we need income to exceed expenses, so that the net income can be reinvested back into The Family Treasury to sustain itself into the future.

Expenses of The Family Treasury include professional fees, investment management fees, insurance premiums, family meeting costs, supplies, etc. When The Family Treasury is large enough, expenses might also include allowances for family members, education costs, and, perhaps (although not an expense, but a cash outlay), regular dividend payments to certain of The Family Treasury members (more about this later).

Sources of income might include additional founder's capital contributions over time, investment earnings, family or privately owned business dividends or interest on loans, and potentially even ongoing contributions offered, or "dues" paid, by other family members.

Assets might include family businesses, liquid portfolio investments, and other private investments such as private equity, real estate, intellectual property, franchises, mortgages, insurance policies, etc. The Family Treasury may also have debts of its own used to leverage the performance of some of these assets.

The following table illustrates what a sample summary of net wealth accumulation targets might look like over a five-year period. Behind the figures are assumptions about

Table 7: Net Wealth Accumulation Targets

Year	2016	2017	2018	2019	2020
Assets					
Rental Real Estate	$ 768,680	$ 784,054	$ 799,735	$ 815,729	$ 832,044
Investment Account	$ 1,707,535	$ 1,713,999	$ 1,618,000	$ 1,720,902	$ 1,721,147
Mortgage Portfolio	$ 151,613	$ 153,129	$ 154,660	$ 156,207	$ 157,769
Family Treasury Meeting Fund	$ 5,000	$ 25,000	$ 45,000	$ 30,000	$ 52,000
Operating Account	$ 5,640	$ 2,696	$ 5,753	$ 10,811	$ 8,869
Subtotal	$ 2,638,468	$ 2,678,878	$ 2,623,148	$ 2,733,649	$ 2,771,829
Ski Condo	$ 597,351	$ 609,298	$ 621,484	$ 633,914	$ 646,592
Total Assets	$ 3,235,819	$ 3,288,176	$ 3,244,632	$ 3,367,563	$ 3,418,421
Liabilities					
Line of Credit	$ (6,417)	$ (3,000)	$ (0)	$ (0)	$ (10,000)
Mortgage	$ (147,033)	$ (139,434)	$ (131,565)	$ (123,416)	$ (114,977)
Subtotal	$ (153,450)	$ (142,434)	$ (131,565)	$ (123,416)	$ (124,977)
Family Treasury Net Worth	$ 3,082,369	$ 3,145,742	$ 3,113,067	$ 3,244,147	$ 3,293,444

income and expense cash flows, investment returns, taxation, inflation, etc. For simplicity purposes, these are not presented here. Again, add or deduct as many zeros as applicable.

Financial planners use software to map out annual expected cash flows and their effect on assets and liabilities. Many assumptions are built into a model such as this, including cash flows in and out of assets due to incomes and expenses, amounts and types of investment returns, savings rates, and the impact of taxation and inflation. The objective is to see the net assets accumulate over time, not deplete. Actual results should be compared to the plan annually so appropriate adjustments can be made to get back on track. Note that in preparing the financial plan, thought went into the likely investment returns, and the type of investment return each type of asset was capable of generating. This becomes important when projecting where to take money from to fund cash flow deficits, and where to invest, or reinvest, cash flow surpluses to maximize growth in high-return investments while at the same time sustaining appropriate diversification into secure but lower-return assets. Leverage is also used prudently, when appropriate, but paid off as soon as appropriate as well.

◢ The Tax-Effective Structure

Long-term wealth creation within The Family Treasury is also assisted by tax planning methods and proper asset protection structures. Two of the most common structures used to house The Family Treasury include trusts and corporations when it has significant financial assets to protect. In Table 8, I illustrate, from a very simplistic, high-level perspective, some of the pros and cons of these two types of structures from a Canadian backdrop as of 2015 (the corporation described below is an investment corporation). You will need advice from your qualified tax and legal practitioners to find the best solution for you.

There is often a role for both structures, but flexibility is required to allow transition from one to the other when the

Table 8: Tax-Effective Structures

Family Trust	
Pros	Cons
Flexible distributions to beneficiaries with no need to treat them equally	Deemed disposition of assets for tax purposes every 21 years
Assets can be protected in case of marital breakdown	Usually must wind up after the end of two generations (except in Manitoba, Nova Scotia and Saskatchewan)
Trustees, not the beneficiaries, have control	Trustees, not the beneficiaries, have control
Income can be split with low tax beneficiaries and reduce tax	Income retained in the trust taxed at the highest rates with no graduated levels
Assets are typically creditor-proof	
Capital gains exemptions on business sale can be multiplied among beneficiaries	
Certain operational expenses deductible	

Corporation	
Pros	Cons
Different classes of shares permitted	All shareholders of same share class get equal dividend
No end life	Value falls into equalization payments upon marital split
Insurance an effective means to pay tax liability on death of a shareholder	Shareholder shares deemed disposed of at their death
Shareholders, not management, usually have control	Shareholder agreements required
Dividends can be paid into investment holding company from operating companies it owns on a tax-deferred basis	Can't pay dividends to children under 18 without adverse tax consequences
Certain operational expenses deductible	With tax equalization, investment income taxed in corporation at close to the same rates as if earned personally

time is appropriate. Further discussion about the technical nature of these structures and how they work is not the subject of this book. However, we will assume that one of these is in place and that the founder's capital has been effectively contributed in order to turn our attention to the appropriate management of The Family Treasury capital.

Tax considerations should never be far from the investment decisions as taxation can have a profound diminutive effect on wealth creation over the long term if proper efforts are not made to minimize its impact. Likewise, attention needs to be paid to asset protection structures to help protect wealth from unwarranted litigious claims.

Looking further into asset productivity, we now consider the manner in which the family members and The Family Treasury invest their capital.

⟁ The Investment Strategy

One of the greatest challenges in meeting your financial plan goals is how to invest your money, whether for your family or The Family Treasury. Of course, you can work hard to accumulate wealth, but it would be nice if the money you have invested works just as hard for you and is protected and secure. However, the world of investing has become over-whelming and, frankly, very volatile. This is an especially important factor when it comes to your family's financial management.

The Strategist and the Specialist

For most people that are not trained money management professionals, figuring out the smart choices with your life savings can be daunting, if not highly stressful. There is an alarming trend of do-it-your-selfers in the area of finance, spurred on by the media and online trading houses and their encouragement of day trading. This is nothing more than gambling. Sure it can be harmless if kept in proportion. But unless finance is your profession, you do not know what you do not know. The complexities of regulation, taxation, high-speed automated trading, and overload of information have made "self-management" of your finances tricky business. Can you really afford to cut corners or make best guesses with your life savings? Would you try to do your own heart surgery? Is not preservation of your hard-earned assets almost as important?

In order to control investment risk and build a strategy that meets your objectives, it is best to seek the advice of both an investment *strategist* and an investment *specialist*. This is not dissimilar from using your family doctor to oversee the complexities and many moving parts of your health care plan, while sourcing and working with best-in-class health care specialists as needed. The strategist is the gatekeeper and generalist, has a strong network, and confirms the credentials and capabilities of any investment specialists who offer their services. The specialist is the master technician asked to implement the specific area of the strategy best suited to their expertise. The main benefits of hiring an investment strategist who is separate and distinct from the specialists is not that different than the reasons for hiring a financial planner who is at arm's length. The success of each family financial plan depends on the productivity of its assets: the investment strategist plays the role of guardian of that wealth with the overriding objective of capital preservation, including protection from the effects of inflation and taxation. The investment strategist is also the keeper of the records. Accountability can only be achieved when results are viewed on a consolidated basis and measured against appropriate, independent benchmarks. Those benchmarks should be set by your financial plan, should belong to you, and should not be the investment manager's benchmarks, which have nothing to do with you. A good investment strategist can also educate you, help you ride through difficult markets (holding your hand if necessary), and ensure you stick with your strategy. An investment strategist should be objective and not sell investment products.

> 66 *It is best to seek the advice*
> *of both an investment strategist*
> *and an investment specialist.*

In summary, an investment strategist offers the following benefits:

- ✔ investment education
- ✔ customized risk adjusted strategic asset allocation
- ✔ customized portfolio design and tax management
- ✔ portfolio risk sensitivity analysis
- ✔ documented investment policy statement
- ✔ manager due diligence

✔ portfolio implementation and administration

✔ customized and consolidated internal rate of return and/or time weighted rate of return performance reporting

✔ market and portfolio analysis

✔ regular meetings and ongoing communications

So where do you find an investment strategist? A fee-based financial planner with a background in investment management is a good choice. If your financial resources warrant it, a family office can play the roles of both financial planner and investment strategist. After all, a suitable investment strategy is guided by your strategic financial plan, cash needs, capital usage, and risk tolerance. I believe success is likely when the investment strategy is customized to your family's values and needs; based on your financial plan; and is robust, disciplined, and free from potential bias. A true family office is free from potential bias, so in my opinion, most suited to this role.

The personal financial plan relies on a prudent investment strategy to grow and conserve financial assets for the family's long-term lifestyle needs. Likewise, The Family Treasury has an investment strategy, based on its financial plan, for a growing foundation of liquid and non-liquid wealth to support the interests, development, enterprises, and experiences of the generations to come. Remember the deep, dark well? This is how you build the ladder.

The Asset Allocation Process

Choosing an investment portfolio that is best for you and The Family Treasury depends on many factors, including risk tolerance, return requirements, income objectives, time horizon, and investment knowledge and aptitude. Once those factors are known, and using the asset allocation process, the investment strategy can be created with the objective of achieving those target returns with the least volatility possible. It is then documented into an investment policy statement that guides your investment decisions going forward and keeps a steady hand on the tiller when markets get choppy.

I grappled with including this section in the book due to its technical nature. However, I want you to know what I know so you can feel confident about your financial management. Our society's approach to wealth management is messed up. Too many people both live in fear of market volatility and abdicate their financial security into the hands of others. You need to know this stuff if you want to take back control of your financial well-being.

So strap on your seat belt, or perhaps go get a stiff drink, and please spend some time with the pages that follow.[38] They outline a long-term approach to investing that has proven time and again to preserve and grow wealth. It did so through the Great Depression of the 1930s and the global financial crisis of 2008, and it will continue to do so. It is built upon the principles that underlie all economic activity and is another reflection of the Law of Cycles discussed earlier.

I am going to show you how to grow your portfolio assets over the long term without fear of capital loss, and without the need to guess what the markets will do tomorrow. I am going to show you a tried-and-true method to obtain good portfolio returns while preserving your financial capital over the long term. This method is usually used by "patient capital" investors, like pension funds, who need income and capital preservation with a long-term focus. The retail investment community, however, is very different, and so this method is not well known in the retail investor marketplace. Driven by media hype, the retail investor most often has a short-term focus and the commissioned trading houses are only too happy to help. Working with the system I describe will change all that. It is better for you, and better for our financial markets. You will still need to work with qualified investment specialists, but you will no longer abdicate control over your decision-making and, with this system, you can expect accountability for results.

Cycles Are Our Friend

The secret to long-term investment success is asset allocation, which works with, instead of against, changing economic cycles. Developed economies move in a cyclical fashion of ups and downs, although the overall trend over time is "up" as growth takes place. According to the research team at Trading Economics, the U.S., for example, had a long-term growth rate in Gross Domestic Product (GDP) that averaged over 3.2%

Figure 8: The cyclical pattern of developed economies

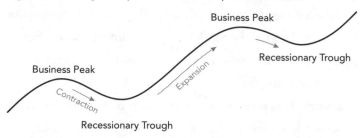

from 1947 to 2015. Canada also achieved an average GDP of 3.2% from 1962 to 2015. Britain saw an average GDP of 2.5% from 1956 to 2015.[39]

> ❝ *The secret to long-term invest-*
> *ment success is asset allocation.*

What we don't know is how deep the troughs or high the peaks will be, or how long each cycle will run, before changing course. Yes, an investment strategy intended to preserve wealth over the long term needs to consider the return and security level of the investments it makes, but more importantly, it needs to set a policy around how money will be directed to a variety of asset classes in order to preserve and grow wealth working with these cycles.

Statistical studies show that the decision on how to allocate total assets among various asset classes will have a far greater impact on overall long-term results (by impacting the portfolio's volatility levels) than security selection and other decisions that affect portfolio performance. *Specifically, between 90–95% of the variability of a portfolio's returns can be attributed to the asset allocation decision.* And yet, in our experience, the vast majority of investors spend 100% of their time and effort on security selection.

Asset allocation works to:

- decrease volatility of returns
- provide capital preservation
- increase opportunity for good, consistent, long-term returns
- reduce tax and administrative costs
- simplify disciplined decision-making

Asset Classes

Asset allocation works through investment in combinations of asset classes to enhance opportunities to consistently achieve good overall portfolio returns. It does so with less volatility than the individual asset classes themselves may experience. This is due to the differences in correlation patterns between asset classes as they respond to certain economic stimuli. Correlation patterns refer to how two asset classes move relative to each other. Those assets that are negatively correlated reduce risk (or volatility) of a portfolio's returns, because the negative returns of one asset class are somewhat offset by the positive returns of another asset class.

What do I mean by asset classes? These represent the general characteristics of certain groups of financial instruments. The asset class universe most commonly used in the Family Office setting is as follows:

- cash and cash equivalents

- fixed income–domestic bonds, mortgages

- fixed income–international bonds

- equities–domestic stocks

- equities–international stocks

- real estate–real estate investment trusts (REITS), limited partnerships, real estate stocks and infrastructure

- specialty (alternative)–gold, oil & gas, resources, emerging markets, hedge funds (managed futures), sector funds, and private equity and other alternative investments

The Efficient Frontier

In my thirty years of experience, I have found that the most efficient asset allocation mix is designed using a process called Efficient Frontier Portfolio Optimization Analysis. The Efficient Frontier (see curved line in Figure 9 on page 282) represents a series of points, each of which is a sample portfolio. Each sample portfolio's dollars are allocated among the main asset classes in differing proportions. However, the allocations were calculated by formulas using an iterative process that *produces a portfolio with the minimum expected volatility for a given level of expected return.* Plotting this "maximum return/minimum volatility" portfolio for every unit of risk creates what we call "the Efficient Frontier curve." Alternatively, for any given return expectation, the portfolio on, or close, to the line is the one whose allocation has the least expected volatility. In other words, it is the most efficient portfolio.

Let's look at the example on page 282 of three different portfolio asset allocations through the lens of the Efficient Frontier. Table 9 shows portfolio P1 has 60% in fixed income and 40% in Canadian and international equities compared to P2, which has 10% in cash, 54% in fixed income, and only 36% in Canadian and international equities. The expected average long-term median return for P2 is somewhat lower as you would expect, but so is the expected level of volatility. Yet the third option, P3, is a much more efficient portfolio. It actually has more in cash than the previous two, less in equities at only 25%, and holds real estate and the much riskier asset class "Specialty." It has a higher expected return than P2 and a significantly lower volatility than both P1 and P2. This is the magic of asset allocation. *It creates efficient portfolios where you can hold riskier asset classes, with higher return potential, while at the same time reducing the overall portfolio volatility.*

Risk is defined here as volatility of expected returns. Therefore, the P3 portfolio is expected to experience an average standard deviation (volatility range) of 7.99%. That means that in any given one-year period, the actual returns achieved

Figure 9: Efficient Frontier Portfolio Optimization Analysis comparison of three portfolios

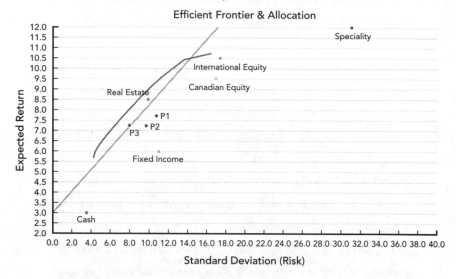

Table 9: Sample Portfolio Asset Allocations

	P1	P2	P3
	%	%	%
Asset Allocation			
Cash	0.0000	10.0000	15.0000
Fixed Income	60.0000	54.0000	45.0000
Canadian Equity	10.0000	9.0000	10.0000
International Equity	30.0000	27.0000	15.0000
Real Estate	0.0000	0.0000	6.0000
Specialty	0.0000	0.0000	9.0000
Expected Return	7.7000	7.2300	7.2650
Standard Deviation (Volatility)	10.7379	9.7032	7.9952

for this portfolio are most likely to land somewhere between -5.36% and 20.90% with 7.26% being only the median (50/50) result. That is quite a band of possibilities. In fact, there is a 95% chance of returns being greater than -5.36% and only a 5% chance they will exceed 20.90% in any one year. However, over periods greater than one year, the range of volatility outcomes narrows as the actual returns converge around the expected 20-year compound return of 6.98%, as demonstrated on the return percentiles chart in Figure 10. Actual 20-year compound results are expected to fall within a probable nominal range of 4.07% to 9.93%.

Another way to say this is that 95% of the time, over a long period of at least 20 years, this portfolio allocation will produce a long-term annualized compound return above 4.07%. It will produce a long-term annualized compound return in excess of 9.93% only 5% of the time.

The aim, through effective asset allocation, is not to maximize returns. The aim is to obtain a good target rate of growth, within the possible "target return range" over the long term, with the least volatility possible. Through continual monitoring and management you can ensure that your changing objectives, required returns, and market realities are addressed and factored into your investment strategy.

> *The aim is to obtain a good target rate of growth, within the possible "target return range" over the long term, with the least volatility possible.*

Figure 10: Return percentiles for portfolio P3 over 20 years

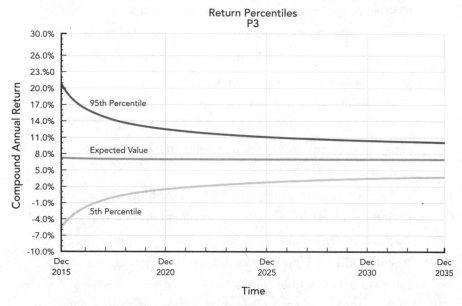

Table 10: Statistics Supporting Figure 10

	Compound Return (%) over			
	1 year	5 years	10 years	20 years
Asset Allocation	**2015**	**2020**	**2025**	**2035**
95th Percentile	20.9000	12.9884	11.1909	9.9371
Expected Value	7.2650	7.0275	6.9979	6.9831
5th Percentile	-5.3581	1.2689	2.9060	4.0796

Ongoing Management and Monitoring

Once the investment selections are made, which in itself is an ongoing process, the performance of the portfolio is monitored on an ongoing basis. It is reviewed at least quarterly for changing assumptions, circumstances, and economic trends.

If such changes are believed to be of a long-term nature, you should make changes to the portfolio investments or asset allocation accordingly. You would also make a change if it is felt that the long-term trend in performance of a specific investment will no longer meet certain targets or requirements. However, I do not advocate market timing.

The success of the asset allocation investment strategy depends on patience and a long-term view, and as such, short-term market timing can destroy its ability to work its "magic." *The risk of trying to guess which asset class to get into and which to get out of, based on short-term projections of market movements, has a far greater cost of being wrong most of the time than the benefit of being right some of the time.*

Figure 11 reflects the dangers of market timing. It measures market results over the period 1926 to 2015 (which includes the Great Depression). It uses the Standard and Poor's U.S. stock market index called the S&P500 to reflect the stock market activity of that period. It shows that $1 invested in that stock market and left for 89 years grew to be worth $5,390 (ignoring the impact of inflation). But if you were attempting to time the market and were out of the market during the best 45 months of the total 1,068 months in that period, you would have ended up with $20.33, less than Treasury Bill returns. Figure 12 reflects the same thing but for the period 1996 to 2015. In that time, $1 invested for 19 years would have grown to be worth $4.82. Yet, if you attempted to time the market and were out of the market for the key 13 months of

Figure 11: Dangers of market timing: hypothetical value of
$1 invested from 1926 to 2015

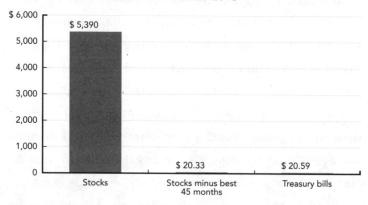

Figure 12: Dangers of market timing: hypothetical value of
$1 invested from 1996 to 2015

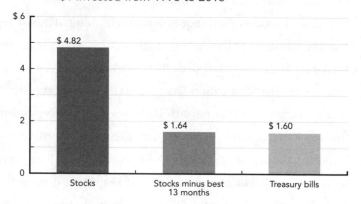

Note: Past performance is no guarantee of future results. These are for illustrative purposes only and not indicative of any investment. An investment cannot be made directly in an index.

the 228-month period, once again you would have ended up with only slightly more than Treasury Bill returns. Of course, the danger with charts is that you can pick any time period you wish, but you get the point: the chances of being wrong far outweigh the likelihood of being right.

Asset allocation is a long-term strategy—not a passive strategy. Time is required for asset classes to respond to correlation patterns. Like pistons of a car engine, the economy moves in cycles, but is propelled forward. From time to time, it may be desirable to amend your investment strategy due to changes in your chosen allocation, or the inputs used to create it. Changing market conditions may cause the portfolio's investment in various asset classes to vary from the target allocation. To remain consistent with the asset allocation strategy established by the investment policy statement (discussed later in the chapter), the portfolio investments should be reviewed on a quarterly basis and rebalanced back to the recommended weighting if the actual weighting varies by 5% or more from the recommended weighting. Rebalancing more often than that is not as effective since it creates unnecessary costs.

Rebalancing is critical to the success of an asset allocation strategy. Without it, the process could, in fact, fail. Figure 13 shows the performance of the various asset classes (as represented by the indices) going into and out of the period of the Great Depression. The U.S. small capitalization stock index lost 90% of its value during the worst of the crisis in 1932. You will see two balanced portfolios modelled and compared with

Figure 13: Effect of rebalancing on portfolio performance going into and out of the period of the Great Depression

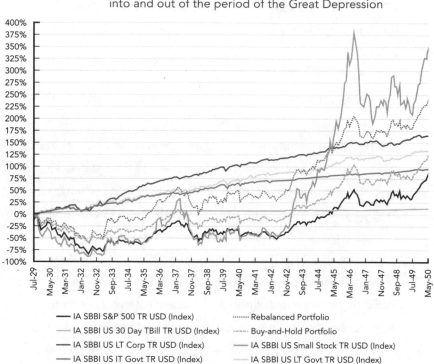

Source: Model designed by Bart Rowe, Director of Investments, First Affiliated Holdings Inc. By permission.

data from that time. Both are invested 50% in fixed income and 50% in equity. Both also declined by around 60% during this tumultuous time. However, the 50/50 "buy-and-hold" portfolio did not permanently regain its ground until 1942 (10 years later). Compare that to the 50/50 "rebalanced" portfolio that was rebalanced back to target each time an asset class moved by more than 5%. It only took 3 years, until 1935, to recover its capital, and after only a short blip in 1937, it went on to be the second highest performing portfolio, behind the small stock index.

> *Rebalancing is critical to the success of an asset allocation strategy.*

Rebalancing allows one the discipline to be a true contrarian investor—buying low and selling high—in a disciplined, unemotional manner, regardless of market conditions.

The same pattern can be seen after the market crash of 2008. Figure 14 shows the behaviour of a portfolio invested 50% in cash and fixed income instruments, and 50% in equity-type instruments. You can see how the equity market value declined almost 45% during the crisis, and by the end of 2012, the S&P/TSX equity market had not recovered to June 2008 values. The actively rebalanced portfolio recovered fully just over 18 months after the lows and was a top performer thereafter. The lesson? Using asset allocation has been proven in the most severe market corrections to maintain and grow capital for those who can take a long-term, patient approach and maintain the discipline to rebalance when the portfolio dictates.

Does asset allocation guarantee against loss? No, it doesn't, as both the models and strategy are still based on human assumptions and input. It also requires a long-term approach

Figure 14: Effect of rebalancing on portfolio performance going into and out of the 2008 global financial crisis

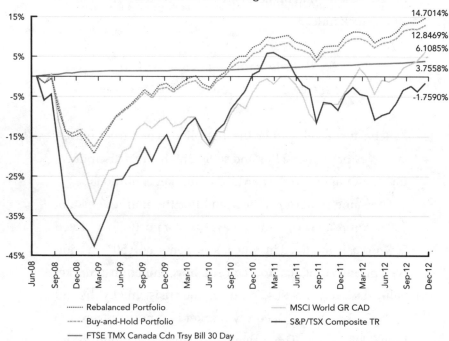

Source: Model designed by Bart Rowe, Director of Investments, First Affiliated Holdings Inc. By permission.

to effectively "do its thing," so there is a risk of loss if there is a forced liquidation too soon due to unforeseen circumstances.

Again, it is worth repeating: asset allocation does not aim to maximize returns. It aims to minimize volatility, preserve capital, and provide good consistent returns over the long term. It is an excellent method for growing and preserving the financial resources of The Family Treasury for the benefit of current and future generations.

Investment Manager Selection

While asset allocation holds a critical role in wealth preservation, the process of choosing investments for the portfolio is also important. Selection of individual securities (individual stocks or bonds) is time-consuming and dependent upon large research capabilities. It is also important, though, to the long-term performance of your portfolio, as is a proper asset allocation mix. Proper investment selection can add additional returns and provide good growth. It is prudent to hire specialists that concentrate on security selection within a specific asset class and have the necessary resources to effectively select individual securities.

> *Proper investment selection can add additional returns and provide good growth.*

Many people fancy themselves armchair investors and, with little to no training, stock pick for their portfolios. They wonder why they should pay an investment manager to do it for them. This does not make any sense to me. A professionally trained portfolio manager has the experience and knowledge to do the job well, and they do it full time. Chances are you don't! Therefore, most likely, they are better at it than you are. They are trained specialists in the field. Would you do your own knee surgery? Professionally managed investment funds offer the following benefits:

✔ broad security diversification

✔ purchasing power

✔ superior investment selection

✔ access to all markets and research

✔ reduced costs

✔ efficient execution and custody

✔ competitive fees

✔ reduced taxes

✔ customized portfolio options

However, as with anything else, there are good investment managers and not-so-good investment managers. So while you may not be well served by managing your investments yourself without professional training, you would be well served to take great care in selecting who does that for you. Here is a list of some issues to look at when completing due diligence on a manager for a particular asset class within your portfolio.

• There should be a **track record** of at least five (and preferably ten years) of performance, allowing you to ascertain how performance behaves given differing business cycles and economic factors. Your objective here is not to identify "top performers" but to identify above-average performers who do so consistently with reduced volatility. After all, the objective of your investment strategy is not to maximize return regardless of risks, but to achieve a target return on average with the most consistency and least volatility possible. Of course to ascertain this, the annual performance numbers over this period must be reviewed, considering fees and comparison to benchmarks, and compared to a global peer group managing in a similar manner. If composite portfolios are used to demonstrate these returns, a full description must be provided as to what makes up the composite and how much of the actual client base is represented by it. "Phantom" track records (based on simulated returns "as if" a strategy was deployed over a past period) should not be acceptable.

- There must be a clear, definable **investment style and process** that is used and consistently followed. The investment style they use must be understandable and consistent with the objectives of both you and those stated by the manager. In addition, it must be suitable to the required portfolio asset allocation strategy that is being implemented.

- In your dealings with the investment supplier, look for a high degree of prompt, accurate **service** and strong **administrative capabilities**. If a firm has poor back-office capabilities, they will likely be spending more time troubleshooting than managing your investments.

- Obtain **references** for smaller "private" managers, where you will be looking for positive feedback.

- **Decision-making** regarding investment management in the firm should be made on the basis of group consensus or centralized management, and generally should not be based solely on power given to one "star" individual. Again, the objective here is to ensure long-term success of the portfolio, not short-term maximized results.

- A potential manager should meet all applicable required **securities legislations**. The adviser must be able to provide written proof of proper registration or exemption. Of course, when looking to acquire a security such as a mutual fund or direct investment, the dealer must have had the product registered as well.

- There must be recognized **professional organizations** supporting the manager. This includes legal, custodial, accounting, brokerage, and trust services. Assets are best held at a separate custodian from the investment manager in either your name or with you nominated as beneficial owner.

- It is preferred that there be over $250 million under the **adviser's management** when you are dealing with a private investment counsel firm. This gives an indication of "staying power" and longevity based on past success. The more "boutique" the firm's approach, the better. Also look for a good **rate of growth of assets** under management over the last five years. That indicates a successful track record.

- In the case of private investment counsel, it is preferred that the majority **ownership** lay with the employees and managers. Again, this leads to a higher level of service and opportunity for success, as there is emotional involvement on the part of the decision-makers. For the same reason, look for low **employee turnover**.

- In all cases, **succession** must be addressed. As your investment strategy is of a long-term nature, you should ensure that plans are in place so there are decision-makers always being "groomed" to take over from older decision-makers holding the same views and philosophy as their predecessor.

- Preferably, greater than 50% of the **investment research** is performed in-house as opposed to outside, which helps encourage originality and intimate knowledge when making decisions. In addition, the decision-making should be based on both quantitative and subjective measures.

Other considerations when choosing an investment manager (including mutual funds, discretionary managers, and limited partnership sponsors) include the following criteria:

- past performance, considered relative to other investments having the same investment objective, taking into consideration both performance rankings over various time frames and consistency of performance

- costs relative to other funds with similar investment styles

- assets under management of the proposed investment fund

- length of time the fund has been in existence and length of time it has been under the direction of the current manager(s) and whether or not there have been material changes in the manager's organization and personnel

- historical volatility patterns of each proposed investment

- how well each proposed investment complements other assets in the portfolio

- The current economic environment and its risks/opportunities

Investment Manager Monitoring

Your return is the most important measure of investment and manager performance. Ongoing monitoring of your investments and managers to appropriate benchmarks is critical to ensure that you continue to have the best-in-class investments. Replacement of an investment or a manager should be considered if they consistently fail to beat their peers and the established benchmarks over a sustained period. In the event of unforeseen turmoil, such as managerial turnover or changes in investment style, you should look at immediate replacement of the manager. For effective monitoring, you will need to consolidate your investments for performance reporting purposes.

" Your return is the most
important measure of investment
and manager performance.

The best measure of performance to your own particular targets is internal rate of return (IRR). It is the actual compounded portfolio return over a time period, annualized, for your particular portfolio, giving effect to the timing of your particular cash flows in and out of the portfolio.

A good measure of performance of one manager to another (which should exclude the impact of your particular cash inflows and outflows) is time weighted return (TWR). It reflects the compound return of portfolio investments after the effect of cash inflows and outflows have been eliminated.

For example, let's say you have $1,000 to invest in mutual funds managed by two fund managers. You put $500 with Manager A and $500 with Manager B, both investments made in June. At the end of the year, Manager A reports a TWR for his fund of 10%. Manager B reports a TWR for his fund of 5%. You would naturally think Manager A outperformed Manager B over that period. And that is true. *But not for you.*

You invested in June. Manager A earned 9% over the period January to May and earned 1% over the period June to December. Manager B earned his 5% in the period June to December. Your IRR with Manager A is 1% and with Manager B, 5%. While a simplistic example, it shows you did better with Manager B over the period in which you invested with him. IRR is your (or The Family Treasury's) return specifically, accounting for your cash flows in and out of investments, and that is the most important measure to use when assessing performance to benchmarks and financial objectives per The Family Treasury financial plan. Unfortunately, to calculate IRR for all your consolidated investments on an ongoing daily basis is not really possible without back office software systems. An investment adviser may be able to provide this, but TWR is their required measure and they do not have access to your other managers' information. I will make a shameless plug for the Family Office firms, who are expert in this area and can work with you to help set the long-term asset allocation strategy, choose and monitor appropriate investments and money managers, and provide you with consolidated performance reporting to measure progress.

Private Property Investments

The previous sections focused on investment in the liquid markets. For many, liquid portfolio investing is their primary focus as they begin the process of wealth creation. This is because anyone can access the markets with as little or as much money as they wish. In addition, as you begin to build wealth, maintaining liquidity is important if you intend that these funds be available for emergencies, to fund lifestyle expenses, or to take advantage of other investment opportunities. Yet as your wealth grows, you will have access to alternative investments that do not offer liquidity but do offer higher return potential. This may include private property, which refers to investments that you have direct control or influence over.

When I use the term "private property," I am speaking not only about real estate, although the definition is inclusive of investment real estate. I also include assets such as mortgage lending, equity or lending interests in private companies, or royalty rights to patents or other intellectual property. The term is being used to denote a specific set of characteristics of the assets themselves; some or all of the characteristics may apply to an asset.

Private property can include assets that:

- are not publicly traded and, therefore, hold relatively stable value

- are typically held for the long term

- are at some level non-liquid for a time

- generally offer higher long-term return potential as compensation for higher concentration and liquidity risk

- benefit from less market-driven risk

- offer the opportunity of significant control in that you are often able to make decisions about the management of the asset, which affects the success of the investment

- allow you to choose who you will hire to help you administer the asset

- usually require additional capital to be invested to preserve the quality of the investment

- often produce both an income and capital appreciation

- offer better price stability than the equity markets, with the result that leverage is more accessible (particularly with real estate)

- give direct control over liquidation decisions and the tax consequences

- play a direct role in economic growth, whereas the public markets really just exchange ownership

- offer a more direct relationship between the investor and the end-user, providing both direct accountability and the pleasure of seeing first-hand the results of your capital commitment

Not all investment real estate, private equity, mortgages, etc. within your portfolio, are necessarily private property, even though they may share some of the characteristics listed above. Assets where the family is actively involved is private property and often not part of the asset allocation strategy outlined previously for the passive and mostly liquid portfolio. Private property investments require personal involvement, should be a direct reflection of your values, and should support your mission. For many families, it is something The Family Treasury will build toward. It most often will include ownership of one or more family or private business interests and private lending opportunities, franchises, direct mortgages, and direct investments in real estate. Private property ownership usually requires high minimum investments, and private property at some point becomes the cornerstone of The Family Treasury investment platform. It provides long-term wealth creation and, at the same time, a platform where the family works and grows together, exercising their leadership and entrepreneurial skills.

> *Private property investments require personal involvement, should be a direct reflection of your values, and should support your mission.*

Let me be perfectly clear. I consider a family with a portfolio of passive and liquid investments to be just as much "in business" as a family that actually owns and operates a private business or other private property. That is because both are earning and saving money for the same reasons: the financial stability and growth of themselves and their family members. The principles of financial stewardship apply to both passive and active investments. Having said that, I do favour The Family Treasury building and preserving family-controlled operating businesses whenever possible. In a perfect world, The Family Treasury will have ownership in a number of these. The reasons are many, but one of the biggest is the control the family has over the business and its ethical, moral, cultural, social, and environmental footprint. In addition, you can better manage the cash flow from the business (through salary and dividends) to ensure it matches the objectives and needs as outlined in your strategic plan for the family members as well as The Family Treasury itself. It also allows you to be more effective with tax planning strategies to minimize tax. And lastly, a family-owned business develops leaders and creates wealth for the family like no other asset can. Do not underestimate the financial power of family business.

KPMG Enterprise released *The Canadian Family Business Guide* in 2012. It states that "over 10 years ago, U.S. researchers found that 92% of the 22 million businesses in the United States were family controlled. The businesses generated 49% of the country's Gross Domestic Product (GDP), employed 59% of the labour force and created 78% of all new jobs."[40] Generally speaking, a family business also gives us more money per unit of LEQ exchanged.

There is a great deal of debate in family-business circles about the prudence of trying to pass on a family business from one generation to the next. That is because of the risk of catastrophic failure of that business, which is often the case due to lack of proper succession planning. Thank goodness there are more experts in this field today who can help increase the chances of successfully passing on that operating business from one generation to the next. With strong returns on capital, these are supercharged funding assets (cash cows often) that can outperform public-market investments by a wide margin.

The Investment Policy Statement

The investment policy statement is a document that records the portfolio objectives regarding risk and return, approved asset classes, the chosen asset allocation strategy, agreed-upon decision-making protocols around investment manager selection, and rules around portfolio monitoring and rebalancing. It also documents how your assets will be protected, how they will be registered, where they will be custodied, and who has decision-making authority. It is very important to record these decisions in order to have a reference during difficult market cycles. It reminds you of the discipline you agreed to follow, which reduces the danger of making potentially destructive, emotionally driven decisions. It should be referred to often and updated regularly if and when the need arises.

⚖ The Succession Plan

The Family Treasury is of greatest service to you, your family, and the world in general when it is built to last. If it can be managed with a view to long-term sustainability, it can be around to support the future generations of your family and can continue to realize its mission and purpose long after the founders have passed on. The Family Treasury ensures that the best of you and your legacy lives on and will not be forgotten. Your contributions of wisdom and experience, creative activity, and selfless love can be celebrated and used as a platform to nurture the same in the following generations. A succession plan, the final process in The Family Treasury System III, enshrines and fosters that path toward the future. That plan will involve achieving certain longer-term objectives such as team culture and leadership, which should begin to be addressed today.

Keys to long-term success in any venture include a strong culture, leadership development, flexibility, and systems to promote sustainability. It is no different for The Family Treasury. If the entire model is carried on the shoulders of the founders without equal sharing of contribution and commitment by the other family members, who are beneficiaries, The Family Treasury will die with the founders. The 3 Root Resources, the triangle upon which The Family Treasury foundation is built, must be consistently brought back into balance if it is to be strong, sustainable, and impactful for the generations that follow. Thankfully, as with any long-lasting business, there are standards and processes that can help The Family Treasury pass its treasures to the next generation and beyond. In effect, we are using much the same principles of succession planning that a business would use:

1. Culture

2. Leadership

3. Structural flexibility and efficiency (and the family office)

4. Sustainability

In his book *The Leader Who Had No Title*, which I mentioned earlier, Robin Sharma offers evolved definitions of business. He suggests that "business is a vehicle to help other human beings. To engage employees so they realize their human potential. And to help your customers achieve their highest aspirations."[41] Furthermore, he says "business really is nothing more than a conversation of sorts. And if the culture of the place where you work forgets to grow that conversation and nurture the human connections between each one of you, the conversation will soon end. And the business will soon fail."[42] He warns that, "with the pace people work at, it's easy to sacrifice relationships in the pursuit of results."[43]

I believe that business at its best is a platform where people gather to learn from and with each other, to secure their financial resources, and to develop ever-increasing competency and stability, confidence and courage, emotional intelligence, wisdom, and personal leadership. We will spend over 60% of our working lives at our place of business, so we must not underestimate the impact it can have on the personal well-being of its people. History shows that the more aligned a business team is, the more it encourages and develops each employee to be a leader in thought and action, the more each individual within the group contributes to the others as well as to those the business serves, the more successful that business is and the more money it earns.

The Family Treasury sees a family as having the same potentials as a business. Society teaches us to think of business and family as separate. We leave our family in the morning to go to work, we do our work, and then we come home to the family for "family time." We feel fortunate if we like our "job," but in most cases, if we didn't have to work for money, we would likely not do it in order to have more time to ourselves and with our family.

> 66 *The Family Treasury sees a family as having the same potentials as a business.*

BUT, if the business where we work can give us financial resources and develop our ever-increasing competency and stability, confidence and courage, emotional intelligence, wisdom, and personal leadership ... why would we not want to go there?

Better yet, if we can get all this for our family members too, would we not want that for them also? In our society, there is little in the way of proven systems, processes, and procedures that can help the business of family be successful. There is plenty of intellectual material available to make businesses successful over the long term. The Family Treasury uses some of that knowledge and successfully applies it to develop the business of family and to sustain its potentials for generations through a succession plan founded on four cornerstone commitments.

Foster a Nourishing Culture

This is an important long term goal that should be part of any Family Treasury strategic plan over the short and long term. What is a nourishing culture? I define the most successful families as those with a balanced use of and harmonious respect for the 3 Root Resources, and enough money, love, and freedom to thrive individually and collectively. In my observation of these families, above all else, I see a number of key qualities that create a nourishing culture:

- ✔ a strong work ethic, actually preferring hard work to leisure or sloth

- ✔ encouragement to learn with practice and to be comfortable with uncomfortable situations

- ✔ respect for themselves as individuals and each other as evidenced in their thoughts, speech, and action

- ✔ a culture of self-responsibility, with each family member responsible for their choices and the consequences (with the blame game not permitted)

- ✔ a continuous practice of self-awareness among family leaders and younger folks, including recognition that emotional challenges with others usually mirror back what needs to be changed within you
- ✔ unwavering loyalty to each other
- ✔ an atmosphere of group sharing and collaboration as opposed to separateness and division, and seeing each other as team members where everyone has everyone else's back
- ✔ absolute forgiveness for each other and for themselves for transgressions, including not ever being afraid to admit they were wrong and to say "sorry"
- ✔ a policy of communication, communication, communication, and then some more communication, with nothing swept under the rug
- ✔ parents who foster curiosity and prudent risk taking in their children, allowing them freedom to stretch into their capabilities, make mistakes, and learn from those mistakes, knowing that failure is not scorned but rather lessons from failure reaped
- ✔ strong value placed on being both independent from and empowered by their part in the family team

What is the number one benefit of fostering a culture like this? Self-esteem. What is the number one rule when fostering a culture like this? Be consistent.

Develop the Next Generation of Leaders

The Family Treasury, which holds and preserves your legacy, will not survive into the next generation without good leaders to take it there. Without leadership there will be no stretching into the next phase of the family's evolution. As such, a plan for building leaders over the short and long term should be built into The Family Treasury Strategic Plan.

> *Without leadership there will be no stretching into the next phase of the family's evolution.*

What is a good leader exactly? Here are some of the qualities of an effective leader:

- ✔ has an inherent drive to innovate and to grow, and enjoys challenges and change

- ✔ usually self-directed and independent

- ✔ emotionally mature, even-tempered, and respectful of others

- ✔ rational and logical but also displays creative and visionary intelligence

- ✔ willing to take prudent risks and is usually optimistic about the outcomes

- ✔ understands that all people are equally but uniquely valuable

✔ has the ability to gather people together and communicate a goal that is worthy enough to inspire others to support it

✔ is clear about appropriate boundaries

✔ their actions follow their words

✔ is knowledgeable in their field and consistently seeks to develop that knowledge and skill

✔ acts with integrity and has excellent relationship skills

✔ takes responsibility for results and is fully committed to achieving them

✔ believes in themselves, their mission, and their ability to deliver results

✔ is able to focus on the priorities and sees them through with self-discipline whether or not they want to

✔ is trustworthy

So how does The Family Treasury grow leaders? How can it ensure that every member fulfills their leadership potential?

The good news is we are all leaders at something. That leadership talent is usually centred around our innate talents. Now, you would think that if we were naturally good at something, we would focus on it and wish to develop it. In reality, what we are best at, what is unique to us, we often take for granted! Frequently, we don't appreciate it and, in some cases, don't even see it because it comes so easily to us. We assume everyone can do it. Which is why we often don't know where our leadership gifts lie. So what can you do to find your unique abilities if you do not have a clear picture of them already? Well ... you can simply walk up to a few friends, offer them a glass of wine to set the tone, and then ask them, "So what do you think is awesome about me?" If you would rather not do that, then I suggest you get a personal coach. They use tools and techniques that can help you identify your unique talents and abilities. After gaining direction with a coach, leaders will usually take it from there. Once you know what your unique talents are, see them as leadership strengths—to be used, developed, and honed with increasing self-confidence.

> The good news is we are
> all leaders at something.

Nurture Leadership Strengths
A core principle of The Family Treasury is that a family is only truly successful when each member thrives. Could there be any better environment where opportunities abound to nurture leadership qualities?

Give Responsibility
As with any business, the existing leaders of The Family Treasury can give each team member the responsibility to

complete a challenge that they alone are best suited to and can take ownership of. This can start at a young age, as children often rise to the occasion when given the responsibility and the trust to accomplish a result under their own steam.

Some points to keep in mind: Clearly define the boundaries within which they are to work and then let them do the work. Show them by example that it is okay to make mistakes if they learn from those mistakes; this is critical in empowering them both to take responsibility for those mistakes and to be willing to take risks and make change without fear of being shamed if they make the wrong move. You are providing them the experience of independence and the opportunity to stretch their decision-making muscles. Give them support and encouragement through regular communication so that they also learn how to ask questions, listen, and voice their perspectives.

In nurturing leaders, remember our discussion about the rope, the ladder, and the elevator. If you do it all for them, you rob them of the self-discovery found in making mistakes and even missing an opportunity. You interfere with them learning about the Law of Cause and Effect. You don't allow them to develop their personal power muscles by striving for some great accomplishment and to experience the joy of achieving it on their own. That is what builds leaders. The elevator creates "needers" and followers. It bears repeating: The Family Treasury can be an excellent place to start developing leadership qualities in young people.

" The Family Treasury can be an excellent place to start developing leadership qualities in young people.

Issue Ongoing Challenges

When members of the family successfully meet and achieve one challenge, give them another one. The next one should be even bigger than the first. Leaders grow by continually being challenged to stretch as they enjoy innovation and self-discovery. It helps them learn to embrace change, seek the new, and continually evolve. It helps them become comfortable with being uncomfortable.

Encourage Education

Education is defined as "the act or process of imparting or acquiring general knowledge, developing the powers of reasoning and judgment, and generally of preparing oneself or others intellectually for mature life."[44] We are educated through our childhood by our parents, our schoolteachers, our peers and, unfortunately too often, also by TV, video games, the Internet, and social media.

The Family Treasury can't control what its young people will learn out in the world, but it can work to ensure the appropriate information is learned and shared within the family. Communicating regularly with young people about world events; their relationship experiences; their social life; their school life; their hopes, dreams, and fears can help you identify what they are perceiving and the judgments they are making. Then you can redirect that thinking in keeping with what you as family leaders feel is healthy and appropriate. The dinner table was the place for this in my family. It created a place every night where cell phones were banished, and we concentrated on each other to help explain the world to our kids as they were experiencing it rather than after the fact. In addition, I would suggest that the best form of family education is not always to tell the kids, but to show them or, better yet, guide them to the discovery themselves.

The Family Treasury Roundtable is another place where family member education can be a central theme. In large family meetings, where multiple generations are in attendance, you can have multiple educational sessions going on based on age and interests. While the older gang is in one area perhaps listening to speakers on business succession, investment management, philanthropy, or world issues, the youngsters could be on a field trip studying local plants and animals and learning about environmental protection. Meanwhile, the teens could be in a workshop learning basic money management skills. If you are avid readers, hold a book club session to review a book or books of interest, or have a speaker come in for a one-hour presentation followed by discussion. If you are a small, single-family group, then pick something that has a something for everyone. Education sessions on anything and everything related to the mission of The Family Treasury will make everyone in the group better at their "job."

The importance of post-secondary education can be written into The Family Treasury Roundtable charter. Consideration should be given to what is meant by education. Do you consider its prime importance to be to further expand the reasoning abilities and maturity of the student? Or is the purpose of post-secondary education to give appropriate skills and competency training for a future career? Is it both? If we are trying to develop leaders, and leadership is most likely to succeed in the areas of calling and purpose for each person (i.e., where their talents lie), then I would suggest reconsidering the old idea that you must have a university education to succeed. In some cases, it can do more harm than good. If a young person's learning style and interests are not suited to the academic university setting, and the family message is you are not worthy if you don't have a degree, this person is unlikely to develop the self-esteem of a leader. Instead, they will likely feel they are not smart enough, so why bother. As behavioural research advances, it is becoming more and more prevalent that too singular a focus on the primary importance of a university education is, these days, leaving many intelligent people out in the cold. Not all intelligence is academic. Not all learning should be academic. A university degree is a great achievement. But let me be clear: education is critical; a university education is not.

Education is critical;
a university education is not.

In addition, some individuals simply learn better by doing. Most entrepreneurs are that way. They are too impatient to wait to be educated before they start their business, so they often get going and learn from hard experience. They, too, are getting a very good education. I would suggest, however, to increase their chances of success, they would benefit from very targeted learning in the areas of finance, marketing, administration, and compliance. This can be done at night school and even over the Internet nowadays, so they can continue to run their business during the day. Although it goes without saying that the business is their schoolroom.

The Family Treasury can play a critical role in financing post-secondary education to make it more affordable, and may even support a private school education if that is what the family values.

Create a Leadership Creed

A leadership creed is a signpost that your family members can refer to when life inevitably throws mud their way. It is a reminder of how to centre on the leadership qualities that can empower you to move through anything with grace and strength. I offer the following example:

- Passionately believe you are worthy and have much to offer.

- Passionately believe you are also worthy of receiving abundant gifts in return.

- Follow through with a step toward your goal each day, whether or not you feel like it.

- Nurture your own well-being, for the more harmonious you are physically, emotionally, and mentally, the more creative power you will have.

- Manage to stay ever more mindful each day and transcend your destructive habits.

- Practice your intuition muscles when making decisions—don't rely solely on reason. The brain often lies; the heart wisdom never does.

- Feel your emotions, then let them go—without blame and without story.

- Conquer fear with courage.

- Work for your well-being but never at the expense of others—as the Dalai Lama says, "For the well-being of all beings."

- Work at a career that uses your unique talents, interests, and abilities to their fullest.

- Work at your calling, which may or may not be your career (a career is a service you perform for income; a calling is a personal interest you are passionate about).

A little more should be said about nurturing oneself. I think most will now agree that the rat race we have created for ourselves is slowly but surely killing us. It kills our spirit first, and then it destroys our bodies. Most of us try to do way too much, cramming too much into one day, and usually live one-dimensional lives of work, work, and more work. We do this so we can have our weekends free, during which we end up working anyway, what with errands and jobs around the house. A truly balanced life is one where every day, not just on weekends, we work some, we play some, we exercise some, we eat-healthy some, meditate some, love some, and we rest some. You cannot lead others if you can't lead yourself and do what is best for yourself and those around you.

> ❝ *You cannot lead others*
> *if you can't lead yourself.*

Build in Structural Flexibility and Efficiency (and the Family Office)

Some would think it very nice, and others have actually tried, to rule from the grave. However, if The Family Treasury is going to remain sustainable and transfer successfully from one generation to the next, it must have structural flexibility. When The Family Treasury is financially large enough to serve multiple generations, the most successful form for this is the investment corporation. We touched on the pros and cons of this structure earlier in the chapter.

Technically, The Family Treasury corporation can have thousands of shareholders with multiple types of share classes with different rights. It can lend money on favourable or commercial terms to family members for house purchases. It can lend money or buy shares in new business ventures proposed by a family member and supported by a business plan. It might elect to lend money on discount terms for members to pursue education or to set up an expense fund for this purpose. It supports those with disabilities who need a helping hand. It provides education forums, career counselling, networking, lifestyle coaching, family vacations, health care or personal counselling, etc. It funds anything and everything that makes the family and its individuals stronger. It tries to do so at a profit, however, so that income exceeds costs and leaves room for dividends to the shareholders who make it all happen. The corporation can hold shares in a family operating business, which is seen as just another investment asset for these purposes. It can invest in other private enterprise as well. In Canada, tax is paid on the growth in value of the shares on the death of each shareholder. So The Family Treasury can buy insurance on each shareholder to fund those taxes, keeping the wealth in the family and avoiding liquidity crisis for a shareholder's estate.

Just like any company, shareholder meetings are held with all shareholders to review performance and make democratic decisions. The largest shareholders will be on the board/ management committee. While everyone may not agree with a decision made by vote, they will stay a shareholder if they believe in the mission of The Family Treasury.

Like any private company, however, the shares are not liquid and thus not easily sold. If the shareholder agreement allows, a shareholder who wants to withdraw can sell their shares to other family shareholders or ask for a redemption, which might have to happen over time. Anything related to shares would be governed by a shareholder agreement.

The shares may pass from one generation to the next, but the core activities of The Family Treasury are preserved under the leadership and management of a centralized team. This centralized team may have their work cut out for them. As The Family Treasury grows in size, it will also grow in complexity. Remember we spoke at great length about the decision to convert LEQ in a balanced and targeted way so as to maximize results? Handling the daily administrative and asset management affairs of The Family Treasury is likely not the best use of the leadership's LEQ. This is where the Family Office comes in. It is best practice for any multi-generational succession plan to either form an in-house "single" family office, or develop a relationship with an outsourced "multi-" family office to guide and manage that process.

Managing significant wealth within The Family Treasury brings great demands and responsibilities with a myriad of time-consuming and complex issues that are often overlooked, misunderstood, or just not managed properly. The Family Office can offer its expertise to support The Family Treasury. It will allow the leadership team to do what they do best while delegating the rest.

With The Family Treasury strategic plan and The Family Treasury financial plan as its road map, the Family Office works with the family to implement the duties required and orchestrate the family's team of advisers in a collaborative process. It will monitor progress and make directional adjustments with discipline and clarity as circumstances dictate. There are more and more financial service providers who now say they offer family office services. However, I am a purist and believe most of them are actually wealth managers, which is just as valuable a service but not a family office. Just saying they offer family office services tells that tale: you don't offer it as a service, you either are or are not a family office. A true multi-family office offers the following distinct attributes:

- a primary relationship with one family office director (FOD) who is responsible for overseeing your entire financial team and the proactive management of your family's finances and strategic plan

- staffed by professionals such as chartered accountants, lawyers, chartered financial analysts, and registered financial planners

- a boutique firm that limits the number of clients any one FOD works with to fifty to sixty families so that the service can be truly comprehensive, which isn't possible with more client families than this (To determine very quickly if the service provider is truly a family office, ask how many clients on average their "relationship managers" have: more than a hundred and they are not a family office.)

- independent and sitting on the same side of the table as you and your family, being compensated for services directly by you and not selling any product (As a second test to determine if a service provider is truly a family office, ask whether they will work with you if you have no liquid cash to invest, as is the case for many wealthy families (e.g., business owners or commercial real estate owners): if they won't, they are a wealth management firm, not a family office.)

- accountability is seen as imperative so uses consolidated asset performance measurement tools and benchmarking to help The Family Treasury stay on track toward the achievement of its long-term strategic goals

> *The family office works with the family to implement the duties required and orchestrate the family's team of advisers in a collaborative process.*

The family office offers The Family Treasury a unique opportunity to have all its wealth, lifestyle, and legacy matters integrated under a single, trusted management team headed by your family office director. This allows you to gain control of your finances, maximize opportunities, and build wealth with accountable results. The family office simplifies the complicated, manages the unmanageable, and brings order to the myriad of financial, legal, and personal administrative matters, which allows you and your family to focus on The Family Treasury priorities of *True* wealth succession.

> " *The family office simplifies the complicated, manages the unmanageable, and brings order.*

Ensure Sustainability

We can develop excellent leadership and a strong team culture within our Family Treasury, but that is still not enough to keep the family legacy intact into the next generations. Succession requires capital growth, not just capital preservation. The current team needs to stay ahead of the ever-growing number of family participants. It needs to stay ahead of change in order to capitalize upon it, grow its wealth at an equal or greater rate than it is consumed, and continually reinvest and reinvent itself so as not to go the way of the dinosaur. This is no different than business. If the business does not invent new services to stay fresh and relevant, if it does not reinvest some of its profits to maintain and strengthen its platform, it will likely not outlive the founders.

Entrepreneurialism

Our society has encouraged the business relationship of the large corporation and the employee. However, just over a hundred and fifty years ago, we were a society of self-employed people. In a Time magazine article, Rick Wartzman quotes renowned management consultant Peter Drucker from an article he wrote, titled "How to Be an Employee," back in 1952: "A hundred years ago only one out of every five Americans at work was employed, that is, worked for somebody else. Today the ratio is reversed, only one out of five is self-employed."[45]

Until relatively recently, we were a society of self-employed tradesmen, farmers, craftsmen, service people and professionals. There has been a transformational shift from an agricultural society to an industrial one and a shift of people from small towns in the countryside to large, crowded cities. Economies of scale lead to small companies morphing into huge, faceless corporate conglomerates. We have experienced great gifts and great pains from these transformations. A great cost has been the loss of the self-employed. I say that because the self-employed typically were that way because they had a particular interest, talent, or ability that was unique to them and that others wanted. Others paid them to express their particular interest, talent or ability. The young man who grew up tinkering with broken-down cars became the local auto mechanic and did what he loved to do for a living. The little girl who liked to play store grew up to open her own shop in town—again getting paid to do what she loved. They were not told to "get their head out of the clouds" and go and find a "safe job" with the huge corporation in the city miles from home. Many parents today tell us they want their children to grow up and get a good job. At election time, the news media is full of promises by our leaders to "create jobs" for us. That is a good enough reason for me not to vote for them. Who the heck just wants a job!

If you must work for someone, is it not better to have a career and/or a profession than a job? A modern definition of career or profession speaks of a blend of technical competence and experience in your particular area of interest that you can "sell" to any company who offers you appropriate compensation for those services. More importantly, you will not work for that company if your particular talents and technical competence is not put to good use. In other words, everyone wants to know their hard work is contributing to a grand purpose of some kind. Being self-employed allows you the flexibility to go wherever that particular interest, talent, or ability is put to the most meaningful use.

So at the very least, The Family Treasury can encourage its younger members to find their particular interests and talents, and become educated in that field of interest so that they can market themselves to others who can make good use of their services. Encourage the young family members to think of themselves as self-employed even if they choose to work for one company for the rest of their life. This requires that they develop the self-esteem and leadership skills spoken of earlier but rewards them with a sense of control over their own lives and empowers their confidence to take risks and make choices that will best enhance their experiences.

I envision a future where firms will hire self-employed persons to fill positions needed within the firm. These persons will offer their services in exchange for a contract as opposed to an employment agreement. The company that hires them respects that self-employed person's freedom to set their own schedule and billing rates. The self-employed person respects the company's right to end that contract if the work is not done on time or is of a poor quality, or if the billing rates become too high. It is a free-market approach that treats both sides as grown-ups and leaders, instead of the current system that treats employees as children who need to be told what to do and how to do it. It ensures a team of people who come together to create something wonderful with the best of their talents directed collaboratively to a common purpose. It is in stark contrast to the way it is today, where most employees feel unheard, undervalued, unappreciated, and uninspired. The self-employed person is mature, in that they view themselves and themselves alone as responsible for their financial security. They also do not have an attitude of entitlement as so many "employees" do. They know that they will not get money, they will not love their work, and they will not experience freedom of expression without first providing a valuable service to another. I see a world where people take back control of their LEQ and offer it for worthy purpose and worthy compensation while enjoying more money, love, and freedom. Isn't this the way the world should work?

But what does this discussion about being self-employed have to do with entrepreneurialism? They are the same but not! Like the self-employed or career professional, entrepreneurs see themselves as self-employed. But there is a critical difference as well. Self–employed persons offer a service. The self-employed person who is also an entrepreneur creates something new. They are visionaries and innovators. They are not satisfied with the status quo. They thrive on change and see working for anyone else to be too risky. They don't see that they need anything, and they want everything. They bring about evolution, as they are the first adopters. They go before. They lead the way. They are a strange bunch, but we need them. And The Family Treasury needs them if it is to transcend time and successfully pass from one generation to the next.

> *Encourage the young family*
> *members to think of themselves*
> *as self-employed.*

> *"The self-employed person*
> *who is also an entrepreneur*
> *creates something new.*

How do you make an entrepreneur? You don't. They are born that way. Yet, strangely, there is usually one in every family. If you don't have one, get one! Marry him, hire her, do whatever you have to do to ensure your team has at least one person on it who is capable of seeing a future that is continuously bigger and grander than the past left behind. Statistics show that a dismal number of family businesses make it to the third generation. This is where the proverb "shirt sleeves to shirt sleeves in three generations" (wealth gained in one generation will be gone by the third) comes from.

Once you identify entrepreneurs, nurture them. How? By fostering a nourishing culture as described above and developing leadership abilities in each member of the family team. And by understanding that entrepreneurs will be different from the rest of you—and that is okay. They will shoot from the hip, they will not administer or manage others well, and they will have less patience than most. They will want to get to the point yesterday and will need a practical reason to do just about anything. They will dream big but sometimes be impractical. That is where the rest of the team can be of support, to help them dream big while keeping their feet firmly planted on the ground.

Their most important role in The Family Treasury, however, is to come up with new and innovative ideas to grow the family wealth at exponential rates in order to protect it throughout time from diminution.

Growth and Profitability

To be sustainable generation after generation, The Family Treasury needs to regenerate capital. It does so by earning income in excess of expenses and by reinvesting that net income to add to capital. It does so by investing in opportunities with high-return expectations. It uses insurance to replace capital lost to taxation of estates. It develops entrepreneurs who will innovate new ways for The Family Treasury to serve and earn money. It works together as a family, united by a common mission.

> ❝ *To be sustainable generation after generation, The Family Treasury needs to regenerate capital.*

Sustainability requires that some basic principles be respected:

- There will be a founder, as with any business, but following generations need to preserve and add to that wealth.
- The founder's original capital should be preserved and never spent.
- Dividends should be set by policy and should never put The Family Treasury into a deficit.

- Tax liabilities should be insured wherever possible.

- Decisions should be made by democratic board majority.

- An independent board of professional advisers should be in place.

- Investments should aim to achieve target returns, take healthy risks, minimize volatility, and be measured and monitored closely.

- Investments should be made in family members, but seldom should there be handouts.

- Protective legal contracts should be in place amongst family members, with service providers, and with investment managers.

- Regular group meetings should be held to make critical decisions in a timely manner.

- Meetings should follow The Family Treasury Roundtable charter (or your version of it) and rules of membership.

- The shareholder agreement should allow for the flexible (but not too flexible) transfer of share ownership.

- The Family Treasury financial wealth should be considered a "family bank" to avoid intergenerational dissipation of that wealth.

- Annual growth of all the treasury resources should be measured using The Family Treasury balance sheet.

Figure 15: Comparison of traditional inheritance and Family Treasury approaches toward keeping wealth intact

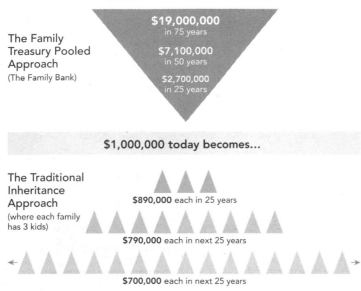

The Family
Treasury Pooled
Approach
(The Family Bank)

$19,000,000
in 75 years

$7,100,000
in 50 years

$2,700,000
in 25 years

$1,000,000 today becomes...

The Traditional
Inheritance
Approach
(where each family
has 3 kids)

$890,000 each in 25 years

$790,000 each in next 25 years

$700,000 each in next 25 years

Note: Assuming a 4% annual growth rate and no capital depletion; reflected in future-value dollars and pre-tax.

Canadians are especially guilty of destroying wealth from one generation to the next with its practice of passing along inherited bequests directly to the next generation through wills. Figure 15 compares this approach to The Family Treasury process of keeping the wealth intact in an investment holding company that provides share ownership for the next generations.

The triangle above the centre line illustrates the growth of wealth intact within The Family Treasury, assuming it is fully invested at a reinvested rate of 4% per annum. The traditional

approach of transferring wealth directly to estate beneficiaries is reflected below the centre line. To illustrate, assume
a $1,000,000 bequest is left to be split among three children
($333,333 each). If they fully invest those funds, reinvest at 4%
per annum, and never spend any of it, they will each have
$890,000 in twenty-five years. They then bequeath their portion
equally among their respective three children, and so on. It may
not be immediately apparent to you which model looks better.
Consider, however, that down the generations, when the money
is given as a bequest directly to beneficiaries, the chances of
all the family members investing the full amount of capital for
twenty-five years is next to nil. They will likely spend most of
it and the wealth disappears. If, instead, the money is passed
down in a centralized manner through share ownership in a
family investment holding company, and that company is managed by capable family wealth stewards, there is a much higher
chance that wealth will be preserved for the benefit of multiple
generations to come. More capital to work with expands the
family's ability to invest into direct assets such as businesses
and commercial real estate, which most often provide higher
return potentials than the securities markets. This supports The
Family Treasury's ability to meet the needs of an ever-growing
number of family members as the generations grow.

I have illustrated this with a Jack and Jill example. It shows
the equality of income potentials, but the reality is that unless
some of the earnings are reinvested, the family bank will
gradually be no more effective than outright bequests. It

must grow its collective assets at a rate greater than they are expended in order to build wealth for the entire group. It needs to build its "purchasing power" to access opportunities that otherwise would not be available to individual beneficiaries on their own. Therefore, the family bank within The Family Treasury, when effectively managed by committed wealth stewards, has a far greater likelihood of providing financial resources for the generations that follow than can be expected when capital is given away to those less prepared or inclined to preserve it.

Let's Look at Jack and Jill

Let's assume that Jack and Jill, still married in this example, pass away leaving behind three children who each receive a bequest of $700,000. A miracle occurs, and they each actually invest the full amount for the next 25 years at a rate of 4% per year. Assuming a tax-free world for a moment, they would each receive income of $28,000 annually from that capital. Alternatively, they could invest the pot of $2,100,000 in the Family Bank and bequest shares, which likewise earn 4% on invested capital and elect to distribute all that income equally to all the shareholders. Again, they would receive $28,000 annually. But now, assuming

each of Jack and Jill's children have three children
when they die, they can pass on their shares in the
same fashion from their estates. Each of the nine children of the next generation would receive an annual
dividend income of $9,333 (4% of $233,333 each) from
the preserved capital pot of $2,100,000. The wealth
is sustained for another generation.

One might be concerned that our children may not agree
or support our plan to pass their inheritance into a centrally
controlled "family bank." It is, therefore, important to point out
to them that it costs them nothing and, in fact, enhances their
life opportunities. They will have access to the same income
potentials with the family bank as they would have if they had
invested their funds directly. This approach only prevents them
from spending the captial! And at the same time, it gives them
more collective power to access a world of investment opportunities they otherwise could not reach. Not to mention the
other *True* wealth benefits available to them through working
collaboratively. Here are some of the benefits of a family bank:

✔ Purchasing power: with more capital, you have access
   to a greater number of unique investment opportunities,
   often with higher-return potential; you can also negotiate
   lower costs, which further enhances returns.

- ✔ You are able to attract and pay for talented professionals to support your ability to reach your goals.

- ✔ You can afford to delegate to others who do what they do best, so you can do what you do best.

- ✔ You can help family members who have large unexpected costs, or special needs.

- ✔ You can support the young entrepreneurs in the family when banks don't take them seriously.

- ✔ You can access leverage to enhance your return potentials.

- ✔ You have a forum to finance Family Treasury gatherings, which help family members grow to be stronger more successful people when united by a common family vision.

- ✔ You have developed a system to preserve your financial legacy for generations to come through wealth stewardship so that a lifetime of your hard work and prudent investment management is not wasted when inherited by those who did not earn it and may not have the acumen or respect to sustain it.

You have provided a financial legacy to help every member of your family, now and into the future, thrive.

I didn't invent the concept of the family bank. It has been around for a long time and is responsible for preserving the wealth of some of the world's wealthiest multi-generational families. It treats the business of family wealth management as just that, a business that is meant to grow over time by reinvesting in itself, its people, and the society that it serves. Why more families with substantial financial resources don't follow their example is beyond my comprehension.

The Family Treasury Balance Sheet

How do we measure our progress toward the realization of our strategic plans? It is a relatively straight-forward process to measure progress toward the achievement of our financial goals. Those goals are quantifiable, and there is sophisticated computer software available that can help us accurately measure progress as long as we have some basic math skills. Measuring progress as it relates to qualitative goals is another matter.

How can The Family Treasury measure its progress toward building *True* wealth and good wealth stewards? How do we know whether we are on track to achieving the personal and group missions? How can the members be accountable for their progress (or lack thereof) in becoming more self-aware and better communicators? How do we measure success in creating family harmony with each member living their best life and expressing their unique potentials?

Can The Family Treasury measure its progress in meeting its strategic plans and can it objectively measure its evolving likelihood of leaving a legacy reflecting a life of many achievements?

Yes.

It does so by keeping The Family Treasury balance sheet, which measures exactly what it says: balance. It is measuring how balanced our results have been in growing our 3 Root Resources, our *True* wealth. Remember that for The Family Treasury to have a strong foundation, it must grow these resources in a harmonious and balanced way. Balance is not a result; it is a dynamic process of moving out of and back into harmonious balance as evolution occurs.

> *Balance is not a result;*
> *it is a dynamic process of moving*
> *out of and back into harmonious*
> *balance as evolution occurs.*

Figure 16 is an example of The Family Treasury balance sheet, although you can design your own to itemize those points of measurement you feel are most important to your Family Treasury model. The system behind this balance sheet is a series of questions that family members measure separately and then collectively collate to provide the rankings associated with each agreed-upon point of measurement. You create the factor measures, the weighting of the factors, and then the overall result for each section to assess relative progress and balance. As an example, let's look at the category "Progress toward the achievement of member mission statements." To assess that progress, you request each member to ask themselves: "How many of my objectives were achieved? Did I achieve them within the planned timeline?" By way of example, as a factor of measure for this category, you ask each member to give themselves one point for each objective met and one point for meeting it on time. Divide the result by the total points that would have been awarded that year had the member met all their objectives and met them on time. Add up all the family results, divide that number by the total family points that could have been awarded for that category, and you get a percentage result for that category.

Each Family Treasury will be unique to the family, as will be the Family Treasury balance sheet, so it is beyond the scope of this book to model all the possible questions and rating systems that a family might use. But keep in mind: this is not meant to be rocket science. You can go through each category relevant to you and your Family Treasury and ask yourself how would you know you have achieved the objectives. You can use a point system to calculate at any given time how far along you are toward achieving that goal, and then express it as a fraction or percentage. Pulling all of this together can be a great family exercise at one of your Roundtable meetings. Just remember that any goal must be measurable and that you and your team are the best ones to decide how to measure it.

Figure 16: Example of The Family Treasury balance sheet

The Family Treasury Balance Sheet	Year Ended XXXX
System I: Wealth Stewardship	*Factor*
❏ How well we have lived by our values and philosophy	.70
❏ Progress toward the achievement of member mission statements	.65
❏ Process 1 – The Family Treasury Mission Statement	.60
System I Progress to Date	65%
System II: Family Development	
❏ Process 2 – The Family Treasury Documentary	1.00
❏ Process 3 – The Family Treasury Roundtable	.50
❏ Process 4 - Mediation and Facilitation	.75
❏ Process 5 – The Family Foundation	.75
System II Progress to Date	75%
System III: Our Legacy	
❏ Process 6 – The Family Treasury Strategic Plan	.60
❏ Process 7 – The Personal Financial Plan	.80
❏ Process 8 – The Family Treasury Financial Plan	.60
❏ Process 9 – The Tax-Effective Structure	.60
❏ Process 10 – The Investment Strategy	.35
❏ Process 11 – The Succession Plan	.40
System III Progress to Date	56%

Progress to Date

The sample report in Figure 16 shows a Family Treasury that is making some progress (just over halfway to their goals) and is relatively in balance.

▲ ▼ ▲

The Family Treasury succession plan incorporates tools that can assist the family to pass on from one generation to the next a culture of positivity, high self-esteem, and teamwork where people want to stay united in their efforts. It focuses on developing leaders from an early age within the next generations. It builds structural flexibility into the system so that it can respond to changing circumstances and regulations. It fosters entrepreneurs and creates a financial model to maintain asset growth and profitability in the face of ever-increasing shareholder demands. It keeps the family on track by measuring our progress, showing how far we have come, and where we are headed.

Are you Ready to Cultivate True Family Wealth and Sustain It for Generations?

▲ ▼ ▲

The Family Treasure seems like a lot of work, right? Is it really worth it for Jack's family, for Jill's family, for your family? Wouldn't it be easier to focus on making money and simply enjoy our family time together without all this formality? Money management is so much simpler: a mental, logical, and analytical process. Family relationships, on the other hand, are emotional and messy, and no one likes conflict. Do we really want to mix money and love in the same conversation?

Well ... Do you want your kids to thrive? Do you want to thrive?

A focus on the *True Family Wealth* within a family can make that happen.

The Family Treasury and its mission can be the tool you use to get there. Jill's kids get to benefit from their mom's experience as a lawyer, learning how to navigate the world of politics and policy. Jack's kids get the opportunity to make extra money farming on land loaned to them by their dad. The kids are empowered to be wealth stewards, instead of wealth consumers. The parents are empowered to be change makers in the world and leave a legacy far greater than their bank account. Together they will learn from each other about finance, accountability, creativity, sales, marketing, and respectful human interaction. They will build networks of influential people. They will learn to be strong leaders and change makers and become good at conflict resolution. Together they will create *True Family Wealth* and protect and encourage each other along the way. The Family Treasury gives you all the tools to develop family leaders, support wealth stewards, and empower a legacy of prosperity and *True Family Wealth* now and into the future.

The Family Treasury is built upon the following core principles:

- The family has many resources, not just financial. They have experiences, networks, histories, knowledge, and love (in its varying forms). All resources should be nurtured and developed in a balanced way or the system will get out of balance and ultimately fail.

- One larger pool of money has more earning potential than a bunch of smaller ones.

- Many minds attuned to the achievement of a common goal are more likely to achieve it than one mind alone.

- Each member of the family comes with their own particular gifts and talents that should be respected, nurtured, and supported for the ultimate success of the individual and their contribution to society.

- To succeed, there must be policies, protocols, and other governance practices in place to guide the family through challenging times so that they may successfully navigate their way through to successful outcomes.

- The family has a common purpose, a vision that inspires them all, for what they can achieve together and the legacy they wish to leave to the following generations and society itself.

Those who have experienced The Family Treasury have said some of its benefits include:

✔ strength and safety in numbers

✔ inspiration through mission and vision

✔ risk minimization

✔ shared rewards and successes

✔ mature conflict resolution

✔ enhanced financial strength and empowerment

✔ development of financial literacy, leadership, and entrepreneurialism

✔ trust, belonging, and expression of individual and group purpose thereby enhancing self-worth and family esteem

The Family Treasury can keep families together in a world that encourages them to separate and lead isolated lives. And it does so while encouraging and celebrating the individuality of each person. It offers the best of both worlds, a place of belonging and mutual support empowering its individuals to shine in the world.

It centralizes and compounds resources to strengthen each member of the family, giving them the ability to express their talents for the benefit of all. It is especially difficult in today's world for young people to develop their independence and highest abilities when (1) they are struggling to make ends meet or (2) they are inappropriately gifted money they did not earn.

The Family Treasury encourages, educates, and finances the young entrepreneurs in the family who would be hard pressed to get this support from a bank.

Where financial wealth has been accumulated, forming a family bank governed by policies based upon *stewardship*, not just management, can ensure that wealth survives into the next generations without being dissipated.

Are you ready for change within yourself and your family?

I believe The Family Treasury is one innovative solution to what ails us in our modern developed society. It reflects what I recognize to be a shift taking place in the world—away from isolating and divisive competitive structures and toward collaborative structures that benefit the group. The psychological and social well-being of a family is essential for building a strong economic foundation, just as it is in a business. And just like a business, the profits achieved are not just financial. They are emotional and spiritual. The unifying objective of The Family Treasury, as with a successful business, is to empower its members to accomplish goals far beyond what each individual on their own could accomplish. It is also a platform to heal the dysfunction in the family dynamic. The formalized processes put into place, just as in a thriving business, serve to provide opportunity to develop strong self-esteem, psychological and social stability, and emotional maturity in its team members. Without these best practices, families tend to operate on self-serving interests and emotional reactivity. *The Family Treasury can introduce you to family members anew. It can reveal to you who your family members really are, not just who they have shown themselves to be in the past within the family dynamics and politics.* The Family Treasury fosters a deeper awareness of that which we are all here to contribute and gives a platform for us to help each other shine.

> 66 *A family is truly wealthy*
> *when each member thrives*

I offer this book and the concepts within it to you as an experiment. There are most certainly bugs that will need to be worked out along the way, but it is offered from a place of thought leadership in the hopes of fostering debate, experimentation, and refinement.

Where can you start?

Hold your first Roundtable meeting and bribe the kids to get them there. Looking at the tools recommended in Chapter 5, one good place to begin is developing your Family Treasury communication model using Kolbe or Prevue. Another good starting point is working together to gain clarity on each person's personal mission and purpose using the tools provided in Chapter 4. Then go on to play with the results of your values and personal mission assessments and see if there is a Family Treasury mission waiting to reveal itself. Then the adventure begins. *We are meeting at the crossroads where money and love intersect and having a new conversation about both!* The Family Treasury can make that crossing a smooth one along the road to an Enriched Family. Want to come along for the ride?

NOTES

1. Statistics Canada, www.statcan.gc.ca/tables-tableaux/sum-som/101/cst01/health26-eng.htm, accessed on December 7, 2016.

2. A family office acts as the client family chief financial officer. It manages the process of managing wealth using integrated financial strategies based on the family's goals and aspirations. It aims to optimize the wealth, lifestyle, and legacy of its clients while simplifying complex matters.

3. Abraham Maslow, *Motivation and Personality* (New York: Harper, 1954).

4. Hermes Trismegistus, *Hermetic Corpus*, an ancient Egyptian–Greek text.

5. Merriam-Webster, www.merriam-webster.com/dictionary/family.

6. Robin Sharma, *The Leader Who Had No Title* (New York: Free Press, 2011), 134.

7. Ibid.

8. Merriam-Webster, www.merriam-webster.com/dictionary/ business, accessed on November 16, 2016.

9. Merriam-Webster, www.merriam-webster.com/dictionary/ enterprise, accessed on November 16, 2016.

10. Financial Post, http://business.financialpost.com/personal-finance/mortgages-real-estate/stubborn-sellers-killing-canada-real-estate-crash, accessed on November 16, 2016.

11. Canada Mortgage and Housing Corporation, www.cmhc-schl.gc.ca/ en/corp/nero/jufa/jufa_025.cfm, accessed on November 16, 2016.

12. Statistics Canada, www.statcan.gc.ca/daily-quotidien/030513/ dq030513a-eng.htm, accessed on November 16, 2016.

13. Statistics Canada, www.statcan.gc.ca/tables-tableaux/sum-som/ l01/cst01/famil108a-eng.htm, accessed on November 16, 2016.

14. Statistics Canada, www.statcan.gc.ca/pub/75-006-x/2015001/ article/14167-eng.htm, accessed on November 16, 2016.

15. *The Globe and Mail*, www.theglobeandmail.com/globe-investor/ personal-finance/household-finances/unlocking-lower-insurance-rates-for-young-drivers/article20883208/, accessed on November 16, 2016.

16. CBC News, www.cbc.ca/news/canada/university-tuition-rising-to-record-levels-in-canada-1.1699103, accessed on November 16, 2016.

17. Workopolis, http://careers.workopolis.com/advice/the-university-degrees-that-earn-the-highest-starting-salaries/, accessed on November 16, 2016.

18. OECD iLibrary, www.oecd-ilibrary.org/sites/health_glance-2013-en/04/10/index.html?contentType=&itemId=/content/ chapter/health_glance-2013-41-en&containerItemId=/content/

serial/19991312&accessItemIds=/content/book/health_glance-2013-en&mimeType=text/html, accessed on November 16, 2016.

19. Kolbe Corp., www.kolbe.com/, accessed on November 16, 2016.

20. Prevue HR Systems, www.prevuehr.com/, accessed on November 16, 2016.

21. Laurie Pick`ard, *Family Business: United We Stand Divided We Fall* (Scottsdale: Avant-Courier Press, 1999), 35.

22. Ibid., 36.

23. Ibid., 45.

24. Ibid., 146 and 147.

25. Jill Bolte Taylor, *My Stroke of Insight: A Brain Scientist's Personal Journey* (New York: Plume and The Penguin Group, 2009), 72.

26. Dan Baker, *What Happy People Know* (New York: St. Martin's Press, 2003), 6.

27. Ibid., 7.

28. Ibid., 12.

29. HeartMath Institute, www.heartmath.org, accessed on November 16, 2016.

30. Andrew Cohen, *Evolutionary Enlightenment* (New York: SelectBooks Inc., 2011), 78.

31. Ibid.

32. Ibid., 80.

33. Ibid., 83.

34. Dirk Junge, Pitcairn Trust Co. Re-produced and edited by permission

35. Miguel Ruiz, *The Four Agreements: A Practical Guide to Personal Freedom* (San Rafael, CA: Amber-Allen Publishing, 1997).

36. These illustrations include non-guaranteed values. The non-guaranteed values are based on the current dividend scale of the

insurance provider. Dividends are not guaranteed and will increase or decrease depending on future dividend scales. Out of pocket premiums may have to continue longer than illustrated or be resumed after starting Premium Vacation. Illustration prepared with the assistance of Canada Gives and a source that prefers to go unnamed.

37.   Institute of Advanced Financial Planners, www.iafp.ca, accessed on November 16, 2016.

38.· With thanks to contributor Bart Rowe, CFA, Director of Investments, First Affiliated Holding Inc.

39.   Trading Economics, www.tradingeconomics.com/about-te.aspx, accessed on November 16, 2016.

40.   KPMG Enterprise, *The Canadian Family Business Guide* (Toronto: Carswell, 2012), 5.

41.   Robin Sharma, *The Leader Who Had No Title* (New York: Free Press, 2011), 135.

42.   Ibid., 137.

43.   Ibid., 135.

44.   Dictionary.com, www.dictionary.com/browse/education, accessed on November 16, 2016.

45.   Rick Wartzman, "Here Is Exactly Why You Wish You Were Self-Employed," *Time*, March 27, 2014, http://time.com/author/rick-wartzman/, accessed on November 16, 2016.

ACKNOWLEDGEMENTS

▲ ▼ ▲

It is with heartfelt gratitude that I wish to thank my team at First Affiliated. You have believed in me, put up with me, and breathed life into this material with the work you do every day. Special thanks to Bart Rowe and Brent Barrie, two brilliant gentlemen who contributed to this book and who are superstars at what they do. To Sabine Abt and Andrea Baker Nash, who always have my back, keep the office running, and in reviewing my early draft, gave birth to Jack and Jill. To Jenny, Dale, Stefanie, thank you for your encouragement and support.

To my teachers, Sara Traub, Donna Mitchell-Moniak, Susan Peltier, Krow Fischer, and "Red." I would have nothing to share if it weren't for you. I depend on you for guidance, inspiration, and the renewal of hope that we are where we all need to be and perfect just as we are.

To Karen and David Keith, who have been lifelong friends. With you I can be completely myself without fear of judgement. You laugh at my jokes and hold me together when I cry. Thank you for your part in editing the early drafts, helping to bring this book to life.

To my business associates who contributed content to this book, a very big thank you. I would like to acknowledge you, who asked to remain nameless, and your team, for your help putting the insurance section together and for your support of our work here at First Affiliated. I am also very grateful to you, Dirk Junge, for your contributions. Your sense of humour is such a joy, and you and the work you do at Pitcairn Trust Company is an inspiration to all of us in the Family Office space. You are a true ambassador. And to my friend and coach, Michael Reddy, who planted the seed for this book and helped give birth to The Family Treasury. You believed in us at a time when we most needed to believe in ourselves.

To my publisher, Sarah Scott, who took a chance on me; to my editors, Eleanor Gasparik and Heather Sangster, who brilliantly turned a manuscript into a book; and to our P.R. gal, Marjorie Wallens, who is putting our message out there— thank you, all! I am grateful you have chosen to lend me your unique talents.

To my great big family: Mom and Dad; siblings and in-laws; aunts, uncles, and cousins; nieces and nephews; and grandparents. Thank you for the years of laughter and joy that have filled this house. You all hold a special place in my heart, and I am grateful you have shared your life with me.

Finally, to my great loves, Karl, Stefan, Erik, and Rachele. I am who I am because of you. Your love and encouragement lets me reach for greater and greater expressions of myself, because I know you will be there to catch me if I fall. Your belief in me lets me believe in me. It is because of you I have written this book. I wish to share with the world everything you have taught me. I am so proud of you all.

Chris Clarke is CEO and co-owner of First Affiliated Family Office Group, which helps families in Toronto, across Canada, and overseas manage their finances. Every day, Chris helps her clients deal with a wide array of wealth, lifestyle, and legacy issues, an approach that has earned her team recognition as one of the world's top multi-family offices from the International Society of Trust and Estate Practitioners.

Chris is a Chartered Professional Accountant, a Trust and Estates Practitioner, and a Registered Financial Planner. She is also certified as a Family Facilitator by the Canadian Association of Family Enterprise. She lives near Thornbury, Ontario.